SOCIAL SCIENCE
PRIMARY 1

TEACHER'S BOOK

BY ME

TABLE OF CONTENTS

Introduction to ByME Social Science

Who the course is for

ByME Social Science is a six-level course for pupils studying the subject of Social Science in a bilingual context. Level 1 is for pupils in year 1 of Primary.

Aims of the course

The course follows the Social Science syllabus as laid out by the LOMCE. It is an introduction to the social sciences, leading learners through their first experiences of Human Geography, Physical Geography and History. *ByME Social Science* aims to develop pupils' scientific knowledge and language skills. Given the challenge of teaching Social Science in a bilingual classroom, it is important that language does not overwhelm the content, nor vice versa. For that reason, this programme was designed to ensure a unique balance between language and content.

The guiding principles are **simplicity** and **motivation** – *ByME Social Science* is interesting and engaging for the pupils and user-friendly for the teacher. It features:

- A simple, fixed unit structure to ensure easy navigation.
- A fresh and clear design with a dynamic mix of age-appropriate illustrations and attractive photography, providing visual aids that facilitate comprehension.
- A focus on **scientific method** in order to develop pupils' **investigative and presentation skills**.
- A real sense of **progression** through the levels with a fun, accessible feel to the early levels – with songs, characters and stories – and a more **mature and scientific approach in higher levels**, a clear **bridge to Secondary**.
- **Flexibility**, with many extra, non-content pages, allowing for easy adaptation to specific teaching situations.
- **Scientific literacy** instruction to support content learning in English through reading, writing, speaking and listening activities.
- A wide range of **additional resources**.

This course also aims to address the children's education beyond the scope of Social Science through:

- Activities designed to prepare children for the question types found in the most common **external exams**.
- **Study skills sections** where children are introduced to techniques for improving their own learning.
- **Cooperative Learning projects** designed to instil collaboration and teamwork as important life skills.
- A strong focus on **ethics** and **values**, encouraging children to engage with the world around them, appreciate its complexities and problems, and develop **social responsibility**.
- Attention to **higher-order thinking skills** to give children opportunities to apply what they know.
- Problem-based activities to encourage **critical thinking**.

Course components

Pupil's materials

Pupil's Book

A 104-page Pupil's Book including:

- a two-page introductory unit introducing pupils to the characters that will accompany them on their learning experience: Sam and Amy in the case of Social Science 1
- six main units of 12-14 pages
- three Cooperative Learning projects and end-of-term review sections
- stickers and a picture dictionary.

Activity Book

An optional 40-page Activity Book comprised of six full-colour pages per unit that offers:

- a range of engaging exercises to consolidate and extend the topics covered in the Pupil's Book
- additional reading and writing practice of the science content
- a mini-project designed to encourage pupils to explore scientific concepts and methods at home or in the classroom
- a bilingual glossary to support language learning.

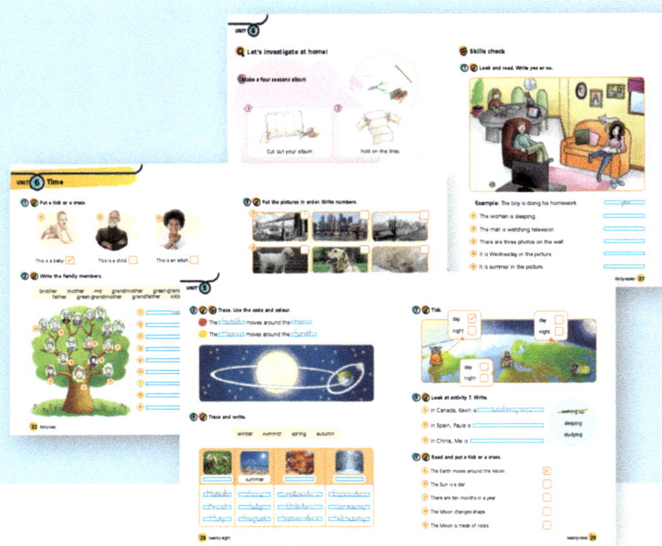

Modules

The modules offer an ideal solution to teaching contexts where only a limited number of hours in English are available. Each module combines a unit of the Pupil's Book with the corresponding Activity Book unit.

Teacher's materials

Teacher's Book

The full-colour Teacher's Book includes easy-to-follow, flexible lesson plans and practical support specially designed for English teachers teaching Science. A clear, simple design helps ease-of-reference even in the most challenging teaching situations. The Teacher's Book fully addresses the new curriculum through:

- careful attention to content, evaluation criteria and learning standards
- treatment of the updated key competences in correlation with the learning standards
- clearly identified key content and extras sections, enabling teachers to focus on minimum content or extend their lessons according to their timetable
- full answer key to all the questions and activities in the Pupil's Book and the Activity Book.

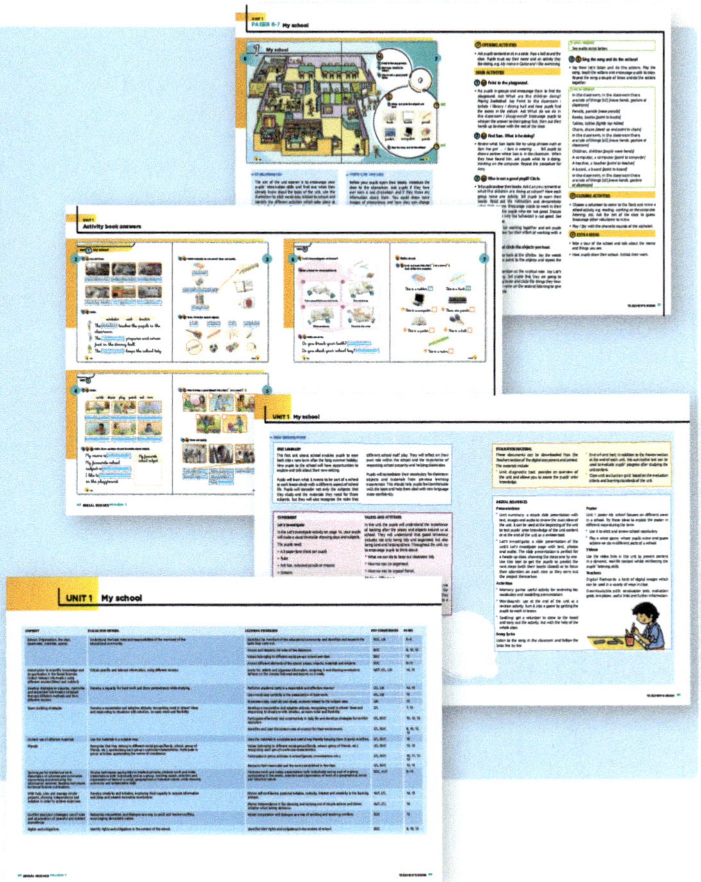

Class audio CD

Included with the Teacher's Book, the Class audio CD offers the key recordings for each Pupil's Book in a traditional, easily accessible format. It can be played on dedicated audio players or on the computer. It includes:

- Stories, songs and chants
- Recordings of the main texts and audio activities

Free access to the complete audio is available through the digital resources, where recordings of all Pupil's Book can be found.

Classroom materials

Digital posters, flashcards and wordcards

Level 1 features several resources to enrich the learning experience. Large-scale interactive posters offer visual support in the classroom. Colourful flashcards provide a flexible tool for revision and games, and wordcards can be downloaded and printed.

Ideas for using these classroom materials are provided in the Teacher's Book.

- Full-colour posters to illustrate the most important topics and vocabulary
- Full-colour flashcards
- A large number of wordcards featuring key content vocabulary for each unit (available for print through the digital resources).

Printable resources

Extra printable resources are provided online through the digital resources. These include:

- Diagnostic tests
- Unit tests
- End-of-term tests
- Evaluation grids
- Letters to family to help involve parents and carers in their children's learning.

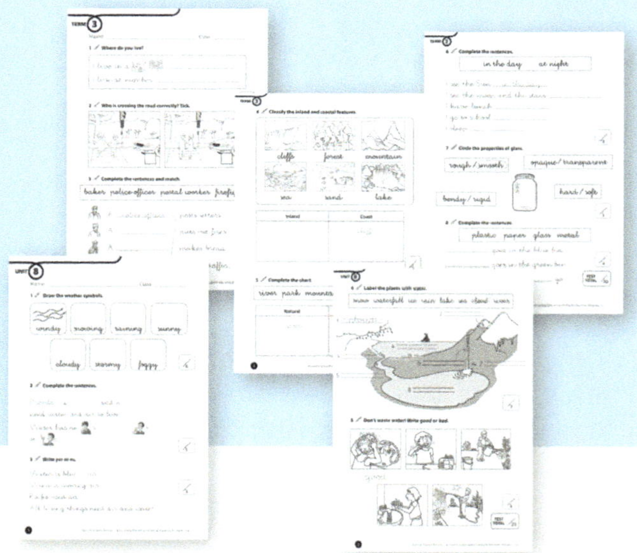

Digital resources

Extensive digital resources are provided. Their focus is a projectable, fully navigable version of the Pupil's Book. This includes a spot-zoom facility to increase ease-of-use and facilitate navigation in dynamic classroom moments. It also provides direct access to all the course audio as well as the Activity Book (with all answers included), Teacher's Book, interactive digital resources and the printable classroom materials.

Interactive digital resources include:

- **Slide presentations:** (two types are provided)
  - Step-by-step experiments and projects from the Pupil's Book.
  - Unit review presentations to be used as an introduction to or revision of key content.
- **Activities:** A variety of activities to revise vocabulary and concepts (Wordsearch, Memory games and Spelling activities).
- **Posters:** Interactive versions of the posters.
- **Flashcards:** Flashcards available in digital format provide a practical image bank.
- **Audio:** All the Pupil's Book reading texts and audio activities.
- **Songs and chants:** All songs and chants are available with a fun and dynamic karaoke effect, to aid and encourage classroom participation.
- **Videos:** Links to useful videos chosen to highlight and expand on key topics in a fun and dynamic way.

bilingualbyme.com

The ByME website is home to a wealth of articles, videos, activities and useful links, updated on a regular basis. It includes all the relevant documentation related to ByME courses.

It also provides support for parents, providing tips and ideas on how to help their children's learning as well as including the songs and chants for listening to at home.

How to use the Pupil's Book

Unit introduction

Opening spread

Each unit opens with a vibrant double-page spread. These introductory pages maximise motivation by showing that pupils' prior knowledge of key topics is often already considerable. Key content and vocabulary is introduced though attractive large-scale illustrations, songs and engaging activities. Don't forget to look for the **chameleon** hiding somewhere in every opening picture!

A **song** with a related activity reviews key vocabulary from the illustration.

A large **illustration** introduces key vocabulary and concepts in an entertaining and accessible way. The illustrations always feature the *Social Science* course characters **Sam** and **Amy**. In some units you can find **Ben** and **Katie**, their *Natural Science* friends, creating a visual link between the two subjects.

Activities can be formulated as group activities or discussions to encourage cooperative learning. They are designed to encourage pupils to think for themselves and draw on their prior knowledge.

Story and external exam practice

Page three features a fun but informative story that follows on directly from the unit opening spread. The action takes place in the same place as the opening illustration and always features the course characters exploring the unit topic and vocabulary in more depth.

A dramatization of the story can be listened to on the class CD or the digital component.

The story activities are designed to reflect the most common activities found in **external exams**.

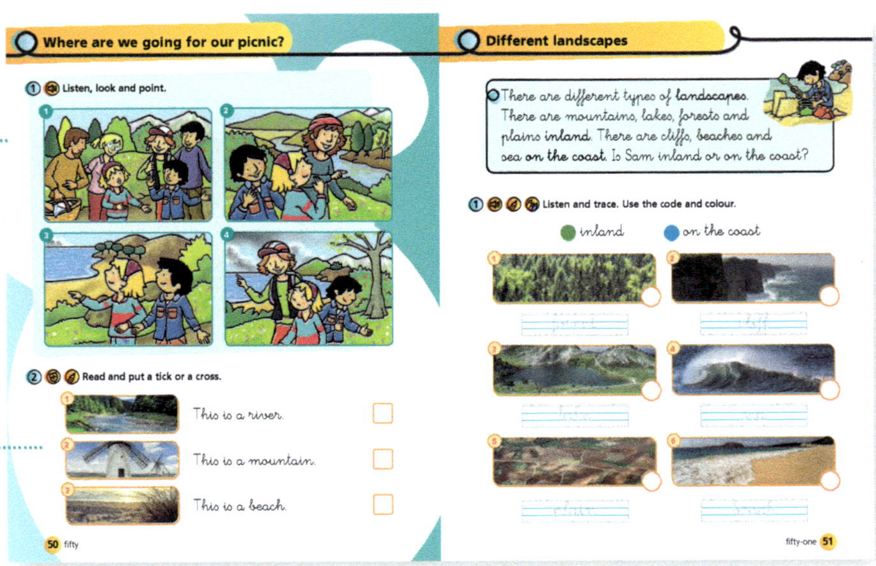

Unit development

The content pages build on pupils' prior knowledge through highly visual content and a wide variety of activities presenting differing levels of cognitive challenge.

Course characters are repeated throughout the unit presenting the key concepts visually in order to facilitate comprehension.

Pupils are introduced gradually and carefully to **reading and writing**.

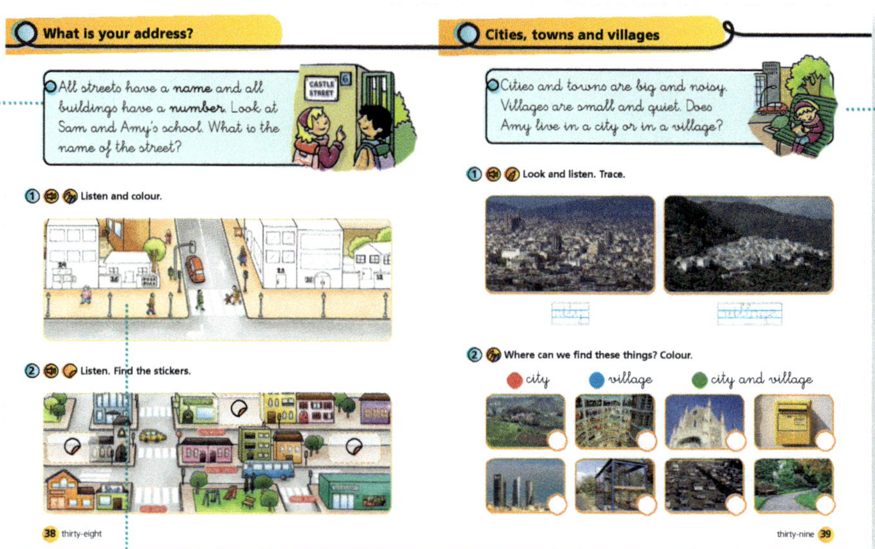

Content pages are richly illustrated with a careful balance of photography and age-appropriate illustration, in order to facilitate comprehension in all learner types and maximise engagement with the content.

Regular sticker activities increase the variety of available activity types.

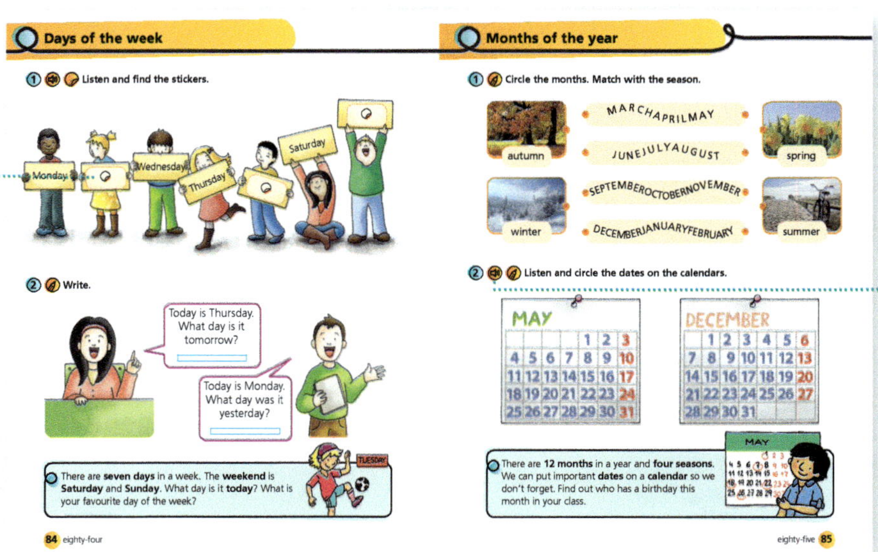

Extensive audio activities provide regular practice of listening skills. Songs and chants in every unit provide a comforting link to pupils' English textbooks.

Unit conclusion

Each unit closes with four pages in which content is extended and revised. The *Let's Investigate and Make a difference* pages give the course added flexibility.

Let's investigate: Fun projects and simple experiments provide children with an age appropriate introduction to **scientific method** (aim, test, conclusion) from the very beginning. Projects are carefully designed to be accessible and appropriate for the youngest children and always use everyday materials. Studio photography including real children of the same age as the pupils helps them relate to the content.

Make a difference: Pupils are introduced to values and ethics in relation to the scientific project. They are presented with situations designed to encourage **reasoning** and an engagement with their immediate surroundings, in order to develop their independence and the beginnings of **social and personal responsibility**. There are also further ideas for projects and class presentations.

Let's remember

Unit revision pages ensure that pupils' **progression is regularly checked and reviewed**. They are also offered the opportunity to carry out some simple **self-assessment**.

Term pages

Four end-of-term pages provide additional progress-checking opportunities as well as the opportunity to practise different communicative skills.

Work together

Cooperative Learning project: A final group project takes these communication and collaboration skills further and gives pupils the opportunity to engage with a key theme from a different point of view while having fun at the same time! These cooperative activities are carefully adapted to the age group. The group dynamics used are fully described in the Cooperative Learning article.

Before doing the activities groups are formed by the teacher. Pupils are given roles and explained the procedures to follow according to the relevant Cooperative Learning structure.

The different activities are conducted following different Cooperative Learning structures that will provide the optimal learning experience for the pupil and guarantee the implication of all group members. Different structures include Round robin, Think-pair-share, Jigsaw, etc.

Term review

Term revision pages ensure that pupils' **progression is regularly checked and reviewed** through a broad range of enjoyable activity types.

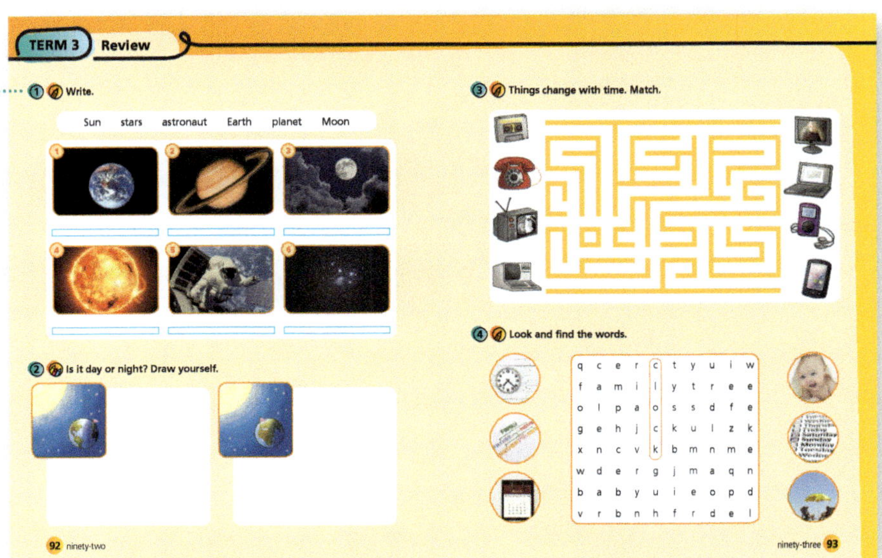

How to use the Teacher's Book

Preliminary pages

The Teacher's Book includes a variety of articles with practical ideas on how to get the most out of the lesson.

Helpful tips & Classroom management

The section *Helpful tips* is set out as a reference resource. Here you will find ideas on setting up reading tasks, maximising the classroom materials and keeping your pupils motivated through a variety of activity types.

The *Classroom management* section provides some general ideas about managing your class in order to create a productive environment in which all pupils are able to flourish.

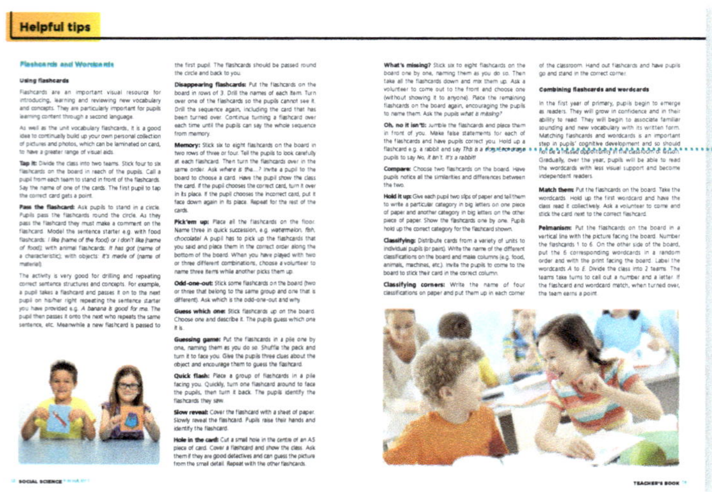

Getting the most out of the classroom materials: posters, flashcards and wordcards are incredibly effective tools if used appropriately. This section offers a wide range of suggestions on how to make these useful resources work for you.

More activities: a host more activities that can be adapted to specific teaching contexts, be it for revision, reinforcement or extension in a mixed-abilities situation, or to occupy fast finishers while the rest of the class finish.

Presenting key content: this section addresses the perennial problem of how to make reading in class dynamic, productive and stimulating.

Classroom organisation: provides clear rules for behaviour which the pupils themselves are asked to help define.

Time management: suggestions for working to a limited timetable. ByME Teacher's Books give teachers the option of focusing on key content, incorporating clearly marked extras only if time allows.

Procedures: ways of sequencing a class session, with suggestions for routines that can be repeated from class to class.

Cooperative Learning

An article on Cooperative Learning (CL) offers an introduction to this innovative method of teaching. This section complements the end-of-term *Work together* sections, explaining in simple language how to set up each CL structure referenced there.

Further reading: a brief bibliography for those who would like to deepen their knowledge on CL.

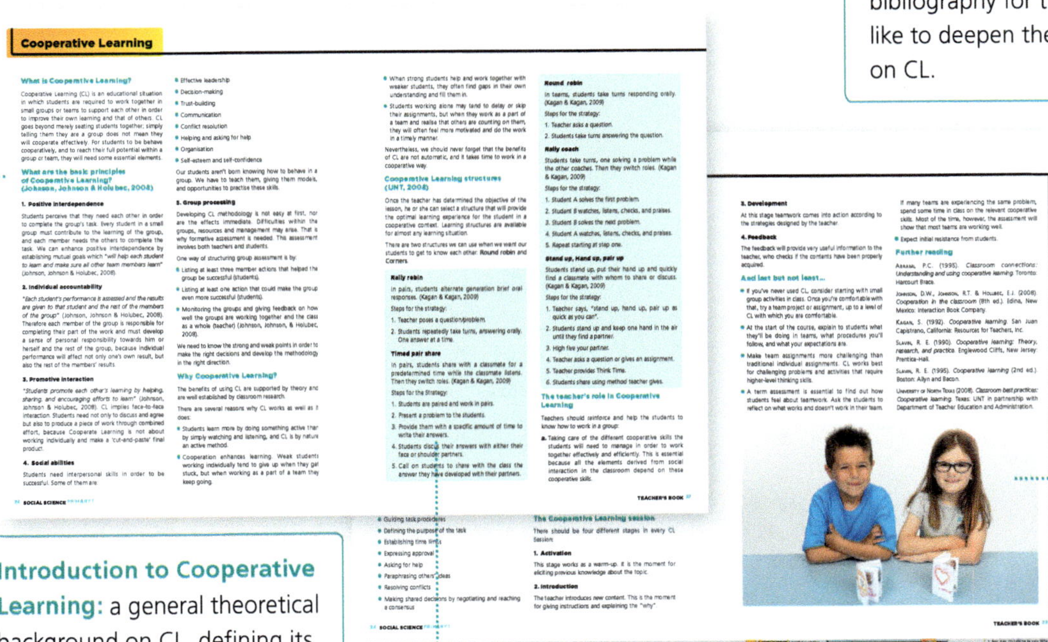

Introduction to Cooperative Learning: a general theoretical background on CL, defining its main principles and benefits.

Cooperative Learning structures: specific information on the different group dynamics referenced in the lesson plans. Here you'll find easy-to-follow instructions on how each CL structure is set up.

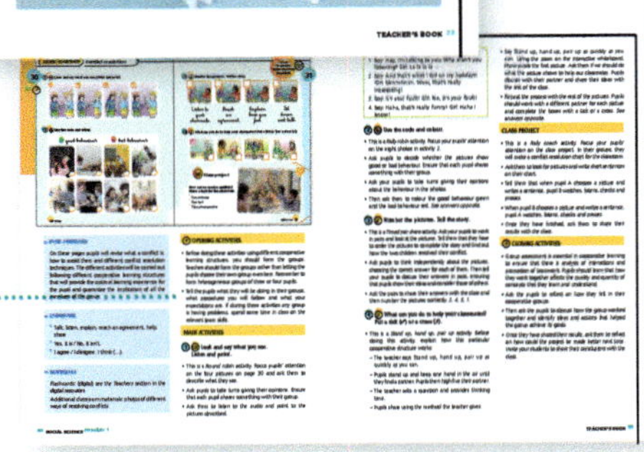

Content maps

Each unit and Cooperative Learning section begins with a content map, fully compatible with the LOMCE curriculum, to help the teacher see at a glance the content, evaluation criteria, learning standards and key competences ahead.

Learning standards, evaluation criteria and content: all key elements of the LOMCE curriculum are clearly mapped out for each unit.

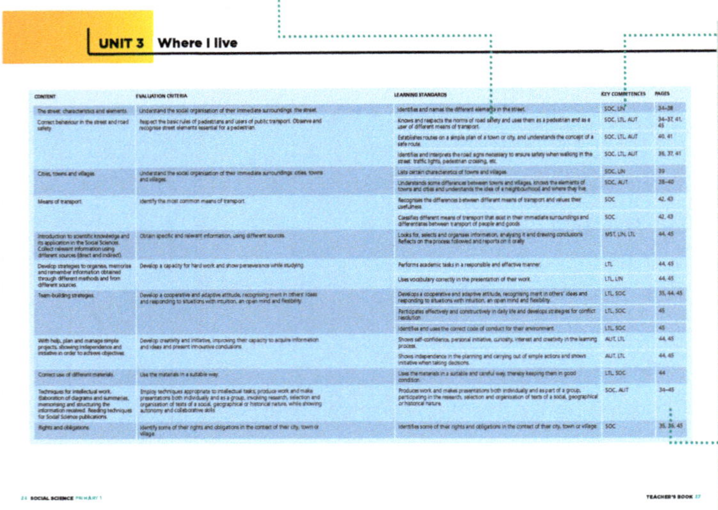

Key competences: related to each learning standard.

LIN: Competence in linguistic communication
MST: Competence in mathematics, science and technology
DIG: Digital competence
LTL: Competence in learning to learn
SOC: Competence in social awareness and citizenship
AUT: Competence in autonomous learning and personal initiative
CUL: Competence in artistic and cultural awareness

Page references: indicate where each learning standard is covered.

Unit information

Unit summary: an overview of the lesson, highlighting the main topics and outcomes, as well as identifying areas that are popular with or difficult for pupils.

Materials: materials required for each lesson and reminders for pupils of materials they should bring from home for upcoming activities.

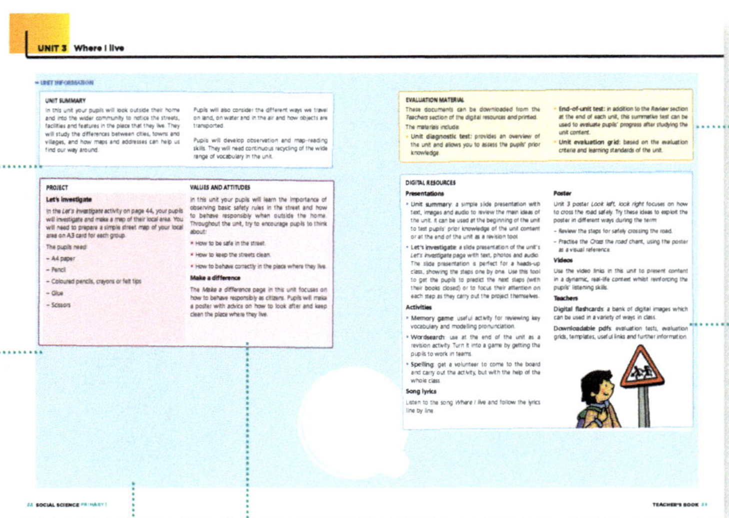

Evaluation material: a short description of the evaluation aids available.

Digital resources: an index of the materials and activities available through the digital resources.

Experiment: helps prepare for the *Let's investigate* project ahead of time. Especially important where experiments require pupils to bring materials.

Values and attitudes: aims to make the content relevant to pupils, helping them to understand how it affects them directly and why it should matter to them.

Lesson plans

There are step-by-step lesson plans for all units and term sections.

Visual page reference: a full-colour image of the Pupil's Book for the teacher's reference.

Lesson information at a quick glance: lesson summary, language focus and materials to help prepare lessons ahead of time.

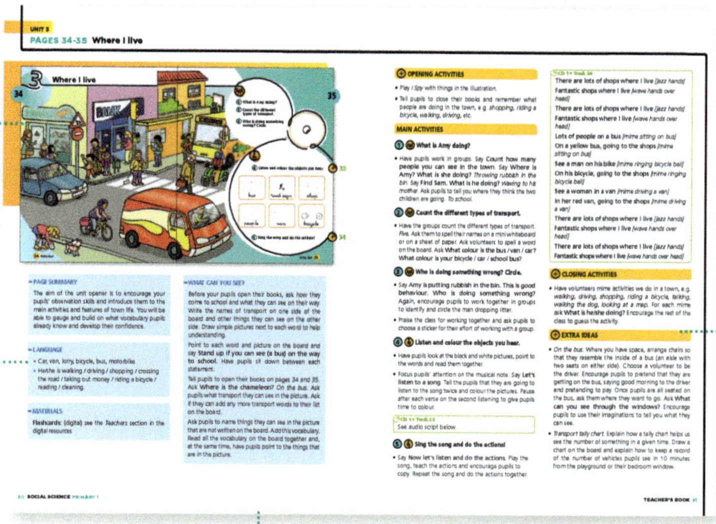

Step-by-step lesson plans: teacher tips on presenting textual and graphic content, and instructions for guiding pupils through the activities.

Extra activities: activities for pupils who finish the lesson early.

Opening and closing activities: each lesson begins and ends with flexible activities that can be reduced or extended according to time available.

Activity Book solutions

Activity Book solutions: provided at the end of the unit making the Teacher's Book a one-stop reference for all the materials of each course.

How to use the digital resources

All teachers using ByME Social Science have free access to the ByME digital resources. Users of the Pupil's Book or Activity Book have access to the complete digital books. Module users have individual access to the specific units they are using of both the Pupil's Book and Activity Book.

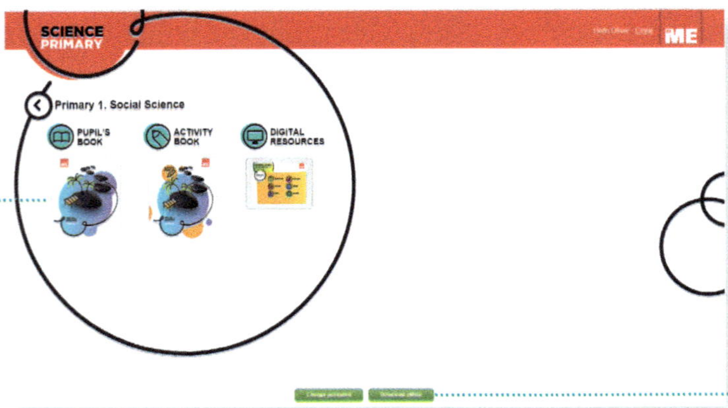

The digital resources are available both on-line and off-line. Both versions are accessed with a specific code that all users will receive.

The digital component also provides easy navigation between the Pupil's Book and the Activity Book and direct access to extensive digital resources.

The user has access to projectable, fully-navigable versions of the Pupil's Book and the Activity Book.

Through an innovative, easy-to-use spot zoom facility, there is ready access to the complete audio.

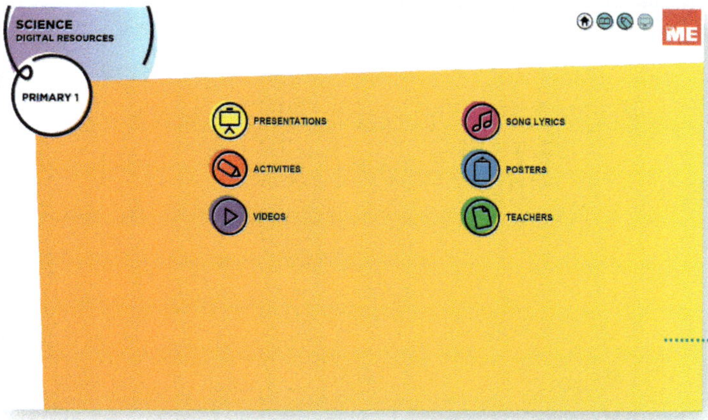

The digital resources include:

- interactive activities (see images below)
- accessible unit review and experiment presentations with integrated audio
- all the songs with the lyrics and a karaoke effect
- access to videos which bring key topics to life
- interactive versions of the course posters
- access to printable resources and a PDF version of the Teacher's Book.

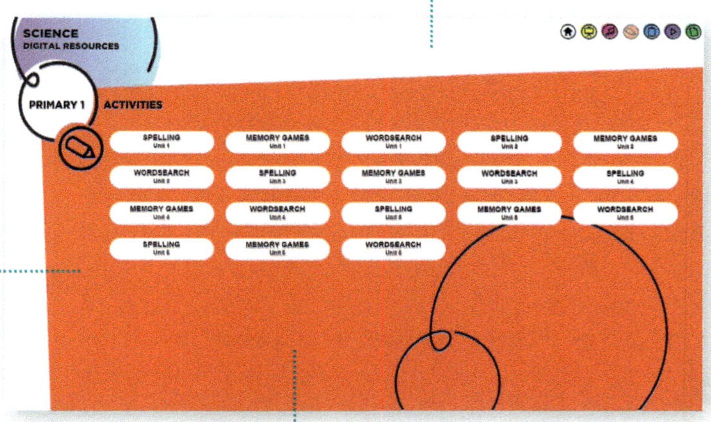

Digital activities to practise key vocabulary vary for each level but include:

- Labelling activities
- Memory games
- Read and reveal activities
- Wordsearches
- Classification and definition activities

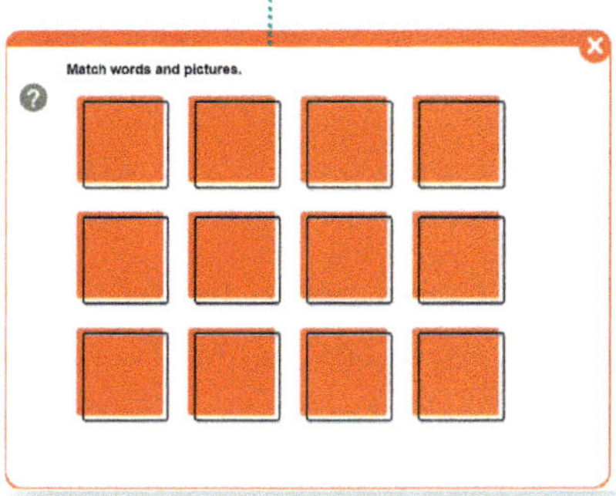

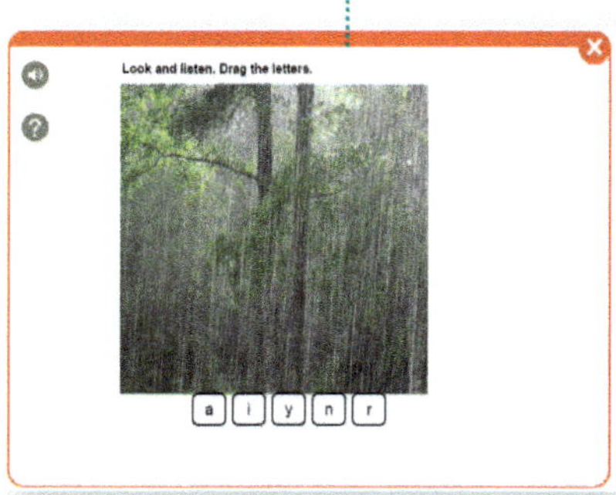

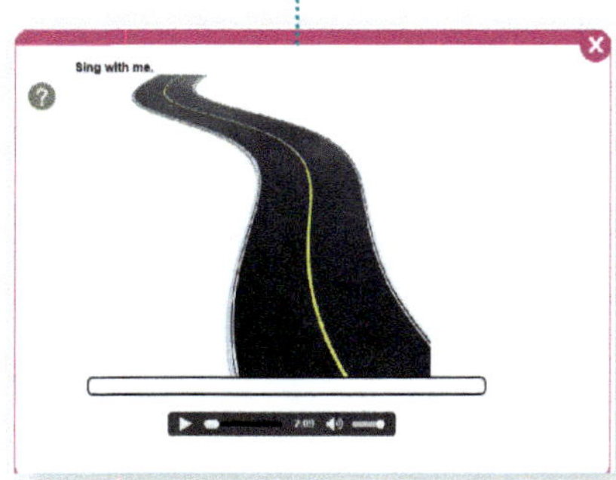

Helpful tips

Flashcards and wordcards

Using flashcards

Flashcards are an important visual resource for introducing, learning and reviewing new vocabulary and concepts. They are particularly important for pupils learning content through a second language.

As well as the unit vocabulary flashcards, it is a good idea to continually build up your own personal collection of pictures and photos, which can be easily laminated on card, to have a greater range of visual aids.

Tap it: Divide the class into two teams. Stick four to six flashcards on the board in reach of the pupils. Call a pupil from each team to stand in front of the flashcards. Say the name of one of the cards. The first pupil to tap the correct card gets a point.

Pass the flashcard: Ask pupils to stand in a circle. Pupils pass the flashcards round the circle. As they pass the flashcard they must make a comment on the flashcard. Model the sentence starter e.g. with food flashcards: *I like (name of the food)* or *I don't like (name of food);* with animal flashcards: *It has got (name of a characteristic);* with objects: *It's made of (name of material).*

The activity is very good for drilling and repeating correct sentence structures and concepts. For example, a pupil takes a flashcard and passes it on to the next pupil on their right repeating the sentence starter you have provided e.g. *A banana is good for me*. The pupil then passes it onto the next who repeats the same sentence, etc. Meanwhile a new flashcard is passed to the first pupil. The flashcards should be passed round the circle and back to you.

Disappearing flashcards: Put the flashcards on the board in rows of three. Drill the names of each item. Turn over one of the flashcards so the pupils cannot see it. Drill the sequence again, including the card that has been turned over. Continue turning a flashcard over each time until the pupils can say the whole sequence from memory.

Memory: Stick six to eight flashcards on the board in two rows of three or four. Tell the pupils to look carefully at each flashcard. Then turn the flashcards over in the same order. Ask *Where is the...?* Invite a pupil to the board to choose a card. Have the pupil show the class the card. If the pupil chooses the correct card, turn it over in its place. If the pupil chooses the incorrect card, put it face down again in its place. Repeat for the rest of the cards.

Pick'em up: Place all the flashcards on the floor. Name three in quick succession, e.g. *watermelon, fish, chocolate!* A pupil has to pick up the flashcards that you said and place them in the correct order along the bottom of the board. When you have played with two or three different combinations, choose a volunteer to name three items while another picks them up.

Odd-one-out: Stick some flashcards on the board (two or three that belong to the same group and one that is different). Ask which is the odd-one-out and why.

Guess which one: Stick flashcards up on the board. Choose one and describe it. The pupils guess which one it is.

Guessing game: Put the flashcards in a pile one by one, naming them as you do so. Shuffle the pack and turn it to face you. Give the pupils three clues about the object and encourage them to guess the flashcard.

Quick flash: Place a group of flashcards in a pile facing you. Quickly, turn one flashcard around to face the pupils, then turn it back. The pupils identify the flashcards they saw.

Slow reveal: Cover the flashcard with a sheet of paper. Slowly reveal the flashcard. Pupils raise their hands and identify the flashcard.

Hole in the card: Cut a small hole in the centre of an A5 piece of card. Cover a flashcard and show the class. Ask them if they are good detectives and can guess the picture from the small detail. Repeat with the other flashcards.

What's missing?: Stick six to eight flashcards on the board one by one, naming them as you do so. Then take all the flashcards down and mix them up. Ask a volunteer to come out to the front and choose one (without showing it to anyone). Place the remaining flashcards on the board again, encouraging the pupils to name them. Ask the pupils *What is missing?*

Oh no, it isn't!: Jumble the flashcards and place them in front of you. Make false statements for each of the flashcards and have pupils correct you. Hold up a flashcard e.g. a rabbit and say *This is a dog.* Encourage pupils to say *No, it isn't. It's a rabbit!*

Compare: Choose two flashcards on the board. Have pupils notice all the similarities and differences between the two.

Hold it up: Give each pupil two slips of paper and tell them to write a particular category in big letters on one piece of paper and another category in big letters on the other piece of paper. Show the flashcards one by one. Pupils hold up the correct category for the flashcard shown.

Classifying: Distribute cards from a variety of units to individual pupils (or pairs). Write the name of the different classifications on the board and make columns (e.g. food, animals, machines, etc.). Invite the pupils to come to the board to stick their card in the correct column.

Classifying corners: Write the name of four classifications on paper and put them up in each corner of the classroom. Hand out flashcards and have pupils go and stand in the correct corner.

Combining flashcards and wordcards

In the first year of primary, pupils begin to emerge as readers. They will grow in confidence and in their ability to read. They will begin to associate familiar sounding and new vocabulary with its written form. Matching flashcards and wordcards is an important step in pupils' cognitive development and so should not be a missed opportunity in the classroom or lesson. Gradually, over the year, pupils will be able to read the wordcards with less visual support and become independent readers.

Match them: Put the flashcards on the board. Take the wordcards. Hold up the first wordcard and have the class read it together. Ask a volunteer to come and stick the card next to the correct flashcard.

Pelmanism: Put the flashcards on the board in a vertical line with the picture facing the board. Number the flashcards *1* to *6*. On the other side of the board, put the six corresponding wordcards in a random order and with the print facing the board. Label the wordcards *A* to *E*. Divide the class into two teams. The teams take turns to call out a number and a letter. If the flashcard and wordcard match when turned over, the team earns a point.

Board snap: Shuffle the flashcards and shuffle the wordcards and place them facing down in two piles. Call two volunteers to turn over the top card of each pile and hold them up. If they match, the class shout *Snap!*

Find a partner: Photocopy wordcards and their corresponding flashcard so there is one for each pupil. Have pupils circulate around the classroom repeating their word until they find a partner or partners with the same word.

Encourage pupils to make a sentence together with their word.

Using wordcards

Run and slap: Divide the class into two teams. Stick the wordcards on the board in reach of the pupils. Call a pupil from each team to stand in front of the wordcards. Say the name of one of the cards. The first pupil to slap the correct card gets a point. (This can also be done with two fly swats.)

Label it: Hand out the wordcards and have pupils label a drawing on the board, a poster, objects on a tray or parts of the classroom, etc.

Find a partner: Photocopy the wordcards so there is one for each pupil. Have pupils circulate around the classroom repeating their word until they find a partner or partners with the same word.

Encourage pupils to make a sentence together with their word.

Now you see it, now you don't: Flash up a wordcard. Have pupils look at it for ten seconds. Hide the wordcard and have pupils spell the word on a mini white board or in their notebooks.

Mix'n'match: Photocopy sets of wordcards from a unit. Cut the words in half. Hand out the sets to groups of pupils who must match the halves correctly.

Hello, goodbye: Stand by the door with the unit's wordcards. Have pupils read a wordcard as they come in or leave your classroom.

Games

Pupils learn in many different ways. The more experiences pupils can have around a new topic, the more likely they will learn and remember concepts and vocabulary. Games offer a wide range of opportunities for pupils to engage with and use what they are learning. They are also a chance to offer movement, a change of focus, and disguised language learning. The competitive element inspires pupils to participate and, what could easily be an uninspiring list of revision questions or words to define, can be transformed into a fun game.

General games

Clever chameleon says: Pupils must carry out an action only when Clever chameleon says. *Clever chameleon says clap your hands,* etc.

I Spy: Use the classroom, the playground, a poster or the opening illustration for a unit to say *I spy with my little eye something beginning with (/k/).* Pupils suggest words beginning with that sound or letter to guess your word. Vary the game by saying instead, I *smell with my little nose...* when reviewing food vocabulary.

Pass the ball: A soft ball is best. The activity encourages turn taking and gives everybody a go at speaking. As pupils pass the ball they must say a word or a statement, depending on what you would like the pupils to practise e.g. *My name is ... / In my bedroom there is ... / In my town there is ...*

Balloon: Divide the class into two and have pupils make two circles. Give each circle a balloon. Pupils must try to keep the balloon in the air by touching it and saying a word in a lexical set you suggest e.g. *school objects, furniture, things we see in the street,* etc. If a pupil touches the balloon without saying a word or the balloon touches the ground before a pupil touches it, that pupil must sit out.

Guess what's in the bag: Use a feely bag to put things inside for pupils to feel and guess, or feel and describe for others to guess.

Pictionary: Divide the class into two teams. Start to draw an item on the board very slowly. In turns, teams have 30 seconds to guess what you are drawing. You'll need a timer! Once pupils are familiar with the game, they can play in threes. One pupil begins to draw an item from the unit or the picture dictionary. The other two pupils in the group must guess what it is. The first to guess, becomes the drawer.

Picture snap: Pupils draw one item from the unit e.g. something they have for breakfast, their favourite animal, a machine in their kitchen. Pupils must keep their picture a secret and must not show others. Provide pupils with the sentence starter you would like them to use e.g. *I go to ... on holiday; In my bedroom there's a ...* Pupils must walk around the classroom repeating their sentence to as many classmates as possible. If they hear somebody say the same item as them, they must shout *Snap!* and show each other their picture. Check at the end how many pupils had the same item as somebody else.

Chain repeating: This game is based on the traditional game: *I went to the market and bought ...*

Begin a sentence, e.g. *In my street, I can see ...* and add an item, e.g. *In my street I can see a road sign.* The next pupil must repeat your sentence and add another item, e.g. *In my street I can see a road sign and a bin.* The game continues until someone makes a mistake or forgets an item.

Stand up if: Pupils listen to the statements you make. If they think your statement is true, they stand up. If they think it is false, they remain seated. Between statements, pupils sit down. The game can also be played with flashcards. Hold up a flashcard and make a true or false statement about what is on the flashcard. Pupils stand up if it is true.

Stand up if it's true for you: Pupils listen to your statement and stand up if it is true for them personally e.g. *I make my bed; I live in a house; I have a red pencil case.*

Repeat if true: Pupils listen to your statements. If they think your statement is true, they repeat it. If they think it is false, they shake their heads and remain silent.

Chinese whispers: Have pupils stand one behind the other, in three lines of equal numbers. Whisper a sentence to the pupil at the end of each line at the same time. They must whisper the sentence to the next person in their line, who whispers it to the next until

it is passed down all the way to the first person in the line. The pupil at the front of the line puts up their hand when they think they know the sentence or runs and circles a flashcard or wordcard on the board.

Backs to the board: Divide the class in half, into two teams. Place two chairs at the front of the class, each chair facing a team. Ask one pupil from each team to come and sit in the chair, facing their team but with their backs to the board. Write a word or put up a flashcard on the board behind the pupil's backs and insist that they do not turn round (ensure the class understand the word you have written). Encourage the teams to mime the word on the board to their team member who must guess what it is. The team member who guesses first gains a point for their team. Two new team members then come to the chairs.

Noughts and crosses: Draw a noughts and crosses grid on the board and write numbers in each square. Divide the class into two teams and choose one team to be *noughts* and one team to be *crosses*. For each number prepare a question or true/false statement. Each team takes turns to choose a number. If they answer your question correctly, a team member can come up to the board and replace the number with a nought or a cross. The winning team is the first to get three noughts (or crosses) in a line.

Bingo: Pupils fold an A5 sheet of paper in half, in half again, and in half one more time. When they open the paper up, they should have a grid with eight squares. Pupils draw (or write) eight items from your lesson (food, animals, machines, etc.). Draw a grid with eight squares on the board. Draw items one at a time in your grid. If pupils have that same item in their grid, they can cross it out. When a pupil has crossed all the items out in their grid that are the same as yours, they can shout *Bingo!* Use the other side of the paper to start a new game.

Clock race: Divide the class into two teams. The first two members come to the front and take a clock each with easily moveable hands. Encourage the rest of the class to chant *What's the time?* Respond with a time e.g. **It's eight o'clock**. Have the two members at the front of the class race to make the time on their clocks. The first to do so gains a point for their team.

One minute, please: Pupils have one minute to carry out a task you set e.g. write their name as many times as possible, write all the letters of the alphabet, write as many numbers as possible, draw a picture. Set the timer or hourglass.

Picture dictation: Pupils listen and draw the things you dictate.

BuzzFizz: Pupils count to 30. Each pupil must say a number but if their number is an even number they must say *Buzz* instead of the number e.g. 1, *buzz*, 3, *buzz*, 5 *buzz*, etc. Another time, have pupils replace the odd numbers with the word *Fizz* e.g. Fizz, 2, fizz, 4, fizz, 6, etc.

Games with movement

Mirror mirror: Two pupils stand opposite each other. They take turns to be the leader and do movements and facial expressions that their partner, the *mirror*, must copy.

Listen and do: Pupils listen carefully to two instructions at the same time e.g. *Pick up a glue stick, point to the door. Ride a bicycle, wash the dishes.* When pupils get good at remembering and following two instructions at a time, increase it to three.

Mime it: Encourage pupils to use mime to accompany new expressions and vocabulary.

Green man, red man: Colour and cut out a green man and a red man (as seen on pedestrian crossings). Hold up the green man and say **Stamp your feet**. Have pupils stamp their feet. When you hold up the red man, pupils must freeze and stop. Repeat with other actions, stopping pupils in mid flow with the red man.

Grandma's footsteps: Play in small groups out in the playground or in the gym. Choose one pupil in each group to be *grandma* (male or female). Grandma must stand and face a wall, while the rest of the group stand behind an agreed line behind them on the other side of the room. They must try to creep up behind grandma and tap her on the shoulder. At any moment, grandma can turn around. If she sees anybody moving, she will point to them and they must go back to the beginning, behind the line. No one must move while grandma is watching. Whoever manages to tap grandma first, without her seeing them, becomes the next grandma and the game starts again.

Games for developing spelling

Letter body shapes: Call out a letter of the alphabet, have pupils make that letter shape with their bodies.

Plasticine and pipe cleaners: Pupils can use these to form the letters you dictate. Review vocabulary from a lesson by asking pupils to make the first letter.

Names: Pupils stand up if their name begins with the letter of the alphabet you say. Ask the pupils who stand up what their name is.

Get in order: Help pupils stand in line in the alphabetical order of their names. Alternatively, give pupils a wordcard and help them stand in the alphabetical order according to the first letter of the word. (It helps pupils at this age to have a visual alphabet somewhere in the classroom they can refer to or write the alphabet on the board.)

A-Z: Write the letters of the alphabet on the board with the pupils' help. In groups of three ask pupils to think of a food item / animal / something in an illustration beginning with each letter of the alphabet. When ideas are drying up, elicit groups' suggestions and write and draw the word next to each letter.

Hangman (man on a raft): Instead of a hanging man, draw a man standing on a raft (ten circles under him on a rough river or sea). Draw a crocodile or shark in a corner of the board. Draw spaces for the letters of a word you want pupils to guess. If pupils guess a letter in the word correctly, write it in the correct space. If the letter does not appear in the word, write it under the crocodile or shark, and rub out a circle of the raft. Pupils must guess the word before the raft is totally rubbed away (and the man is eaten by the shark or crocodile!).

Colour it: Pupils write new vocabulary in their notebooks in different sizes and different colours. Encourage them to draw small pictures to accompany the words, or draw a picture and then label it.

Guess the word: Begin to write up a word from the day's class slowly, one letter at a time. Ask pupils to guess the word you are spelling before you finish writing it and help you complete the spelling.

Scrabble: Have sets of plastic alphabet letters, scrabble letters, and/or letter sets cut up on card. Divide the class into small groups. Give each group a set of letters. The groups spell the word you tell them.

Ready, steady, spell: Mini whiteboards are a great learning aid! Say a word and have pupils spell it on their mini whiteboard and hold it up to show you. The boards also provide an easy opportunity for pupils to practise spelling a word before writing it in their books.

Let's spell: Make sure pupils are familiar with the vowels the *a, e, i, o, u.* Write vocabulary items from the lesson on the board but with the vowels missing (*k_tch_n*). Pupils write the complete word with a partner on a mini whiteboard or in their notebooks. Encourage them to use colours for the vowels.

Run and spell: Divide the class into three teams. Have a member from each team stand in front of the board with a board pen. Ask pupils to spell a word (use short words, pupils have seen a lot). The first team member to spell the word correctly gains a point for their team.

Classroom management

Classroom routines

Teaching this age group a hands-on subject, including group and pairwork, in a second language, makes classroom management vitally important from the outset.

Classroom routines

From the very first class, make sure you establish the boundaries and norms of the behaviour you expect, so that pupils know what is and isn't acceptable in the classroom.

Procedures and routines should be introduced gradually throughout the first term and practised on a regular basis. Positive reinforcement can help the acquisition of these procedures and routines. Encourage pupils with positive statements. For example, *Let's talk with our indoor voices; Let's walk nicely*, instead of *Don't shout, Don't run*.

Have simple rhymes or chants to focus pupils' attention:

Let's begin routine: Have pupils stand up and say **Touch the sky, way up high. Touch your toes. Now we're ready to go.** Motion with your hands for the pupils to sit down and say **One. Two. Three. Four. Five. Six. Seven. Eight. Look, listen and sit up straight.**

Listening routine: Teacher: **1, 2, 3. Look at me.** Pupil: *1, 2. I'm looking at you.*

Try to give one instruction at a time for pupils to carry out otherwise they may quickly forget. When pupils are not sure what they need to do, this can be a cause for disruption. Make sure you accompany instructions with demonstrations, mime or other visual support. Pupils learning through English need more support than pupils learning in their own language.

Sometimes during class, you may need to stop the pupils in order to give them further instructions. Many pupils find it difficult to stop working and choose to keep colouring, cutting, painting, etc. Use a tambourine, a small bell, or a maraca, to get pupils' attention. Place your hands on your head and wait for the class to do the same. Place your hands on your shoulders, then fold your arms and have pupils follow. They should now all be focused on you.

Strategically-placed signs with an illustration can help to regain control or focus pupils' attention non-verbally. Talk with pupils about your expectations when using these signs:

- Hands up!
- Look.
- Listen.
- Share.
- Speak English!
- Quiet please!
- Sit properly.
- Tidy up!

Remember pupils are learning through a language that is not their own. Positive reinforcement can be very effective in the bilingual classroom. Praise pupils who attempt to express themselves through English and try not to over-correct but instead recast what they want to say with the correct phrase or use of vocabulary. Keep language simple.

Some pupils will be shier and less confident than others when contributing in class. These pupils will benefit from having more listening time. Using a *hands up* approach allows you to see when pupils are ready and feel more confident to contribute. Make sure that pupils who do not or cannot contribute very much are given other opportunities to take an active role e.g. by being in charge of classroom resources, designing titles for displays, etc. Be aware of who these pupils are in your class so that you build their confidence in other ways and give praise for art work, group work, tidiness, etc.

Useful techniques which may serve as a guide to ensure your pupils participate equally, include:

- Writing pupils' names on ice-lolly sticks, and keeping them in a pot on your desk. Pull out a name stick when you want a volunteer, want to form new pairs or groups, or want pupils to help with resources, etc.
- Having small pots of pebbles on each group of tables. As pupils participate orally, they may take a pebble and place it in front of them. The pebbles provide a visual record, showing you who has participated, thus enabling you to encourage pupils who do not yet have a pebble. In following activities or sessions, you can focus more attention on this group of pupils.

Materials

Another important dimension to classroom management is being prepared and having the materials you need, ready and at your fingertips. Look ahead at the lessons so that you have the resources to make posters and displays and to carry out experiments and investigations. If pupils need to bring items from home, make sure they are given time to do so and that parents are also aware.

Design a procedure for passing out materials. A helper(s) can be selected every week to help hand out materials. Keep a chart so that everybody has a turn during the term.

Design a cleaning up procedure too and allow time for this in your lesson. Encourage pupils to be tidy and to throw rubbish in the bin. Helpers can be useful in this procedure. There are many cleaning up songs on the internet. You can choose one and play it while pupils clean up.

Insist on good sharing from the start of the first term and on pupils asking politely for materials.

Group and pairwork

Pupils are encouraged throughout the units to work together in pairs and in groups. This will take time for pupils of this age to get used to. Praise pairs and groups who work well together. The opening pages of each unit also encourage pupils to reflect on how well they have worked in a group and to reward themselves with a sticker for good collaboration. The *Work together* pages, every second unit, encourage pupils to make decisions together.

As you get to know the class you may want to consider how you would prefer to group pupils and who works best together. As much as possible, try to keep pupils mixed in ability and encourage collaboration. There may be times, however, where pupils working in ability groups will enable you to better address learning needs.

Seating arrangements

Group work has an impact on seating arrangements in the classroom. Try to design a seating arrangement that will require the least amount of moving. Have pupils practise moving their desks quickly, quietly and carefully from rows to groups and back to rows again.

Pupils at this age need to move around, therefore, having a space in the classroom where pupils or small groups of pupils can sit in a circle on the floor and do a variety of the activities presented in each lesson (opening activities, talking about experiences, observing and passing round objects, etc.) would be ideal.

Space for miming, action chants and language games, is very important. If you don't have space in the classroom, try to make going out to the playground for short bursts, at least once a week, part of your routine.

Time

Managing time is a key factor in covering any syllabus. If you have short sessions (less than 45 minutes) be selective when planning what to cover and don't try to do everything. Opening and closing activities can be shortened and lengthened depending on your time.

Be realistic when planning, this will help you manage your time expectations. At this age, pupils' fine motor skills are still developing and they will need more time for writing and drawing. Until pupils are into a good routine for using and putting away materials, this can be slow in the first term. Teaching in a bilingual context also has time implications. Pupils need more reinforcement in learning a new language as well as understanding the concepts in that language. Time for recycling vocabulary, new language and concepts must be an important aspect of your lesson plan.

Make sure that you move from once activity to another quickly and smoothly. Distracted and undesirable behaviour can quickly ensue if there is too much waiting between activities. Having your material and resources at the ready can cut down unwanted disruptions. Having pupils sing the unit chant, do a breathing exercise, or a simple miming game can help shift focus and change the pace of the class. Keep them engaged!

There are pupils who will be faster at completing tasks than others. Have ready short simple activities for them to do. These can include helping with displays, tidying up, labelling, helping others, spelling practice on mini whiteboards, etc. Visiting a corner or area in the classroom with resource books relevant to the topic pupils are studying, is also a good habit for pupils to get into.

Lessons that include taking pupils out of the classroom need to be carefully planned and perhaps completed over two sessions in order to collect all the necessary results and discuss the pupils' observations. However, if it is not possible for you to take your class outside, slide presentations are suggested as an alternative.

Cooperative Learning

What is Cooperative Learning?

Cooperative Learning (CL) is an educational situation in which pupils are required to work together in small groups or teams to support each other in order to improve their own learning and that of others. CL goes beyond merely seating pupils together; simply telling them they are a group does not mean they will cooperate effectively. For pupils to behave cooperatively, and to reach their full potential within a group or team, they will need some essential elements.

What are the basic principles of Cooperative Learning? (Johnson, Johnson & Holubec, 2008)

1. Positive interdependence

Pupils perceive that they need each other in order to complete the group's task. Every pupil in a small group must contribute to the learning of the group, and each member needs the others to complete the task. We can enhance positive interdependence by establishing mutual goals which *"will help each student to learn and make sure all other team members learn"* (Johnson, Johnson & Holubec, 2008).

2. Individual accountability

"Each student's performance is assessed and the results are given to that student and the rest of the members of the group" (Johnson, Johnson & Holubec, 2008). Therefore each member of the group is responsible for completing their part of the work and must develop a sense of personal responsibility towards him or herself and the rest of the group, because individual performance will affect not only one's own result, but also the rest of the members' results.

3. Promotive interaction

"Students promote each other's learning by helping, sharing, and encouraging efforts to learn" (Johnson, Johnson & Holubec, 2008). CL implies face-to-face interaction. Pupils need not only to discuss and agree but also to produce a piece of work through combined effort, because Cooperative Learning is not about working individually and make a 'cut-and-paste' final product.

4. Social abilities

Pupils need interpersonal skills in order to be successful. Some of them are:

- Effective leadership
- Decision-making
- Trust-building
- Communication
- Conflict resolution
- Helping and asking for help
- Organisation
- Self-esteem and self-confidence

Our pupils aren't born knowing how to behave in a group. We have to teach them, giving them models, and opportunities to practise these skills.

5. Group processing

Developing CL methodology is not easy at first, nor are the effects immediate. Difficulties within the groups, resources and management may arise. That is why formative assessment is needed. This assessment involves both teachers and pupils.

One way of structuring group assessment is by:

- Listing at least three member actions that helped the group be successful (pupils).
- Listing at least one action that could make the group even more successful (pupils).
- Monitoring the groups and giving feedback on how well the groups are working together and the class as a whole (teacher) (Johnson, Johnson, & Holubec, 2008).

We need to know the strong and weak points in order to make the right decisions and develop the methodology in the right direction.

Why Cooperative Learning?

The benefits of using CL are supported by theory and are well-established by classroom research.

There are several reasons why CL works as well as it does:

- Pupils learn more by doing something active than by simply watching and listening, and CL is by nature an active method.
- Cooperation enhances learning. Less confident pupilsworking individually tend to give up when they get stuck, but when working as a part of a team they keep going.

- When strong pupils help and work together with less confident students, they often find gaps in their own understanding and fill them in.
- Pupils working alone may tend to delay or skip their assignments, but when they work as a part of a team and realise that others are counting on them, they will often feel more motivated and do the work in a timely manner.

Nevertheless, we should never forget that the benefits of CL are not automatic, and it takes time to work in a cooperative way.

Cooperative Learning structures (UNT, 2008)

Once the teacher has determined the objective of the lesson, he or she can select a structure that will provide the optimal learning experience for the student in a cooperative context. Learning structures are available for almost any learning situation.

Rally robin

In pairs, pupils alternate generation brief oral responses. (Kagan & Kagan, 2009)

Steps for the strategy:

1. Teacher poses a question/problem.
2. Pupils repeatedly take turns, answering orally. One answer at a time.

Timed pair share

In pairs, pupils share with a classmate for a predetermined time while the classmate listens. Then they switch roles. (Kagan & Kagan, 2009)

Steps for the strategy:

1. Pupils are paired and work in pairs.
2. Present a problem to the pupils.
3. Provide them with a specific amount of time to write their answers.
4. Pupils discuss their answers with either their face or shoulder partners.
5. Call on pupils to share with the class the answer they have developed with their partners.

Round robin

In teams, pupils take turns responding orally. (Kagan & Kagan, 2009)

Steps for the strategy:

1. Teacher asks a question.
2. Pupils take turns answering the question.

Rally coach

Pupils take turns, one solving a problem while the other coaches. Then they switch roles. (Kagan & Kagan, 2009)

Steps for the strategy:

1. Pupil A solves the first problem.
2. Pupil B watches, listens, checks, and praises.
3. Pupil B solves the next problem.
4. Pupil A watches, listens, checks, and praises.
5. Repeat starting at step one.

Stand up, hand up, pair up

Pupils stand up, put their hand up and quickly find a classmate with whom to share or discuss. (Kagan & Kagan, 2009)

Steps for the strategy:

1. Teacher says *Stand up, hand up, pair up as quickly as you can.*
2. Pupils stand up and keep one hand in the air until they find a partner.
3. High five your partner.
4. Teacher asks a question or gives an assignment.
5. Teacher provides thinking time.
6. Pupils share using method teacher gives.

The teacher's role in Cooperative Learning

Teachers should reinforce and help the pupils to know how to work in a group:

a. Taking care of the different cooperative skills the pupils will need to manage in order to work together effectively and efficiently. This is essential because all the elements derived from social interaction in the classroom depend on these cooperative skills.

b. Turning social interaction into promotive interaction. Teachers should make pupils reflect on the way they address their group mates: what they mean and how they sound.

c. Creating opportunities for inter-individual information intake (or processing) making them aware of their individual accountability.

d. Contemplating group assessment as an instrument for cooperative reflection to ensure the improvement of the cooperative structure. Teachers should help pupils identify their weak and strong points as a group and take the necessary actions.

Cooperative skills

Cooperative skills can be classified as (Johnson, Johnson, & Holubec, 2008):

Organisation skills: those related to group formation and organisation as well as establishing behavioural rules.

- Encouraging every member to participate
- Turn-taking
- Forming groups quickly with minimum noise
- Staying in the group
- Managing noise level
- Respecting other members' personal space
- Taking care of materials
- Paying attention to the person talking
- Respecting everybody's opinions

Working out skills: those devoted to completing the tasks and keeping efficient working relationships within the group.

- Reflecting on more efficient procedures
- Guiding task procedures
- Defining the purpose of the task
- Establishing time limits
- Expressing approval
- Asking for help
- Paraphrasing others' ideas
- Resolving conflicts
- Making shared decisions by negotiating and reaching a consensus

Formulation skills: those needed for a deep understanding of the concepts the pupils have acquired.

- Summarising
- Correcting others and adding information
- Scaffolding with previously-seen concepts
- Creating memorisation strategies
- Checking understanding
- Explaining how the task should be done

Processing skills: those targeted as raising socio-cognitive awareness to cultivate a more in-depth understanding. For example:

- Discussing ideas
- Integrating different ideas in one conclusion
- Improving the answers of other group members
- Verifying and contrasting the work produced with the instructions given

Group formation

Teachers should form the teams rather than letting the pupils to choose their own group members.

One of the fundamental aspects in structuring CL activities is the size of the groups. Ideally, form groups of three or four pupils. Pairwork doesn't usually produce the diversity of ideas and approaches common to CL. In groups of five or more, some pupils are likely to be inactive.

Make the groups heterogeneous in ability level. In heterogeneous groups, the less confident students learn from others, and the stronger students gain a deeper understanding of the subject by teaching it to their peers.

The Cooperative Learning session

There should be four different stages in every CL session:

1. Activation

This stage works as a warm-up. It is the moment for eliciting previous knowledge about the topic.

2. Introduction

The teacher introduces new content. This is the moment for giving instructions and explaining the 'why'.

3. Development

At this stage teamwork comes into action according to the strategies designed by the teacher.

4. Feedback

The feedback will provide very useful information to the teacher, who checks if the contents have been properly acquired.

And last but not least...

- If you've never used CL, consider starting with small group activities in class. Once you're comfortable with that, try a group project or assignment, up to a level of CL with which you are comfortable.
- At the start of the course, explain to pupils what they'll be doing in groups, what procedures you'll follow and what your expectations are.
- Make group assignments more challenging than traditional individual assignments. CL works best for challenging problems and activities that require higher-level thinking skills.
- A term assessment is essential to find out how pupils feel about teamwork. Ask the pupils to reflect on what works and doesn't work in their group. If many groups are experiencing the same problem, spend some time in class on the relevant cooperative skills. Most of the time, however, the assessment will show that most groups are working well.
- Expect initial resistance from pupils.

Further reading

ABRAMI, P.C. (1995). *Classroom connections: Understanding and using cooperative learning*. Toronto: Harcourt Brace.

JOHNSON, D.W., JOHNSON, R.T. & HOLUBEC, E.J. (2008). *Cooperation in the classroom* (8th ed.). Edina, New Mexico: Interaction Book Company.

KAGAN, S. (1992). *Cooperative learning*. San Juan Capistrano, California: Resources for Teachers, Inc.

SLAVIN, R. E. (1990). *Cooperative learning: Theory, research, and practice*. Englewood Cliffs, New Jersey: Prentice-Hall.

SLAVIN, R. E. (1995). *Cooperative learning* (2nd ed.). Boston: Allyn and Bacon.

UNIVERSITY OF NORTH TEXAS (2008). *Classroom best practices: Cooperative learning*. Texas: UNT in partnership with Department of Teacher Education and Administration.

UNIT 0

PAGES 4-5 Meet Sam and Amy

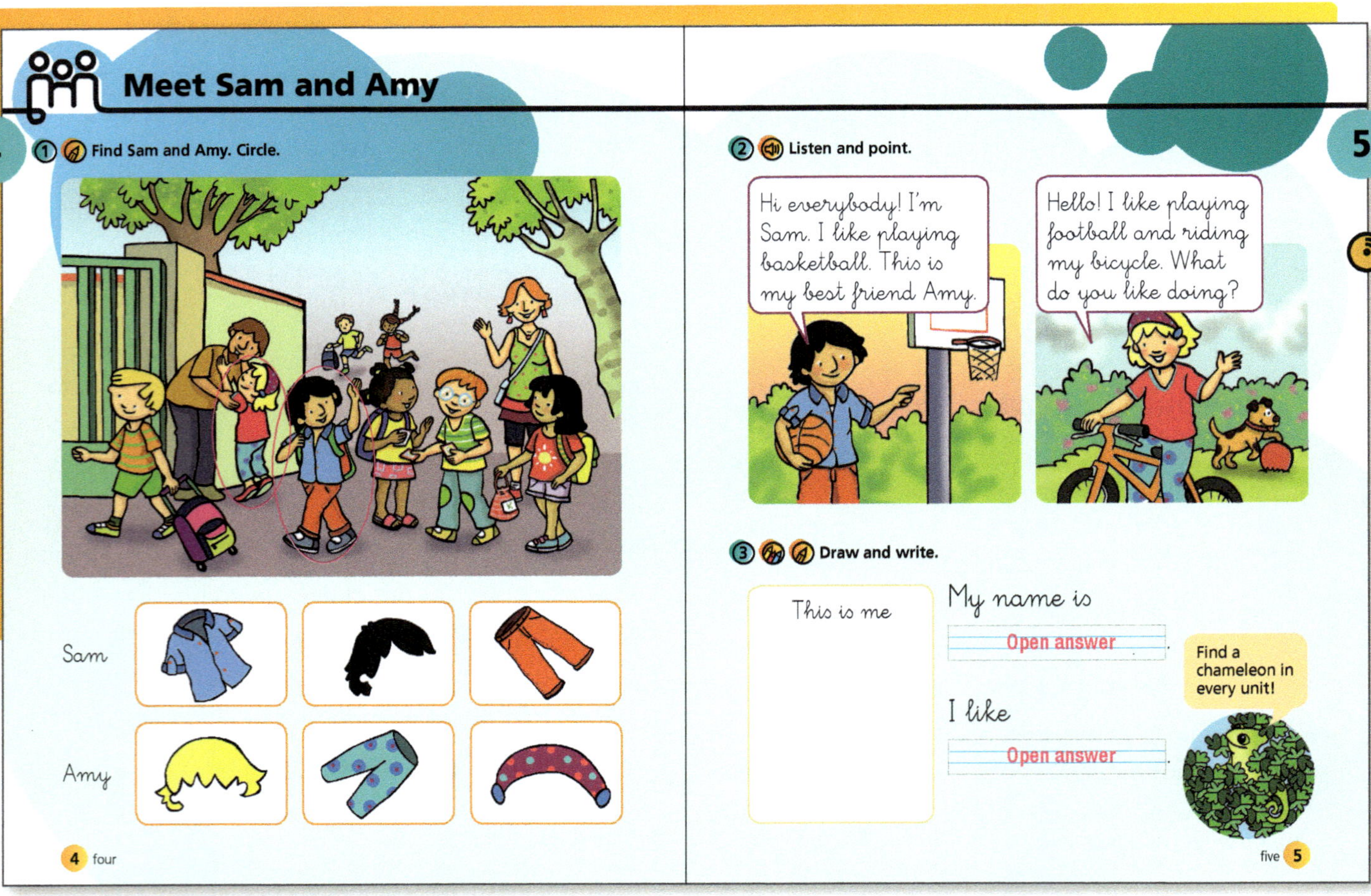

PAGE SUMMARY

Use these opening pages to introduce the pupils to the two main course characters and to familiarise yourself and the pupils with each other's names. Review classroom vocabulary and instructions and find out what vocabulary pupils know from prior learning (alphabet, numbers 1-20, colours, clothes).

LANGUAGE

- Hair, trousers, shirt, hair band, school, playground, gate, school bag, pupils, teacher
- Red, blue, yellow, green, orange, pink, purple, brown, black, white
- My name is (...). What's your name?
- I like playing basketball / riding my bicycle.
- Point to, touch, show me, stand up, sit down

MATERIALS

Flashcards: (digital) see the *Teachers* section in the digital resources

A NEW SCHOOL YEAR

It may be the first time you have this class for Social Science and some pupils may also be new to the school or have been regrouped from pre-school classes, so it's important to spend some time getting to know each other.

It is the beginning of the school year and the opening illustration is a good opportunity for pupils to show you what vocabulary they know for school, and for you to review and check pupils' understanding of simple classroom instructions.

It is important to use these first classes to set up your classroom rules and routines whilst also creating a relaxed and fun environment for pupils to learn in. Emphasise the importance of respecting the classroom environment and each other. Encourage pupils to think about how they should behave in class, how they can help each other and how they can best learn.

⊕ OPENING ACTIVITIES

- Wave and mouth the word **Hello**. Can pupils guess what you are saying? Encourage them to say *Hello* in different ways (slowly, loudly, quietly, quickly).
- Introduce yourself. Say **My name is (...).** Show pupils you have an imaginary ball. Throw the ball to a pupil and ask **What's your name?** Encourage them to catch the ball and answer *My name is (...).* Gesture for the pupil to throw the ball to another pupil. Pupils should say their name and throw the ball to another classmate. Continue in this way until everyone has had a chance to say their name. If you have space you can play the name game with pupils sitting in a circle on the floor and rolling a real ball to each other.

MAIN ACTIVITIES

1 Find Sam and Amy. Circle.

- Do a stick drawing of a boy on the board and write the name *Sam.* Say **This is Sam**. Ask pupils to repeat the name. Point to the letter S and ask pupils to tell you what letter it is. Do a stick drawing of a girl on the board and write the name *Amy.* Say **This is Amy**. Ask pupils to repeat the name. Point to the letter A and ask pupils to tell you what letter it is.
- Focus pupils' attention on the three pictures to help identify Sam on page 4. Use the zoom if using the interactive whiteboard. Point to the different children and say **Find Sam**. Walk around the classroom and praise the pupils for finding Sam. Repeat the step but this time to find Amy. *See answers opposite.*
- Focus on the smaller pictures and describe the two main characters. Say **Look, Sam has got brown hair. He is wearing a blue shirt and orange trousers. Amy has got blonde hair. She is wearing blue trousers and a pink hair band.**

2 Listen and point.

- Ask pupils to look at page 5. Point to Sam and ask **What can you see?** Ask pupils what other sports they know that need a ball.
- Say **Listen and point to Sam**. At the same time touch your ear and point to your book. Listen to Sam. Then do a stick drawing of a boy and draw a big speech bubble. Write *Hello. I'm ...* and encourage pupils to help you complete the information about Sam. Continue writing *I like ...* and again ask pupils for the missing information. Say **Now listen and point to Amy**. Repeat the steps above for Amy.

CD 1 • Track 04

Sam: **Hi everybody! I'm Sam. I like playing basketball. This is my best friend Amy.**

Amy: **Hello! I like playing football and riding my bicycle. What do you like doing?**

- Point to your stick drawings or the pictures of the two characters and repeat the sentences **I like playing basketball / I like playing football and riding my bicycle**. Throw an imaginary ball to a pupil and ask **What do you like doing?** Help them with their reply and write each activity on the board: *I like (rollerskating).* If an activity is repeated, simply put a tick beside it on the board. At the end, ask pupils to help you count the ticks to see how many pupils like playing football, riding bicycles, etc.

3 Draw and write.

- Draw a box on the board and write the incomplete sentences from activity 3. Draw yourself in the box and see if pupils can guess who it is! Read each sentence out loud and complete with your name and your favourite activity. Ask pupils to look at the activity in their books and see what materials they need (a pencil and coloured pencils). Encourage pupils to draw themselves and complete the sentences with their own information.

⊕ CLOSING ACTIVITIES

- Write a pupil's name on the board and have pupils read out the name. Say **Where is (María)?** Pupils point to that person. Ask them to read out their sentences from activity 3: *My name is (María), I like (playing tennis).*
- Call out the letters of the alphabet. Have pupils stand when they hear the first letter of their name. Those standing must tell you something else beginning with that letter.
- Ask pupils to listen and stand up if their answer to your question is *Yes!* (e.g. **Are you wearing blue trousers? Have you got a bicycle? Is your name Monica? Are you a boy?** etc.)

UNIT 1 My school

CONTENT	EVALUATION CRITERIA
School. Organisation, the class, classmates, materials, spaces.	Understand the basic roles and responsibilities of the members of the educational community.
Introduction to scientific knowledge and its application in the Social Sciences. Collect relevant information using different sources (direct and indirect).	Obtain specific and relevant information, using different sources.
Develop strategies to organise, memorise and remember information obtained through different methods and from different sources.	Develop a capacity for hard work and show perseverance while studying.
Team-building strategies.	Develop a cooperative and adaptive attitude, recognising merit in others' ideas and responding to situations with intuition, an open mind and flexibility.
Correct use of different materials.	Use the materials in a suitable way.
Friends.	Recognise that they belong to different social groups (family, school, group of friends, etc.), appreciating each group's particular characteristics. Participate in group activities, appreciating the norms of coexistence.
Techniques for intellectual work. Elaboration of diagrams and summaries, memorising and structuring the information received. Reading techniques for Social Science publications.	Employ techniques appropriate to intellectual tasks; produce work and make presentations both individually and as a group, involving research, selection and organisation of texts of a social, geographical or historical nature, while showing autonomy and collaborative skills.
With help, plan and manage simple projects, showing independence and initiative in order to achieve objectives.	Develop creativity and initiative, improving their capacity to acquire information and ideas and present innovative conclusions.
Conflict resolution strategies: use of rules and appreciation of peaceful and tolerant coexistence.	Recognise cooperation and dialogue as a way to avoid and resolve conflicts, encouraging democratic values.
Rights and obligations.	Identify rights and obligations in the context of the school.

LEARNING STANDARDS	KEY COMPETENCES	PAGES
Identifies the members of the educational community and describes and respects the tasks they carry out.	SOC, LIN	6–8
Knows and respects the rules of the classroom.	SOC	9, 10, 13
Values belonging to different social groups: school and class.	SOC	12
Knows different elements of the school: places, objects, materials and subjects.	SOC	6–11
Looks for, selects and organises information, analysing it and drawing conclusions. Reflects on the process followed and reports on it orally.	MST, LTL, LIN	14, 15
Performs academic tasks in a responsible and effective manner.	LTL, LIN	14, 15
Uses vocabulary correctly in the presentation of their work.	LTL, LIN	15
Expresses orally, carefully and clearly, contents related to the subject area.	LIN	15
Develops a cooperative and adaptive attitude, recognising merit in others' ideas and responding to situations with intuition, an open mind and flexibility.	LTL	7, 15
Participates effectively and constructively in daily life and develops strategies for conflict resolution.	LTL, SOC	10, 12, 13
Identifies and uses the correct code of conduct for their environment.	LTL, SOC	9, 10, 12, 13
Uses the materials in a suitable and careful way thereby keeping them in good condition.	LTL, SOC	10
Values belonging to different social groups (family, school, group of friends, etc.) recognising each group's particular characteristics.	LTL, SOC	12, 13
Participates in group activities in school (games, conversations, etc.)	LTL, SOC	10, 11, 12, 13
Respects their classmates and the norms established in the class.	LTL, SOC	12, 13
Produces work and makes presentations both individually and as part of a group, participating in the research, selection and organisation of texts of a social, geographical or historical nature.	SOC, AUT	6–15
Shows self-confidence, personal initiative, curiosity, interest and creativity in the learning process.	AUT, LTL	14, 15
Shows independence in the planning and carrying out of simple actions and shows initiative when taking decisions.	AUT, LTL	14
Values cooperation and dialogue as a way of avoiding and resolving conflicts.	SOC	12
Identifies their rights and obligations in the context of school.	SOC	9, 10, 13

UNIT INFORMATION

UNIT SUMMARY

This first unit about school enables pupils to ease back into a new term after the long summer holiday. New pupils to the school will have opportunities to explore and talk about their new setting.

Pupils will learn what it means to be part of a school as each lesson deals with a different aspect of school life. Pupils will consider not only the subjects that they study and the materials they need for those subjects, but they will also recognise the roles that different school staff play. They will reflect on their own role within the school and the importance of respecting school property and helping classmates.

Pupils will consolidate their vocabulary for classroom objects and materials from previous learning experiences. This should help pupils feel comfortable with the topic and help them deal with new language more confidently.

PROJECT

Let's investigate

In the *Let's investigate* activity on page 14, your pupils will make a visual timetable showing days and subjects.

The pupils need:

- A3 paper (one sheet per pupil)
- Ruler
- Felt tips, coloured pencils or crayons
- Scissors
- Glue

You may wish to help pupils with the timetable grid by photocopying a template onto A3 paper or by folding the A3 paper so pupils have a guide to help them draw the grid lines.

VALUES AND ATTITUDES

In this unit the pupils will understand the importance of looking after the places and objects around us at school. They will understand that good behaviour includes not only being tidy and organised, but also being kind and helping others. Throughout the unit, try to encourage pupils to think about:

- What we can do to keep our classroom tidy.
- How we can be organised.
- How we can be a good friend.

Make a difference

The *Make a difference* page in this unit links what we do in school with what we do outside school. In the pairwork activity the pupils review the activities they need to do to get ready for school by listening to a chant and drawing pictures.

EVALUATION MATERIAL

These documents can be downloaded from the *Teachers* section of the digital component and printed.

The materials include:

- **Unit diagnostic test:** provides an overview of the unit and allows you to assess the pupils' prior knowledge.
- **End-of-unit test:** in addition to the *Review* section at the end of each unit, this summative test can be used to evaluate pupils' progress after studying the unit content.
- **Class unit evaluation grid:** based on the evaluation criteria and learning standards of the unit.

DIGITAL RESOURCES

Presentations

- **Unit summary**: a simple slide presentation with text, images and audio to review the main ideas of the unit. It can be used at the beginning of the unit to test pupils' prior knowledge of the unit content or at the end of the unit as a revision tool.
- **Let's investigate**: a slide presentation of the unit's *Let's investigate* page with text, photos and audio. The slide presentation is perfect for a heads-up class, showing the steps one by one. Use this tool to get the pupils to predict the next steps (with their books closed) or to focus their attention on each step as they carry out the project themselves.

Activities

- **Memory game**: useful activity for reviewing key vocabulary and modelling pronunciation.
- **Wordsearch:** use at the end of the unit as a revision activity. Turn it into a game by getting the pupils to work in teams.
- **Spelling**: get a volunteer to come to the board and carry out the activity, but with the help of the whole class.

Song lyrics

Listen to the song *In the classroom* and follow the lyrics line by line.

Posters

Attractive and informative posters to display in class. You can use them to review key concepts and vocabulary.

Videos

Use the video links in this unit to present content in a dynamic, real-life context whilst reinforcing the pupils' listening skills.

Teachers

Digital flashcards: a bank of digital images which can be used in a variety of ways in class.

Downloadable pdfs: evaluation tests, evaluation grids, templates, useful links and further information.

PAGES 6-7 My school

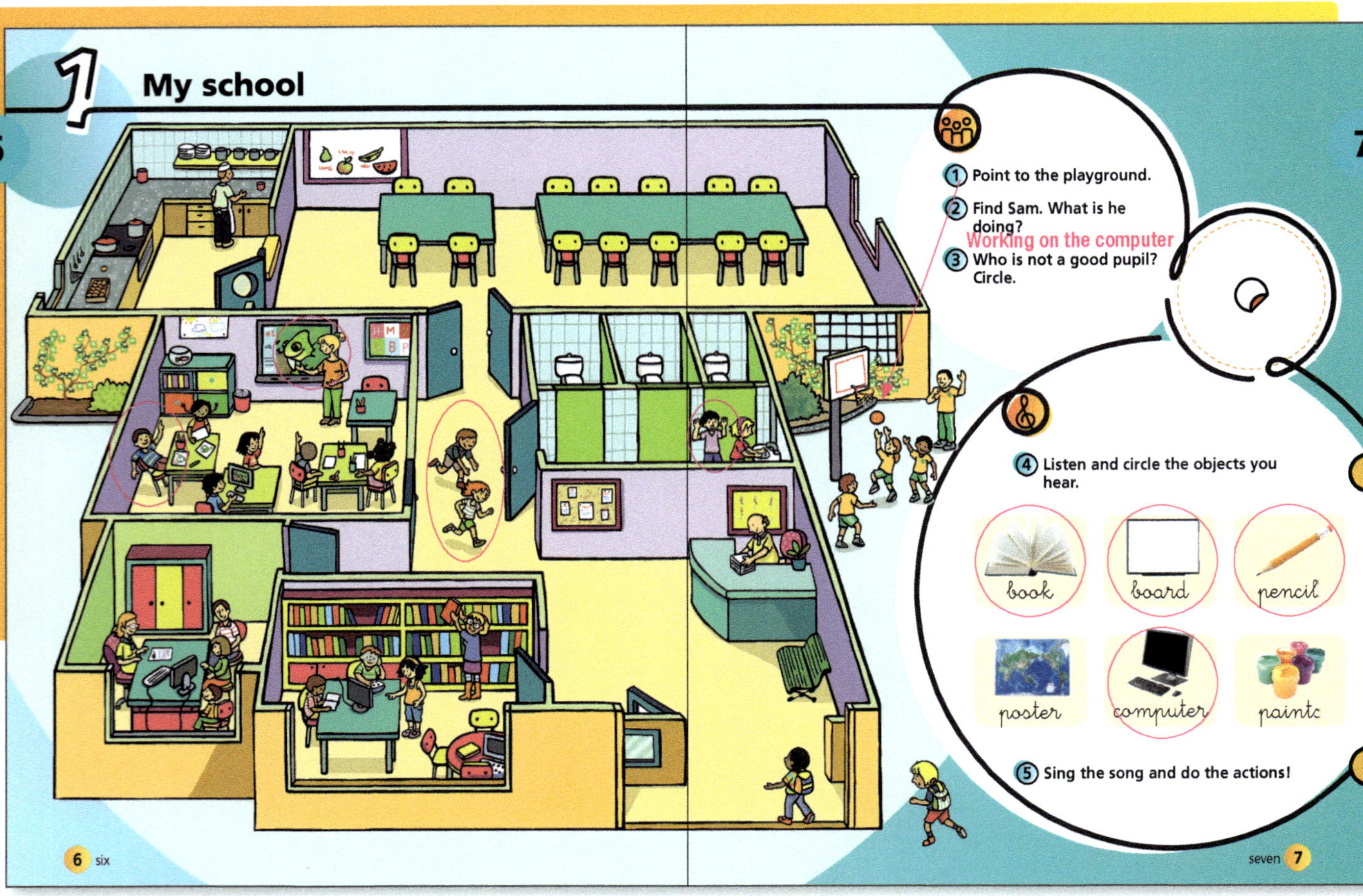

PAGE SUMMARY

The aim of the unit opener is to encourage your pupils' observation skills and find out what they already know about the topic of the unit. Use the illustration to elicit vocabulary related to school and identify the different activities which take place at school. Pupils answer the questions in groups then learn the actions to the song.

LANGUAGE

- Book, board, pencil, poster, computer, paints
- Playground, library, toilets, classroom, gym, dining hall
- What is it? What do you do in a library?
- What is he/she doing? He/she is running / playing / reading / listening.

MATERIALS

Flashcards: (digital) see the *Teachers* section in the digital resources

Additional classroom materials: soft ball

WHAT CAN YOU SEE?

Before your pupils open their books, introduce the class to the chameleon. Ask pupils if they have ever seen a real chameleon and if they know any information about them. You could show some images of chameleons and how they can change colour to fit their background. Ask pupils to close their eyes, put their heads down on folded arms and count to 12 slowly together. Hide a picture of a chameleon (or a soft toy chameleon if you have one) in the classroom but where pupils will be able to see it. Tell pupils to open their eyes and ask **Where is the chameleon?** When he has been found, tell pupils to open their books on pages 6 and 7. Repeat the question **Where is the chameleon?** *On the board.*

Hold up flashcards for places in a school and ask if pupils know the names. Put the flashcards around the classroom and name them as you do. Say **Point to the playground**. Then choose a volunteer and say **Go to the gym**. The pupil should go to this flashcard. Praise the pupil and ask the rest of the class **What can we do in the gym?** Repeat the activities with other volunteers and flashcards.

OPENING ACTIVITIES

- Ask pupils to stand or sit in a circle. Pass a ball round the class. Pupils must say their name and an activity they like doing, e.g. *My name is Carlos and I like swimming.*

MAIN ACTIVITIES

1 Point to the playground.

- Put pupils in groups and encourage them to find the playground. Ask **What are the children doing?** *Playing basketball.* Say **Point to the classroom / toilets / library / dining hall** and have pupils find the rooms in the picture. Ask **What do we do in the classroom / playground?** Encourage pupils to whisper the answer to their group first, then put their hands up to share with the rest of the class.

2 Find Sam. What is he doing?

- Review what Sam looks like by using phrases such as *Sam has got … / Sam is wearing …* Tell pupils to show a partner where Sam is. *In the classroom.* When they have found him, ask pupils what he is doing. *Working on the computer.* Repeat the procedure for Amy.

3 Who is not a good pupil? Circle.

- Tell pupils to close their books. Ask **Can you remember what the children are doing at school?** Have each group name one activity. Tell pupils to open their books. Read out the instruction and demonstrate what *circle* means. Encourage pupils to work in their groups to find the pupils who are not good. Discuss with your pupils why the behaviour is not good. *See answers opposite.*
- Praise the class for working together and ask pupils to choose a sticker for their effort of working with a group.

4 Listen and circle the objects you hear.

- Ask the pupils to look at the photos. Say the words and ask pupils to point to the objects and repeat the words with you.
- Focus pupils' attention on the musical note. Say **Let's listen to a song.** Tell pupils that they are going to listen to the song twice and circle the things they hear. Pause after each verse on the second listening to give them time to circle.

CD 1 • Track 05

See audio script below.

5 Sing the song and do the actions!

- Say **Now let's listen and do the actions.** Play the song, teach the actions and encourage pupils to copy. Repeat the song a couple of times and do the actions together.

CD 1 • Track 06

In the classroom, in the classroom there
are lots of things [x2] *[wave hands, gesture at classroom]*

Pencils, pencils *[wave pencils]*

Books, books *[point to books]*

Tables, tables *[lightly tap tables]*

Chairs, chairs *[stand up and point to chairs]*

In the classroom, in the classroom there
are lots of things [x2] *[wave hands, gesture at classroom]*

Children, children *[pupils wave hands]*

A computer, a computer *[point to computer]*

A teacher, a teacher *[point to teacher]*

A board, a board *[point to board]*

In the classroom, in the classroom there
are lots of things [x2] *[wave hands, gesture at classroom]*

CLOSING ACTIVITIES

- Choose a volunteer to come to the front and mime a school activity, e.g. *reading, working on the computer, listening,* etc. Ask the rest of the class to guess. Encourage other volunteers to mime.
- Play *I Spy* with the phonetic sounds of the alphabet.

EXTRA IDEAS

- Take a tour of the school and talk about the rooms and things you see.
- Have pupils draw their school. Exhibit their work.

PAGE 8 Is this my classroom?

PAGE SUMMARY

Use the story to identify different places in a school and recognise the roles of school staff. The stories are a good opportunity to focus on the course characters.

LANGUAGE

- Classroom, dining hall, office, library, playground, gym
- Head teacher, cook, teacher, caretaker
- Who is this? Where does he/she work?

MATERIALS

Flashcards: (digital) see the *Teachers* section in the digital resources

Additional classroom materials: photos of different staff members relevant to your pupils

OPENING ACTIVITIES

- Play the unit song and have pupils join in.
- Play *Quick flash*. Flash a flashcard or picture of *library* very quickly and ask pupils which room they saw. If they are correct, say **Yes, that's right. It's the library**. If the pupils guess incorrectly, say **No, try again** and flash the card again. Play with the remaining cards.
- Point to the *library* flashcard. Ask the pupils **What do we do in the library?** Mime reading and say **Read**. Encourage the pupils to join in with the mime, repeating the word as they do so. Repeat with the remaining places in a school: *dining hall (eat), gym (run), playground (play, either football or a clapping game), toilets (wash our hands) and classroom (write).*

MAIN ACTIVITIES

- Look around your classroom and ask pupils **Is this your classroom?** When they all shout *Yes!* ask pupils how they know. *Their bags are in the classroom, their work may be on the wall, the class name / number is on the door,* etc.

1 Listen, look and point.

- Ask pupils to open their Pupil's Books on page 8.
- Point to frame 1 and say **Look at the picture**. Ask **Who can you see?** Encourage pupils to say *Sam and Amy.* Point to the third person in the picture and ask **Who is this?** Say **It's the cook.** Say **Look. Where is the cook? In the classroom? In the gym?** Elicit *dining hall.* Say **Yes, that's right.** Place the *cook* picture and the *dining hall* picture together on the board.
- Repeat the procedure with the head teacher, the caretaker and the teacher, placing the picture of the person together with picture of the place they work on the board.
- Say **Let's listen to the story.** Play the audio.

CD 1 • Track 07

Is this my classroom?

Sam and Amy are looking for their classroom.

Frame 1

Amy: **Is this our classroom?**

Sam: **Hmmm ... I don't think so!**

Cook: **Hello children. This is the dining room.**

Frame 2

Sam: **Is this our classroom?**

Head teacher: **No, sorry children. This is the head teacher's office.**

Frame 3

Amy: **Oh no! This isn't our classroom!**

Caretaker: **No, but don't worry children. I know where your classroom is.**

Frame 4

Sam: **Phew! This is our classroom.**

Amy: **Hurrah!**

Teacher: **Welcome Sam. Welcome Amy. Sit down and let's start the class.**

- Focus pupils' attention on each frame of the story or use the zoom on the interactive whiteboard. Point to the cook and say **This is the ... He works in the ...** Pause after each sentence and encourage pupils to finish it for you. Repeat for the remaining three frames.

2 Match.

- Focus pupils' attention on activity 2 and read the instruction. Encourage pupils to trace a line with their finger from each person to their corresponding area. Encourage pupils to say *A cook works in the dining hall.* Repeat the procedure with the *teacher* and *caretaker* before asking pupils to match with a pencil. *See answers opposite.*

CLOSING ACTIVITIES

- Put flashcards or pictures of the school staff in a vertical line on one side of the board. Jumble flashcards or pictures of the places in a school and put them in a vertical line on the other side of the board. Point to the first flashcard and say **Who is this?** Point to each of the flashcards opposite, asking **Does he/she work in the dining hall / the gym / the office?** Draw a line to the correct flashcard. Repeat the procedure with the other staff flashcards.
- Hold up a flashcard of a place in the school, say the name and have pupils mime an activity they do there.

EXTRA IDEAS

- Take photos of different staff members (the cook, caretaker, P.E. teacher, librarian, secretary, nurse, etc.). Show the photos to your class and elicit / introduce their job titles. Ask pupils where they work in the school. Visit these staff members and have pupils ask their names. Write down their names and later make a *Who's who* poster to display in class.
- Use the photos to revise descriptions: *He/she has got brown hair. He/she is wearing glasses / black trousers,* etc.

PAGE 9 Write, play, run!

PAGE SUMMARY

Your pupils will establish what we do at school and where. They will identify different classroom materials and equipment, and learn the importance of looking after these items.

LANGUAGE

- Classroom, dining hall, gym, playground, bathroom, head teacher's office
- Coloured pencils, paints, books, chair, desk, basketball net, cat, duck, frying pan
- Show me, point, touch, pick up, stand next to
- Where do we eat / play / read?

MATERIALS

Flashcards: (digital) see the *Teachers* section in the digital resources

Additional classroom materials: slide presentation showing different areas of your school

OPENING ACTIVITIES

- Write the vowels *a, e, i, o, u,* on the board and explain that these letters are called *vowels*. Write the word *classroom* on the board with the vowels missing *(cl _ ssr_ _ m)*. Point to each space and elicit the missing vowel. Repeat with other school words, e.g. *playground, library.*
- Play *Where am I?* Look at one of your pictures of a place in a school, e.g. *library.* Do the corresponding mime (mime reading) and ask the pupils **Where am I?** Pupils should answer *In the library.* Repeat for a different area. After a couple of turns, show one of the flashcards to a volunteer and encourage them to perform the mime for the rest of the class to guess. Repeat with the remaining flashcards and different volunteers.
- If you took photos of school staff members for the previous lesson, identify again who they are, where they work and what their names are.

MAIN ACTIVITIES

1 Listen and colour.

- If you made a slide presentation of the different areas in your school, show it and have pupils identify the different places. Elicit what activities they do in each place.
- Ask pupils to open their Pupil's Books on page 9. Focus on each picture and ask **What is he/she doing?** After each picture, say **Show me how you skip / wash your hands,** etc.
- Draw pupils' attention to the different coloured circles. Say **Blue circle** and have pupils mime what the child is doing in that picture. Repeat with the other coloured circles.
- Focus pupils' attention on the photos. Point to each one in turn and ask **Where is this?** Elicit the name and what pupils do in these areas at school.
- Explain that pupils are going to match the photos with the activities. Play the audio. Pause after each description and ask **What colour is the gym?** etc. Play the audio again, pausing so pupils have time to colour. *See answers opposite.*

CD 1 • Track 08

We do exercise in the gym. Can you see the gym? Colour the gym blue.

We wash our hands in the toilets. Can you see the toilets? Colour the toilets green.

We eat lunch in the dining hall. Can you see the dining hall? Colour the dining hall orange.

We play with our friends in the playground. Can you see the playground? Colour the playground purple.

We write in the classroom. Can you see the classroom? Colour the classroom red.

2 What can you see in your classroom? Circle.

- Walk around the classroom and elicit the names of some classroom features or materials. Touch the board and say **What is this?** or **Is this a window?** Elicit the names of the bookshelves, desks, a rubbish bin, a classroom cupboard, sink, etc. Ask for other information. **What do we keep on the bookshelves? What do we put in the bin?** etc.
- Say **Point to the bookshelves / bin / cupboard.** Extend the activity by calling on volunteers and asking them to stand next to / touch / pick up the items you name.
- Focus pupils' attention on the photos in activity 2. Point to each photo in turn and ask **Is this in our classroom?** If pupils answer *Yes,* say **Show me** and ask pupils to point to or hold up the item.
- Read the instruction and have pupils follow in their books. Ask pupils to circle the objects in their classroom. *See answers opposite.*

Reading (CD 1. Track 09)

- Ask pupils to look at the reading box. Say **Let's listen and read.** Play the audio and encourage pupils to follow in their books. Make sure that pupils understand what *looking after* means and demonstrate, for example, by putting the tops on your marker pens and saying **I'm looking after my pens.** Ask pupils if Sam is looking after his classroom materials. *Yes, he is.*

CLOSING ACTIVITIES

- Ask pupils to show you different ways they can look after their classroom materials (e.g. *putting things back in their pencil cases, washing paint brushes,* etc.)
- Play Clever *chameleon says (point to / touch classroom materials).* Hold up the chameleon picture or soft toy and explain that when the clever chameleon says an instruction they must do it, but if he doesn't then they mustn't move.

EXTRA IDEAS

- Play *Guess my word.* Start to write one of the classroom words on the board e.g. *bookshelves.* Encourage pupils to say what the word is before you finish spelling it. Repeat with other classroom words (*cupboard, sink, bin, desk, clock, computer, poster,* etc.).
- Have pupils choose a word and make a label for the objects in their classroom (make sure pupils don't all write the same word by asking which word they want to write and putting a tick by the word). Look around the class and read the labels together once they are in place.

PAGE 10 My classroom

PAGE SUMMARY

Your pupils will identify classroom equipment and materials, identify responsible behaviour at school and learn the importance of a tidy classroom.

LANGUAGE

- Pencil case, pencil, sharpener, rubber, crayons
- Keep tidy, look after, put away, hang up, pick up, throw in the bin
- Is this in your pencil case? Yes, it is. / No, it isn't.
- Can you see a desk in the classroom? Yes, we can. / No, we can't.

MATERIALS

Flashcards: (digital) see the *Teachers* section in the digital resources

Additional classroom materials: six copies of a chameleon picture, cloth bag with classroom items inside

OPENING ACTIVITIES

- Play *Where is the chameleon?* Before pupils enter the classroom, place six pictures of the chameleon (numbered 1-6) in different places around the classroom, e.g. on the bookshelves, next to the bin, on a cupboard, etc. Ask pupils to look around the classroom and tell you how many chameleons they can see. Ask **Where is chameleon number 1?** Encourage pupils to describe where he is, e.g. *He's on the cupboard.* Ask another information question, e.g. **What is in the cupboard?** Continue for all the chameleons.
- Ask pupils questions about their classroom. Ask **Can you see a bicycle in the classroom? Can you see a desk in the classroom?** Encourage pupils to answer *Yes, we can. / No, we can't.*
- Play *I Spy* with classroom items using the phonetic sounds of the alphabet.

MAIN ACTIVITIES

1 What is in your pencil case? Draw lines.

- Play *What is in my pencil case?* Before the start of the lesson, hide the following objects in a big pencil case: pencil, rubber, pencil sharpener, scissors, glue stick, crayon. Create interest by asking **What is in my pencil case?** Take out the first item and elicit its name, e.g. *a pencil.* Say **Show me a pencil** and have the children hold up their own pencil. Repeat for the other items in your pencil case.
- Ask pupils to open their Pupil's Books on page 10 and look at the photos. Say **Point to the rubber.** Check that pupils are pointing to the rubber. Say **Now let's read the word.** Encourage pupils to run their finger under the word as they read. Repeat with the other photos and words.
- Point to each photo again and ask **Is this in your pencil case?** If the answer is *Yes,* have pupils draw a line from the item to the pencil case. *See answers opposite.*

2 Who is a good pupil? Tick (✔).

- Take some pieces of scrap paper, scrunch them up and theatrically throw the pieces onto the floor. Ask them **Is that right?** The pupils will say *No!* and (hopefully) point you in the direction of the bin. Say **Yes, that's right! We need to keep our classroom tidy.** Empty the contents of your pencil case onto your desk and pretend to leave the class, waving goodbye. Ask again **Is that right?** Pupils should tell you to put your things in your pencil case. Say **Yes, that's right! We need to look after our things and keep the classroom tidy.**
- Focus pupils' attention on the first picture in the activity. Ask **Is he a good pupil?** *Yes.* Explain that the pupil is very good because he is putting the rubbish in the bin. Point to the second picture and ask **Is she a good pupil?** *No.* Elicit the reason why and explain that we mustn't throw rubbish on the ground, inside or out. Repeat for the remaining two pictures. *See answers opposite.*

Reading (CD 1. Track 10)

- Ask pupils to look at the reading box. Say **Let's listen and read.** Play the audio and encourage pupils to follow in their books. Ask pupils **Is Amy is keeping the classroom tidy?** *Yes.* Elicit or explain that she is hanging up her coat.
- Ask pupils where they hang up their coats, where they keep their pencils and rubbers, where they put their school bag in class, where they put rubbish, where they store classroom materials, and where they keep their books. Say **Remember, it's important to look after your things and keep the classroom tidy.**

CLOSING ACTIVITIES

- Play *Find the classroom materials.* Place classroom materials into a cloth bag, naming each one as you do so. Choose a pupil and say **Find the book.** The pupil must put their hand into the bag and pull out the requested item.
- With more confident classes you can give out all the classroom materials to pupils sitting in teams. Pupils take turns to pick up the items you request. At the end of the game, have pupils put the items away, making sure they remember where each item goes.

EXTRA IDEAS

- Give each pupil a sheet of paper and say **This is the classroom.** Tell them they are going to draw the things you say. Demonstrate first on the board by drawing the first object you say. Say **Draw a pencil. Draw two rubbers. Draw a pencil sharpener,** etc.
- Set up a simple role play, where pupils have to ask each other politely for classroom items, e.g. *Can I have the glue, please? Yes, here you are. Thank you.*

PAGE 11 School subjects

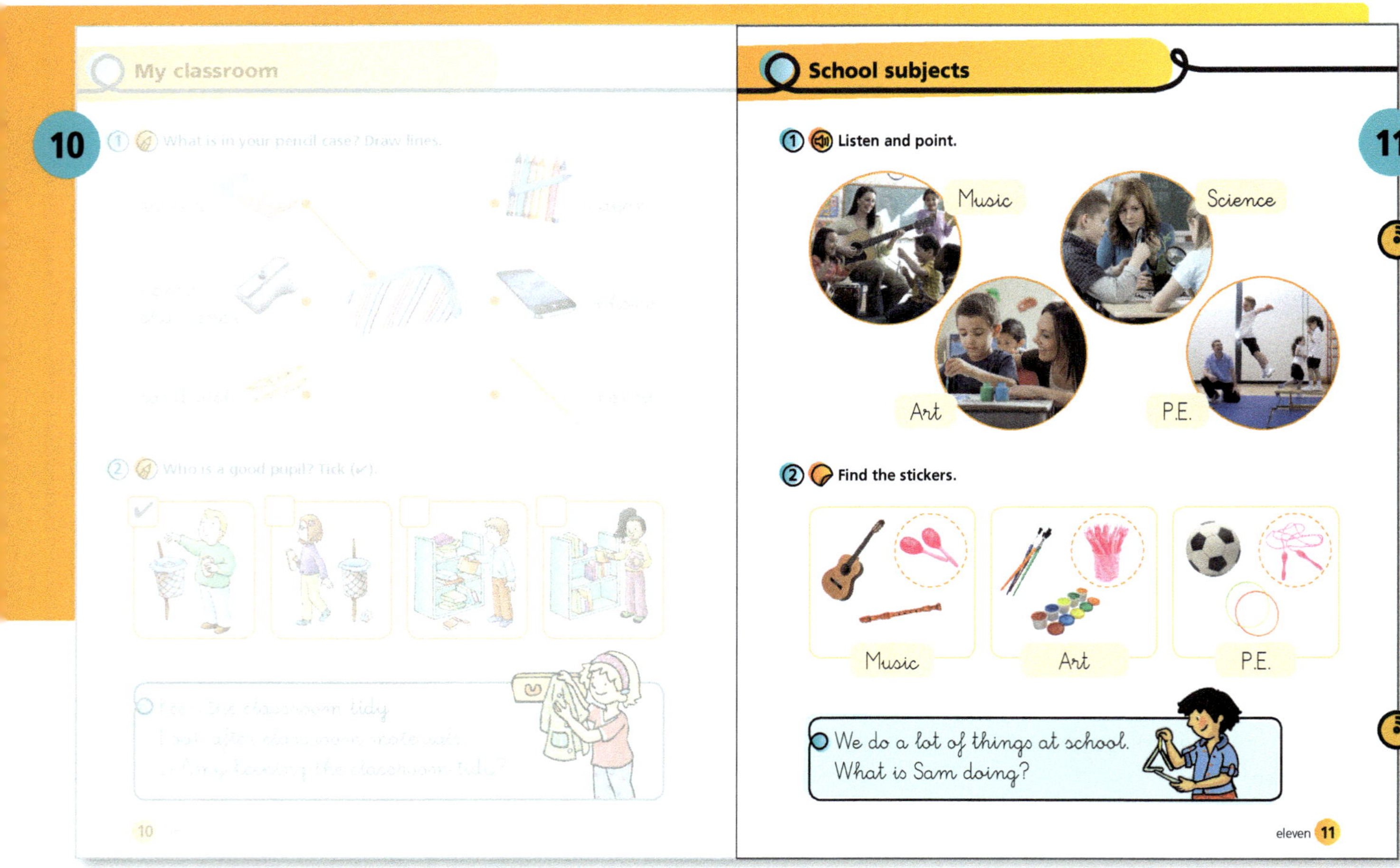
My classroom

10

① What is in your pencil case? Draw lines.

② Who is a good pupil? Tick (✓).

10

School subjects

11

① Listen and point.

Music

Science

Art

P.E.

② Find the stickers.

Music

Art

P.E.

We do a lot of things at school.
What is Sam doing?

eleven 11

PAGE SUMMARY

Your pupils will establish what we do at school, recognise that we study different school subjects and identify the materials we need to study different subjects.

LANGUAGE

- Music, Science, Art, P.E.
- Paint, draw, write, run, jump, play an instrument
- What is he/she doing? He/she is playing an instrument.

MATERIALS

Flashcards: (digital) see the *Teachers* section in the digital resources

Additional classroom materials: some equipment used in Science (e.g. magnifying glass, ruler, tweezers, camera, jar, etc.)

OPENING ACTIVITIES

- Play *Guess what this is*. Choose a volunteer and say **Close your eyes.** Put one of the classroom materials in their hands. The volunteer should try to guess which object they are holding. Repeat with a different volunteer.
- Play *Clever chameleon says.* Have pupils stand up. Instruct pupils to touch / pick up / point to different items in the classroom. If they do the action without hearing the words *Clever chameleon says,* they must sit down.
- Mime good behaviour, e.g. cleaning the board. Ask **Is this good behaviour?** *Yes.* Ask pupils to work with a partner and think of good behaviour they can mime or demonstrate to the class (e.g. *putting rubbish in the bin, asking for items politely, putting books back on the shelves, sharpening pencils over the bin, not throwing things across the classroom,* etc.). At the end of the activity, praise pupils for knowing how to behave in class and around school.

MAIN ACTIVITIES

1 Listen and point.

- Show a picture or flashcard of *school* and ask pupils to help you spell the word *school* on the board. Elicit from pupils all the things they do at school. Use mime to help them remember if necessary. Encourage them to say *We read / write / play / run / listen / walk / sing / tidy up / wash our hands / speak English,* etc.
- Tell pupils that we study different subjects at school. Ask them which subject they are studying at the moment. Ask **What is this subject?** *Science.*
- Ask pupils to open their Pupil's Books on page 11 and look at activity 1. Focus their attention on the Music class and read **Music.** Repeat for the other photos.
- Play the audio and ask pupils to listen to the sounds in the classroom and then to point to and name the correct subject as they listen.

CD 1 • Track 11

Music. In Music we sing songs and play instruments.

Science. In Science we do experiments and learn about the world.

Art. In Art we paint pictures and make crafts.

P.E. In P.E. we run, jump and play. Hooray!

- Focus pupils' attention on the photo of the Music class once again and ask **What do we do in Music?** Elicit activities that pupils do in Music, e.g. *In Music we sing / play a recorder / clap / dance,* etc. Repeat the procedure for the other subjects, e.g. *In Art we draw / paint / cut out. In P.E. we run / jump / play football.* Finally, focus the pupils' attention on the Science picture and elicit as many activities as possible, e.g. *In Science we write / read / draw / think / colour / cut out / investigate.*

2 Find the stickers.

- Focus pupils' attention on the three boxes of items. Point to each one in turn and encourage pupils to name the subject. Ask pupils to read the word underneath to check.
- Point to *Music* and ask **What do you need?** Point to and name the guitar and recorder. Ask pupils to find the missing sticker (at the back of the book). Ask **What is it?** Elicit or teach the name of the missing instrument. *Maracas.*
- Repeat the procedure for the remaining boxes and subjects. *See answers opposite.*
- Hold up and name some things you might use in a Science class, e.g. a magnifying glass, a tape measure, a camera, tweezers, a jar, etc. and describe how we use them.

Reading (CD 1. Track 12)

- Ask pupils to look at the reading box. Say **Let's listen and read.** Play the audio and encourage pupils to follow in their books. Ask pupils what Sam is doing. *Playing a triangle.* Ask pupils what instruments they can play.

CLOSING ACTIVITIES

- Repeat the question from the beginning of the class **What things do we do at school?** This time, encourage pupils to name the subjects they study and the activities they do in those subjects.
- Mime the school subjects and encourage pupils to name the subject you are miming, e.g. *Music* (mime singing), *P.E.* (mime jumping or running), *Art* (mime painting a picture), *Science* (mime observing something).

EXTRA IDEAS

- Ask pupils **What is your favourite subject?** Encourage them to name the subject they like best. If you have a confident class, allow the pupils to perform a survey in small groups. Record the results in a bar chart on the board.
- If you have a confident class, teach the vocabulary for the remaining subjects pupils study at school, e.g. *English, Maths, Language, Religion, French, German,* etc.

PAGE 12 My new friends

PAGE SUMMARY

Encourage your pupils to consider how to be a good friend to others and to recognise kind and helpful acts.

LANGUAGE

- My name is (...). I'm six years old.
- How many children are there? How many boys / girls are there? Thereare 10 boys.
- Be kind / a good friend.
- I'm sorry. Let's play.

MATERIALS

Flashcards: see the *Teachers* section in the digital resources

OPENING ACTIVITIES

- Mime a school activity (painting, jumping, playing the recorder, writing, etc.). Have pupils guess what you are doing and name the subject (there may be more than one possibility). Encourage volunteers to mime in front of classmates.
- Play *Repeat if true.* Tell pupils you are going to tell them some things about their school. Ask them to repeat your sentences if they think they are true. For example, say **There is a gym / playground / cinema / music room / swimming pool / dining room / library / shop at our school.**
- Play a counting game. Tell pupils that they must listen carefully to carry on the counting when you point to them. Say **One.** Point to a random pupil and encourage them to say *Two,* point to another pupil and encourage them to say *Three*, etc. Tell pupils it is important that they are listening and paying attention. See how far you can count to.

MAIN ACTIVITIES

1 Write and draw a picture of you.

- Ask pupils to say the alphabet. Write the letters one under the other on the board.
- Point to A and **say Stand up if your name begins with /a/.** Write the names of any pupils whose names begin with /a/ on the board next to the letter A. Run through the alphabet asking for names in the same way. Once you have all the names on the board (some may be repeated), read through the list together.
- Call out random letters and say **Stand up if your name begins with /t/, /r/, /k/,** etc. When pupils stand up, ask them **What is your name? How old are you?** Encourage pupils to answer *My name is (...), I'm (six) years old.* Have pupils sit down after they have answered.
- Count the pupils one by one. Ask **How many children are there?** Encourage the pupils to count with you. Then ask **How many boys are there?** This time, count only the boys. Draw a simple boy's face on the board and write the number of boys. Ask **How many girls are there?** Count only the girls. Draw a girl's face and write the number of girls under the number of boys. Ask the pupils to help you do the sum.
- Ask pupils to open their Pupil's Books on page 12 and focus their attention on the instruction. Have pupils follow as you read it out. Draw a box on the board and draw a picture of yourself. Read and write the sentence *My name is ...* on the board and add your name. Continue with the second sentence *I'm ... years old.* Add your age. Finally, write the last sentence and ask how many pupils they counted in the class. Write the number in your sentence.
- Say **Now it's your turn. Write your name** (point to the first line), **how old you are** (point to the second line) **and how many children are in the class.** Have pupils draw a picture of themselves in the box.
- Walk round and make sure pupils are filling in the information correctly.

2 Who is a good friend? Circle.

- Ask **Are you a good friend at school?** Encourage pupils to give you examples of being a good friend.
- Focus pupils' attention on the first picture of activity 2. Read the instruction. Point to the first picture and ask **Is the boy a good friend?** *Yes.* Say **Yes, that's right, the boy is helping the girl. He is a good friend.** Point to the next picture and ask **Is the girl a good friend?** *No.* Say **That's right. The girl isn't a good friend. She isn't sharing her ball / playing with the other girl.** Repeat the questions and procedure for the remaining two pictures.
- Ask pupils to circle only the good friends. *See answers opposite.*

Reading (CD 1. Track 13)

- Ask pupils to look at the reading box. Say **Let's listen and read.** Play the audio and encourage pupils to follow in their books. Ask pupils **Is Amy a good friend?** *Yes.* Encourage pupils to explain why. *She is sharing with her friends.*

CLOSING ACTIVITIES

- Ask the pupils how they feel when somebody is not being a good friend: happy or sad?
- Have pupils walk around the class, smiling to each other, asking *How are you today?* And responding *I'm great, thank you!*

EXTRA IDEAS

- Ask pupils to work in pairs to act out a scene showing how to be a good friend. Encourage pupils to use expressions such as *I'm sorry / Let's be friends / Let's play / Let me help you.*
- Have groups play a simple board game to promote politeness and turn-taking, e.g. *It's my / your turn, well done.*

PAGE 13 My new school

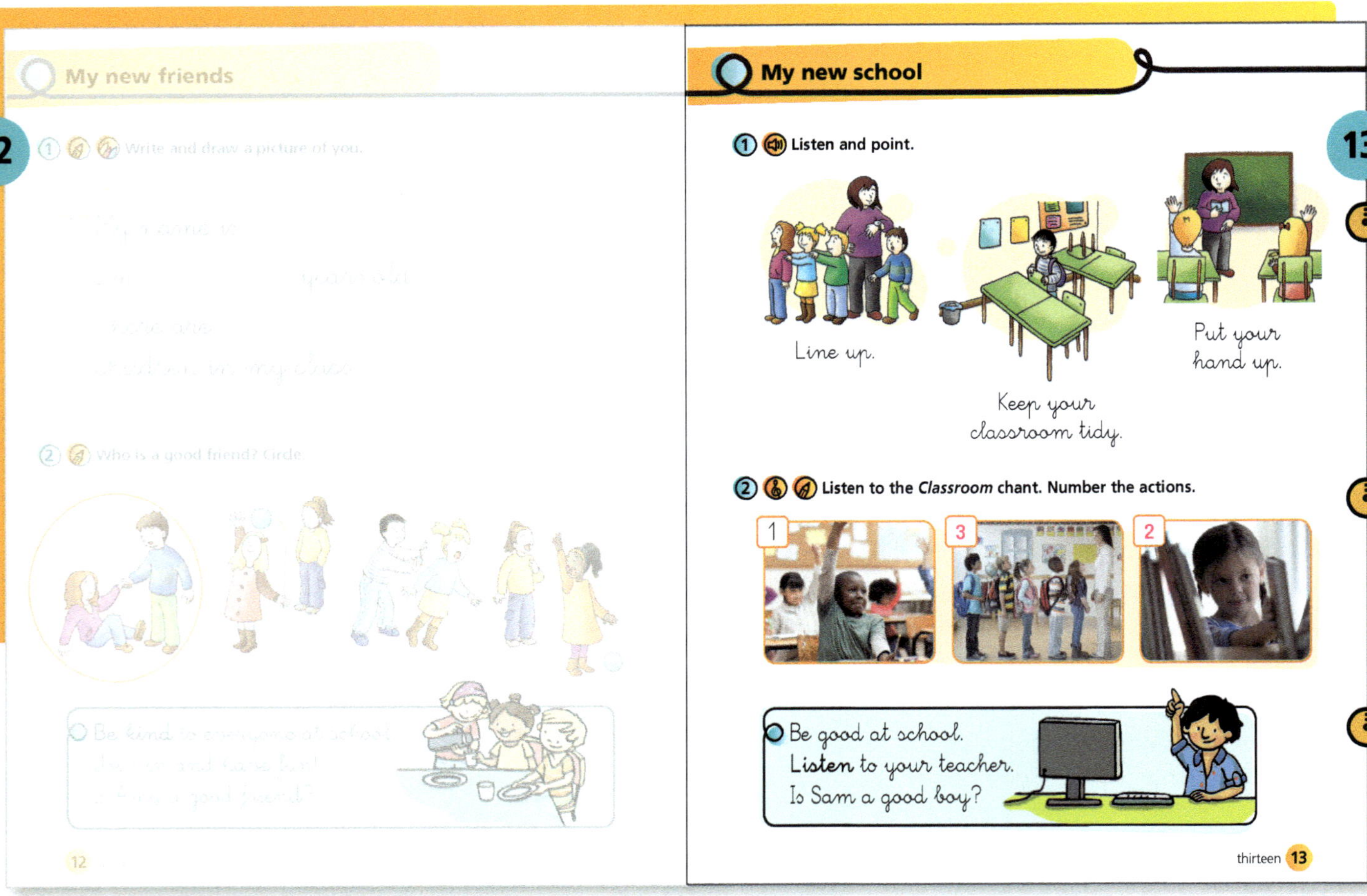

My new friends

12

1 Write and draw a picture of you.

My new school

13

1 Listen and point.

Line up.

Keep your classroom tidy.

Put your hand up.

2 Listen to the *Classroom* chant. Number the actions.

1 3 2

Be good at school.
Listen to your teacher.
Is Sam a good boy?

thirteen 13

PAGE SUMMARY

Pupils learn about good behaviour in the classroom and the importance of behaving properly.

LANGUAGE

- Line up. Put your hand up. Keep your classroom tidy.
- Listen to your teacher. Be good at school.

MATERIALS

Flashcards: (digital) see the *Teachers* section in the digital resources

Additional classroom materials: long strips of coloured card, digital camera

OPENING ACTIVITIES

- Play *Clever chameleon says*. Have pupils stand up. Give instructions for pupils to touch / pick up / point to different items in the classroom. If they do the action without hearing *Clever chameleon says,* they must sit down.
- Practise lining up. Say **Let's practise lining up.** Practise taking pupils around the school from one area to another.

  Note: Getting children into the class in an orderly manner can cut down on control problems once in the classroom. If children walk in calmly, they will be ready to start straight away and you can gain valuable time.
- Remind pupils about being a good friend. Encourage them to ask each other for different objects around the classroom, e.g. *Can I have some paper / a pencil / a rubber / glue / a pencil sharpener?* etc. Encourage pupils to use this language throughout the classes and always share their things with each other.

MAIN ACTIVITIES

1 Listen and point.

- Walk around the class and say **Let me see who is behaving well.** Praise different pupils as you walk around, e.g. **I can see (Juan) is paying attention, (Lucía) is sitting properly, (Roberto's) desk is very tidy, (Sofía) is listening,** etc.
- Tell pupils you are going to name some classroom materials. Explain that you are not going to speak, only mouth the word. Tell pupils to put their hands up when they think they know the word. The activity must be done in silence, with no shouting out. Mouth the word *paper*. Point to one pupil and ask **What is my word?** Check with the rest of the class **Is that right?** Repeat with different classroom materials.
- Tell pupils to open their Pupil's Books on page 13. Point to each picture and ask **What can you see?** Focus pupils' attention on the sentence under each picture. Read each one and have pupils follow with their fingers. Say **Listen and point.** Play the audio.

CD 1 • Track 14

Line up. Line up.

Keep your classroom tidy. Keep your classroom tidy.

Put your hand up. Put your hand up.

- Talk about the importance of behaving well, respecting turn-taking and keeping the classroom tidy.

2 Listen to the *Classroom* chant. Number the actions.

- Look at each photo and ask pupils **What can you see?** Focus pupils' attention on the musical note. Say **Let's listen to the *Classroom* chant.** Play the audio and have pupils point to each picture as they hear the action. Ask **Which picture is number 1?** Play the audio again and pause after the first action. Focus on the number 1 in the box and say **That's right.** Ask **Which picture is number 2?** Have pupils point to a picture and then play the audio to check. Ask pupils to write the number 2. Repeat for number 3. Play the audio one more time and encourage pupils to join in with chant. *See answers opposite.*

CD 1 • Track 15

Put your hand up, put your hand up. Up, up, up!

Keep your classroom tidy, keep your classroom tidy. Tidy, tidy, tidy!

Line up, line up, line up. Everyone line up!

Reading (CD 1. Track 16)

- Ask pupils to look at the reading box. Say **Let's listen and read.** Play the audio and encourage pupils to follow in their books. Ask pupils **Is Sam a good boy?** *Yes.* Ask why. Ask pupils if they are good boys and girls. Elicit why (*they pay attention, put their hands up, put their things away, help their friends,* etc.)

CLOSING ACTIVITIES

- Play *Hands up!* Ask questions and pupils listen and put their hands up, without speaking. Say **Put your hand up if you have a pencil case / a black bag. Put your hand up if you are a good friend / six years old / tidy / happy. Put your hand up if you can run fast / ride a bicycle,** etc.
- Practise lining up. Divide the class into four groups. Give each group one minute to come to the front and line up. The rest of the class should say if the group was good at lining up or not. Check that the group weren't shouting, pushing or turning round to each other. Praise pupils for their efforts.

EXTRA IDEAS

- Make a *Good pupil* display. Stick long strips of card on the board. On one strip, write the title *We are good pupils.* Elicit how the class can be good pupils and write each idea on a separate strip in big writing, e.g. *We put our hands up; We line up nicely,* etc. Hand out a strip to each group and a sheet of A5 paper for each pupil to illustrate that behaviour. Display the strips and pictures in class as a constant reminder of good behaviour.
- Ask pupils to mime an example of good behaviour. Take photos and add them to the display.

PAGES 14-15 Let's investigate and Make a difference

LET'S INVESTIGATE: **Timetables**

14

Project:
Make a school timetable.

Instructions:

Step 1
Write the days.

Step 2
Write numbers.

Step 3
Make pictures for your timetable.

① Count and write. Open answer

How many days are there in your timetable?

How many school subjects are there?

Which is your favourite day at school?

14 fourteen

MAKE A DIFFERENCE: **Ready, steady, go!**

15

① Look at the pictures. Tick (✓) the things you do every day. Open answer

Eat a good breakfast.
Brush your teeth.
Brush your hair.
Check your school bag.
Do some exercise.
Sleep well.

② Listen to the *Ready for school* chant. Draw pictures.

1

1. Say the four actions you hear in the chant.
2. Draw pictures of the actions.
3. Do the actions and say the chant!

fifteen 15

PAGE SUMMARY

Your pupils will learn how to make a school timetable. They will also practise following instructions and working independently.

LANGUAGE

- Monday, Tuesday, Wednesday, Thursday, Friday, Saturday, Sunday
- Science, Art, P.E., Music, Maths, English
- On Monday I have P.E, Maths and Science.
- There are five days on my timetable.
- My favourite day is Friday.

MATERIALS

Flashcards: (digital) see the *Teachers* section in the digital resources

Additional classroom materials: A3 paper (one sheet per pupil)

Pages 14 and 15 allow pupils to reflect on daily routines at school and at home. The ***Let's investigate*** page makes pupils aware of the structure and organisation of their school week by getting them to produce their own visual timetable. The activity encourages pupils to review the names of the days of the week and different school subjects. They learn how a timetable helps teachers and pupils be organised.

The ***Make a difference*** page links what we do in school with what we do outside school. Pupils review the essential routines that we take part in every day, outside our school timetable, that keep us healthy and organised.

LET'S INVESTIGATE

⊕ OPENING ACTIVITIES

- Put wordcards for days of the week in a random order on the board. Ask pupils to help you order the week. Put the cards in order as they call out the days.
- Ask **What day is today? What day was yesterday? What day is tomorrow?**
- Hold up pictures or flashcards of school subjects one at a time and elicit the name of the subject.
- Show pupils examples of visual timetables from the internet and talk about what subjects they can see on the different days.
- Talk about pupils' own timetable of classes.

MAIN ACTIVITIES

- Tell pupils to open their books on page 14. Say **Let's make a school timetable.** Draw the grid for a timetable on the board with five columns and six rows (depending on the number of periods your school timetable is divided into).
- Elicit the days of the week and write these in the row along the top. You may want to show pupils how we abbreviate each day (e.g. *Mon. / Tues.* etc.). Write numbers in the squares in the first column indicating the number of periods. Decide whether you will include lunch and break times.
- Demonstrate how to fill in the timetable. Say **On Monday, period 1, I have ...** Elicit a subject from the pupils and draw a picture to represent that subject. Continue until pupils understand.
- Hand out materials. Pupils will need a lot of help drawing the actual grid (see unit introduction).

1 Count and write.

- Focus pupils' attention on the questions. Have pupils follow as you read them out and give them time to find and write their answers.

⊕ CLOSING ACTIVITIES

- Have pupils talk about their favourite day and show each other their timetables.

MAKE A DIFFERENCE

⊕ OPENING ACTIVITIES

- Mime getting up out of bed and ask pupils what they do in the morning before they go to school. *Brush my teeth, have breakfast,* etc. Ask pupils what they eat for breakfast. Say **Hands up if you have milk / orange juice / cereal,** etc.

MAIN ACTIVITIES

1 Look at the pictures. Tick (✔) the things you do every day.

- Tell pupils to open their books on page 15. Read the instruction and have pupils follow.
- Point to the first picture. Elicit what the girl is doing. Point to the sentence under the photo and encourage pupils to read with you. Ask **Do you eat breakfast every day?** Tell pupils to put a tick if they do. Repeat for the other activities in the photos.

2 Listen to the *Ready for school* chant. Draw pictures.

- Focus pupils' attention on the musical note. Say **Let's listen to the *Ready for school* chant.** Play the audio and mime the actions in the song, then play again and have pupils join in.

CD 1 • Track 17

Get ready for school. Brush your hair! [x2]
Get ready for school. Eat your breakfast! [x2]
Get ready for school. Brush your teeth! [x2]
Get ready for school. Check your school bag! [x2]
Now you're ready for school!

- Ask pupils to name the four actions. Have pupils work with a partner to draw pictures for the actions.

⊕ CLOSING ACTIVITIES

- Play the audio and have one pupil hold up the correct picture while the other mimes the action. Have partners change roles and play the chant again.

PAGES 16-17 Let's remember

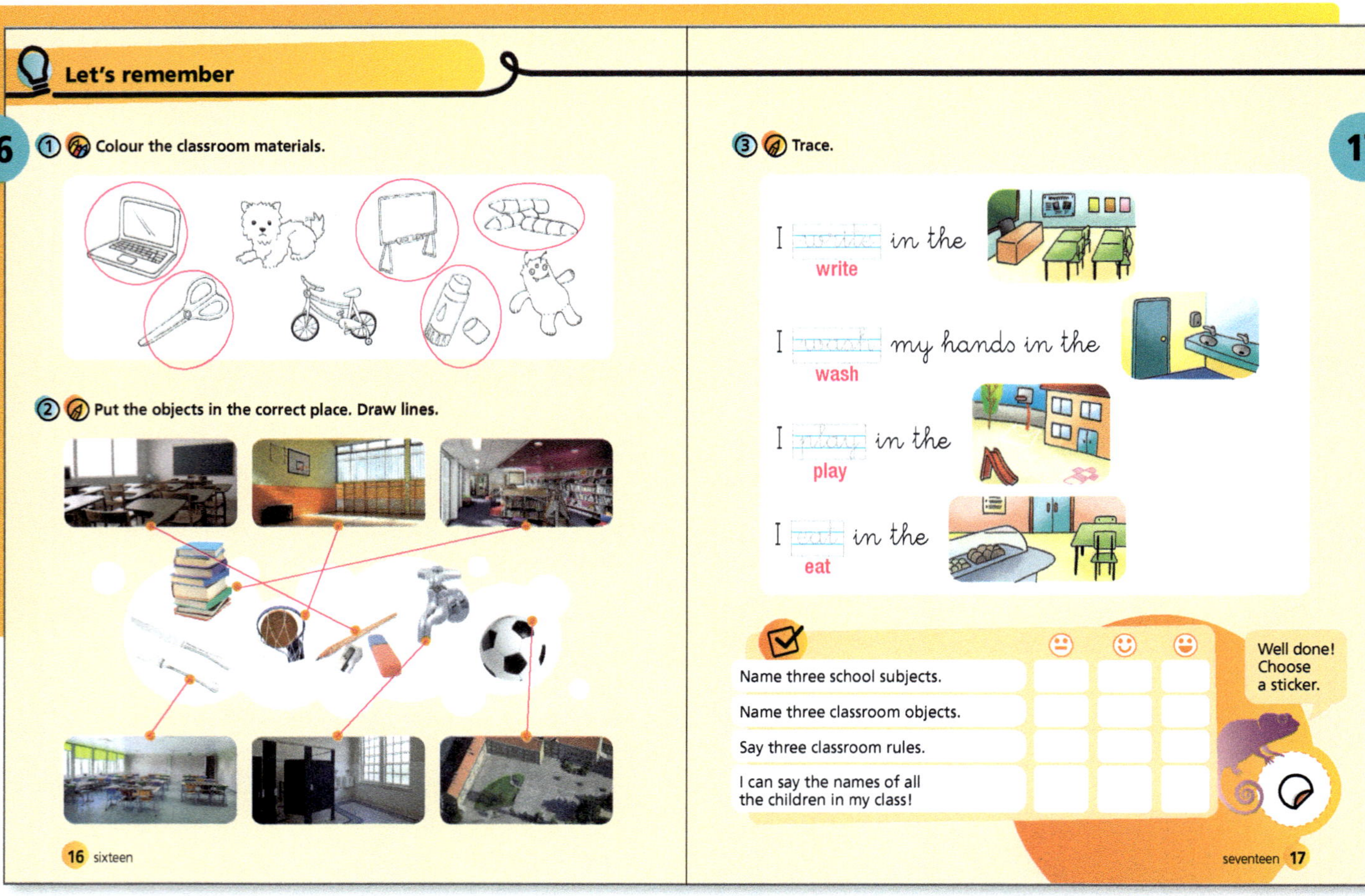
Let's remember

16

1 Colour the classroom materials.

2 Put the objects in the correct place. Draw lines.

16 sixteen

3 Trace.

I write in the

I wash my hands in the

I play in the

I eat in the

Name three school subjects.			
Name three classroom objects.			
Say three classroom rules.			
I can say the names of all the children in my class!			

Well done! Choose a sticker.

seventeen 17

PAGE SUMMARY

Pupils review unit content and undertake a simple self-assessment on the unit content.

LANGUAGE

- Book, pencil case, pencil, rubber, sharpener, scissors, glue, computer, crayons
- Science, P.E., Music, Art, Maths, English
- Classroom, library, toilets, dining hall playground, gym

MATERIALS

Flashcards: digital flashcards for the unit

Additional classroom materials: displays and timetables made during the unit

MAIN ACTIVITIES

1 Colour the classroom materials.

- Play *Pictionary.* Start to draw one of the classroom materials on the board, e.g. *pencil.* Stop after you have drawn only a small part of the object and ask the pupils if they can guess what it is. Say **What do you think it is?** Allow pupils time to guess, then continue drawing, until it becomes clear which object it is. Say **That's right! It's a pencil.** Repeat for the other materials.
- Put pupils in pairs and ask them to draw a classroom material for their partner to guess.
- Tell pupils to open their books on page 16. Point to each item and ask **Can we see this in the classroom?** Read the instruction and have pupils colour the classroom materials. *Computer, scissors, board, glue stick, crayons.*

② Put the objects in the correct place. Draw lines.

- Ask pupils to name the school areas they can see in the photos. Focus pupils' attention on the pictures in the centre. Point to the books and ask **Where do these go?** *In the library.* Repeat the question for the other objects.
- Read the instruction and have pupils draw lines from the objects to the correct school areas. *See answers opposite.*
- Extend the activity by asking pupils to tell you what we do in the different areas, e.g. *We eat in the dining hall.*

③ Trace.

- Encourage pupils to take turns miming an activity they do at school for their partner to guess.
- Ask pupils to name the school areas they can see on page 17. Ask **What do we do in the classroom?** Elicit pupils' ideas.
- Say **Let's read.** Read each sentence with the pupils. Encourage pupils to run their finger under each word as they read it. Have pupils trace the words and read the sentences to a partner when they have finished.
- Ask pupils to close their books. Distribute a small whiteboard or some recycled paper to each pair. Ask **Can you spell *play?*** Encourage partners to help each other spell the word and hold it up when they have finished. Walk round and check spellings. Repeat with the spelling of *eat, wash* and *write.* Point out how the *w* in *write* is a silent friend.
- Play *Run and slap!* Write words from the unit around the bottom half of the board. Divide the class into two teams. Have a member from each team stand a metre away from the board. Call out a word. The first pupil to run and slap the word gains a point for their team. Remind pupils that good behaviour means no pushing or shouting.

Self-assessment

- Write *My school* on the board. Hold up the unit flashcards or pictures quickly, one by one, and pupils shout out what they see. Stick them on the board.
- Focus pupils' attention on the self-assessment table. Read the first sentence together: *Name three school subjects.* Ask pupils to whisper the subjects to a partner. Elicit the subjects.
- Now read the sentence: *Name three classroom objects.* Ask pupils to take out items from their pencil case and ask their partner to name them.
- Read the sentence: *Say three classroom rules.* Encourage pupils to count on their fingers as they name three things to a partner.
- Finally, read the sentence together: *I can say the names of all the children in my class!* Have pupils stand up one at a time while the rest of the class chant their name.
- After reading each sentence, the pupils should tick the boxes according to whether they have learned a lot (*very happy face*), some things (*happy face*) or a little (*disappointed face*) about their school.
- Ask pupils to choose a sticker to show how they feel about their learning in the unit.
- Give individual attention to any pupils who choose the *disappointed* sticker.

⊕ EXTRA IDEAS

- If there is time, review and talk about any displays the class have done during the unit (review the *Good pupil* display, look at the *School staff* poster, hand out pupils' timetables for different groups to look at and talk about, etc.).
- Distribute wordcards to groups and have them label the flashcards on the board.

Activity book answers

UNIT 1 My school

2

① Say and trace.

classroom | playground | library

playground | library

dining hall | gym | toilets

dining hall | gym | toilets

② Write.

caretaker cook ~~teacher~~

The teacher teaches the pupils in the classroom.

The cook prepares and serves food in the dining hall.

The caretaker keeps the school tidy.

2 two

3

③ Which materials do you need? Trace and match.

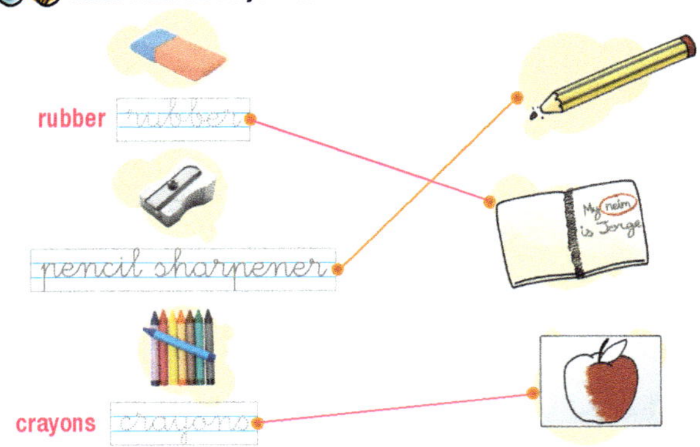

④ Trace. Circle the correct objects.

Art | Music | P.E. | Science

Music | P.E. | Science

three 3

UNIT 1

4

⑤ Write.

write draw play paint eat ~~run~~

run | play | draw

play | draw

write | eat | paint

⑥ Write. Draw a picture of your favourite school subject. Open answer

My name is ________.

My favourite school subject is ________.

I like to ________ in the playground.

My favourite school subject

4 four

5

⑦ Who is being a good friend? Put a tick (✓) or a cross (✗).

⑧ Trace and match.

Put your hand up. | Keep your classroom tidy. | Line up.

Keep your classroom tidy. | Line up.

five 5

UNIT 1

Let's investigate at home!

Make a *Ready for school* mini book

1

Cut out and fold your mini book.

2

Draw pictures.

3

Write sentences.

4

Decorate the cover.

1 Write *yes* or *no*. Open answer

Do you brush your teeth? ______

Do you check your school bag? ______

Skills check

7

1 Look and read. Put a tick (✓) or a cross (✗).
Look at the two examples.

This is a rubber. ✓

This is a book. ✗

1 This is a computer. ✓

2 These are paints. ✓

3 This is a poster. ✗

4 This is a ball. ✗

5 This is a ruler. ✓

UNIT 2 My home

CONTENT	EVALUATION CRITERIA
The family. Family types and relationships.	Recognise the basic family relationships. Express their understanding and appreciation of belonging to a family with its own characteristics and belonging to a particular social group, in this case a family. Names and surnames.
The home.	Understand the social organisation of their close surroundings: the home.
Introduction to scientific knowledge and its application in the Social Sciences. Collect relevant information using different sources (direct and indirect).	Obtain specific and relevant information, using different sources.
Develop strategies to organise, memorise and remember information obtained through different methods and from different sources.	Develop a capacity for hard work and show perseverance while studying.
Team-building strategies.	Develop a cooperative and adaptive attitude, recognising merit in others' ideas and responding to situations with intuition, an open mind and flexibility.
Use of different text types and graphic languages.	Obtain, analyse and adapt the information received from a variety of different textual and graphic formats.
With help, plan and manage simple projects, showing independence and initiative in order to achieve objectives.	Develop creativity and initiative, improving their capacity to acquire information and ideas and present innovative conclusions.
Techniques for intellectual work. Elaboration of diagrams and summaries, memorising and structuring the information received. Reading techniques for Social Science publications.	Employ techniques appropriate to intellectual tasks; produce work and make presentations both individually and as a group, involving research, selection and organisation of texts of a social, geographical or historical nature, while showing autonomy and collaborative skills.
Conflict resolution strategies: use of rules and appreciation of peaceful and tolerant coexistence.	Recognise cooperation and dialogue as a way to avoid and resolve conflicts, encouraging democratic values.
Rights and obligations.	Identify rights and obligations in the context of the family.

LEARNING STANDARDS	KEY COMPETENCES	PAGES
Identifies family relationships and understands the different family roles.	SOC	24–27
Understands belonging to a family with its own particular characteristics.	SOC	24, 27
Values belonging to certain social groups (family, school, group of friends) and recognises their characteristics.	SOC	24, 27
Respects the norms established in the family.	LTL, SOC	25–27
Identifies different types of home and can describe each one of them orally.	SOC, LIN	21
Knows and can describe orally the different elements of the home.	SOC, LIN	18–23
Looks for, selects and organises information, analysing it and drawing conclusions. Reflects on the process followed and reports on it orally.	MST, LIN, LTL	26, 27
Performs academic tasks in a responsible and effective manner.	LTL	26, 27
Uses vocabulary correctly in the presentation of their work.	LTL, LIN	26, 27
Develops a cooperative and adaptive attitude, recognising merit in others' ideas and responding to situations with intuition, an open mind and flexibility.	LTL, SOC	19, 25–27
Participates effectively and constructively in daily life and develops strategies for conflict resolution.	LTL, SOC	25–27
Identifies and uses the correct code of conduct for their environment.	LTL, SOC	25–27
Analyses information related to the subject area and handles images, tables, graphs, diagrams and summaries using both traditional supports and Information and Communication Technologies.	AUT, LTL	26
Shows self-confidence, personal initiative, curiosity, interest and creativity in the learning process.	AUT, LTL	26, 27
Shows independence in the planning and carrying out of simple actions and shows initiative when taking decisions.	AUT, LTL	26, 27
Produces work and makes presentations both individually and as part of a group, participating in the research, selection and organisation of texts of a social, geographical or historical nature.	SOC, AUT	18–27
Values cooperation and dialogue as a way of avoiding and resolving conflicts.	SOC	27
Identifies their rights and obligations in the context of the family.	SOC	25–27

UNIT INFORMATION

UNIT SUMMARY

In this unit your pupils will learn about what makes up a home. They will study the internal parts of a house, specifically rooms and furniture, as well as the external parts of a house.

Pupils will consider who they live with in the home. They will review the names of family members and understand how we can help each other with household jobs.

There is a lot of vocabulary in the unit. Pupils will have used some of the vocabulary orally in previous learning situations but may be unfamiliar with its written form. It is important to support new language visually and provide opportunities for pupils to familiarise themselves with the written words.

PROJECT

Let's investigate

In the *Let's investigate* activity on page 26, pupils will carry out a simple survey to see how many pupils help out with different jobs in the home.

The pupils need:

- A4 coloured card (one sheet per pupil)
- Magazines (with household jobs)
- Felt tips, coloured pencils or crayons
- Scissors
- Glue

If it is difficult to obtain magazines showing photos of household jobs, pupils can take photos of themselves doing a job at home or draw a picture. Alternatively, you could amplify and photocopy the photos of the different household jobs on page 25.

VALUES AND ATTITUDES

This unit develops the concept of helping others and being tidy from the previous unit. It will raise awareness about helping at home and the household jobs pupils can do. Throughout the unit, try to encourage pupils to think about:

- What we can do to help out at home.
- How we can be kind to family members.

Make a difference

The *Make a difference* page aims to make pupils aware of the importance of behaving well and being kind to other family members in the home. The pairwork activity encourages pupils to draw and talk about their family to classmates. Pupils can also be encouraged to bring in family photos.

EVALUATION MATERIAL

These documents can be downloaded from the *Teachers* section of the digital resources and printed.

The materials include:

- **Unit diagnostic test:** provides an overview of the unit and allows you to assess the pupils' prior knowledge.
- **End-of-unit test:** in addition to the *Review* section at the end of each unit, this summative test can be used to evaluate pupils' progress after studying the unit content.
- **Unit evaluation grid:** based on the evaluation criteria and learning standards of the unit.

DIGITAL RESOURCES

Presentations

- **Unit summary**: a simple slide presentation with text, images and audio to review the main ideas of the unit. It can be used at the beginning of the unit to test pupils' prior knowledge of the unit content or at the end of the unit as a revision tool.
- **Let's investigate**: a slide presentation of the unit's *Let's investigate* page with text, photos and audio. The slide presentation is perfect for a heads-up class, showing the steps one by one. Use this tool to get the pupils to predict the next steps (with their books closed) or to focus their attention on each step as they carry out the project themselves.

Activities

- **Memory game**: useful activity for reviewing key vocabulary and modelling pronunciation.
- **Wordsearch**: use at the end of the unit as a revision activity. Turn it into a game by getting the pupils to work in teams.
- **Spelling**: get a volunteer to come to the board and carry out the activity, but with the help of the whole class.

Song lyrics

Listen to the song *My home* and follow the lyrics line by line.

Posters

Attractive and informative posters to display in class. You can use them to review key concepts and vocabulary.

Videos

Use the video links in this unit to present content in a dynamic, real-life context whilst reinforcing the pupils' listening skills.

Teachers

Digital flashcards: a bank of digital images which can be used in a variety of ways in class.

Downloadable pdfs: evaluation tests, evaluation grids, templates, useful links and further information.

PAGES 18-19 My home

PAGE SUMMARY

The aim of the unit opener is to encourage your pupils' observation skills and find out what they already know about the topic of the unit. Use the illustration to elicit vocabulary related to the home. Pupils answer the questions in groups then learn the actions to the song.

LANGUAGE

- Living room, kitchen, bedroom, bathroom, dining room
- Table, chair, bed, sofa, fridge, shower, bath, television, lamp, bookshelves
- He/she is cooking / reading / listening / washing her hands / talking / laying the table.

MATERIALS

Flashcards: (digital) see the *Teachers* section in the digital resources

WHAT CAN YOU SEE?

Draw a big square on the board and ask pupils for suggestions as to what it might be. When they suggest *house,* say **Yes!** Draw on a triangular roof. Try to see what vocabulary pupils already know about rooms and furniture. Divide the house into five rooms (bedroom and bathroom upstairs, kitchen, living room and dining room downstairs). See if pupils can name the rooms, label them, then read each name together. Point to the living room and ask **What can I see in the living room?** Draw in any furniture pupils suggest. Now ask pupils what activities they do in the different rooms. **What do you do in the living room / kitchen?** etc. Encourage pupils to say *I wash in the bathroom, I eat in the dining room,* etc.

Tell pupils they are going to look at a house in their books. Ask pupils where they think the chameleon could be hiding and listen to their ideas. Tell pupils to open their Pupil's Books on pages 18 and 19. Ask **Where is the chameleon?** *On the window blind.* Ask pupils if they can find the furniture they suggested on the board in the illustration. Tick the items on the board as they find them.

⊕ OPENING ACTIVITIES

- Hold up pictures or flashcards of objects and furniture one at a time. For each flashcard say **What is it? Point to it in the picture. Which room is it in?**
- Ask pupils to listen and look carefully at the picture in their books. Say true or false sentences about the objects, e.g. **The television is in the bathroom.** Pupils should answer *No, it isn't. It's in the living room.*

MAIN ACTIVITIES

1 Circle Amy. Which room is she in?

- Put pupils in groups and ask them to count the people in the house. Read the instruction and have pupils circle Amy. Ask pupils to name the room she is in. *Bedroom.* Ask **What is Amy doing?** *She is listening to a story.*

2 Name four objects in the house.

- In their groups, pupils see how many objects they can name. Can they name more than four? Tell them to use their fingers to count.
- Ask each group to name an object and write them on the board. Encourage pupils to listen to each other so they don't repeat objects. Praise pupils for all the words they know.

3 Is Sam doing something wrong?

- Ask **Where is Sam?** Tell pupils to look closely and decide with their group if Sam is doing something wrong. *Yes, he isn't wiping his feet.*
- Praise the class for working together and ask pupils to choose a sticker for their effort of working with a group.

4 Listen and tick (✔) the objects you hear.

- Encourage pupils to read the word under each photo with you. Focus pupils' attention on the musical note. Say **Let's listen to a song.** Tell pupils they will listen to the song twice and tick the pictures they hear.

CD 1 • Track 18

See audio script below.

5 Sing the song and do the actions!

- Say **Now let's listen and do the actions.** Play the song, teach the actions and encourage pupils to copy. Repeat the song a couple of times and do the actions together.

CD 1 • Track 19

My home has different rooms, yes *[dance]*
My home, please visit soon *[dance]*
Where's the sofa? In which room? *[shrug]*
Where's the sofa? In the living room! *[mime sitting]*
Where's the bed? In which room? *[shrug]*
Where's the bed? In the bedroom! *[mime sleeping]*
My home has different rooms, yes *[dance]*
My home, please visit soon *[dance]*
Where's the table? In which room? *[shrug]*
Where's the table? In the dining room! *[mime eating]*
Where's the fridge? In which room? *[shrug]*
Where's the fridge? In the kitchen! *[mime cooking]*
My home has different rooms, yes
My home, please visit soon! [x2] *[dance]*

⊕ CLOSING ACTIVITIES

- Ask more questions about the illustration, e.g. **How many windows are there? What colour is the door? How many books are there in the bedroom? What animal can you see on the television?**
- Mime an activity, e.g. brushing your teeth. Ask pupils to name the activity and room.

⊕ EXTRA IDEAS

- Review the use of prepositions of place (*in, on, under, next to, behind*) by hiding a chameleon picture or soft toy and asking **Where is the chameleon?** Encourage answers using a preposition. *He's on the window. He's under your desk,* etc.
- Do a *Funny picture* dictation. Have pupils draw a house with the five rooms. Write the room names on the board for pupils to copy. Ask pupils to listen carefully and draw the object. Say **There is a fridge in the bathroom. There is a bed in the kitchen.** When you have finished, talk about what is wrong with the picture.

PAGE 20 Everybody helps

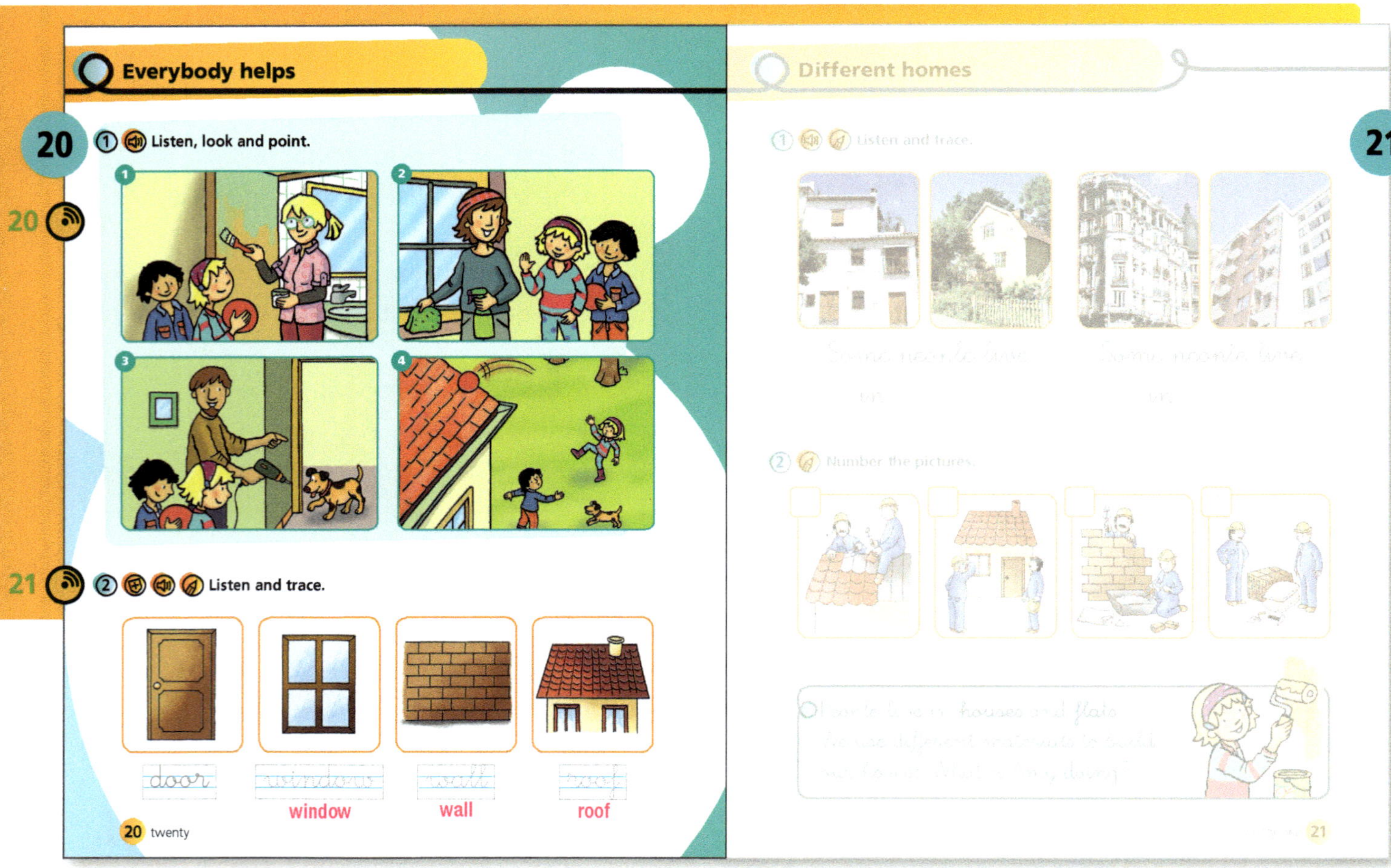

PAGE SUMMARY

The story provides a context for identifying the different parts that make up a house. Use the story to make pupils aware of the different jobs that we need to do to look after the house. The stories are also a good opportunity to focus on the course characters.

LANGUAGE

- Door, window, wall, roof
- I'm cleaning / painting / hanging a picture.
- Do you want to play with us?

MATERIALS

Flashcards: (digital) see the *Teachers* section in the digital resources

Additional classroom materials: magazines (with houses and furniture), wooden blocks, plasticine, cereal boxes

OPENING ACTIVITIES

- Play the unit song again and have pupils join in with the actions.
- Have pupils look at the opening pages of the unit (or show them on the board) and play *I Spy* with household objects.
- Ask pupils to tell you all the different activities they do at home. *Eat, sleep, play, watch TV, read,* etc.
- Ask pupils how they get from home to school. **Do you walk / take the bus / come in a car to school? Do you live near or far from school?**

MAIN ACTIVITIES

- Draw the outline of a house again and elicit the names of the rooms. Write the name of the room in each area. Elicit one activity for each room. *Sleeping, eating, washing,* etc.
- Tell pupils they are going to listen to a story about jobs around the house.

1 Listen, look and point.

- Ask the pupils to open their Pupil's Books on page 20.
- Point to frame 1 and say **Look at the picture.** Ask **Who can you see?** Encourage pupils to say *Sam and Amy.* Ask who they think the other person in the picture is. *Amy's mother.* Ask pupils **What is Amy's mother doing?** *She is painting the door.* Try to elicit what Amy and Sam want. Tell pupils they will be able to listen to find out. Ask similar questions for the other three frames, asking who pupils can see and what they are doing.
- Say **Let's listen to the story.** Play the audio.

> **CD 1 • Track 20**
>
> Everybody helps
>
> The children are looking for someone to play with.
>
> Frame 1
>
> Amy: Hi mum! Do you want to play football with us?
>
> Mum: Sorry children, I'm busy. I'm painting this door.
>
> Frame 2
>
> Sam: Hi Penny! Do you want to play football with us?
>
> Penny (Amy's sister): Sounds great! But I can't. I'm cleaning these windows.
>
> Frame 3
>
> Amy: Dad! Do YOU want to play football with us?
>
> Dad: I can't children, I'm hanging this picture on the wall. But I DO know someone who wants to play football.
>
> Frame 4
>
> Sam: This is fun!
>
> Amy: Yes. Whoops!
>
> Sam: Oh no! The ball's on the roof!

- After listening, say **Oh dear! What happens to the ball?** Elicit that it goes on the roof.
- Ask pupils what Sam and Amy ask in each frame. *Do you want to play football?* Play the audio one more time. Ask pupils if they can name any parts of the house mentioned. *Door, window, wall, roof.*

2 Listen and trace.

- Hold up pictures or flashcards and elicit what part of the house they are. Ask **What is this?** *It's a wall / door / window / roof.*
- Focus pupils' attention on the pictures and words in their book. Play the audio and have pupils point to each word as they hear it.

> **CD 1 • Track 21**
>
> Door – door; window – window; wall – wall; roof – roof.

- Have pupils read each word again together. Ask pupils to trace each word and read them to their partner when finished.

+ CLOSING ACTIVITIES

- Mime the activities from the story (*painting a door / cleaning windows / putting up a picture / playing football*). After each one ask **What am I doing?**
- Put pupils into groups of three and encourage them to act out the scenes from the story.

+ EXTRA IDEAS

- Make a *House* collage. Working in pairs, have pupils cut out different windows, doors, walls and roofs from magazines and stick them on card to make their own house.
- Give pupils different materials to build houses with, such as wooden blocks, plasticine, cereal boxes, etc. Encourage them to include roofs, windows and doors. Take photos of their models.

PAGE 21 Different homes

PAGE SUMMARY

Pupils will talk about the different types of homes they live in. Some pupils may live in houses, others in flats. Pupils will also consider the different materials houses are made of and the sequence of building of a house.

LANGUAGE

- House, flat
- Door, window, wall, roof, chimney
- Bricks, tiles, cement
- What is he/she doing?

MATERIALS

Flashcards: (digital) see the *Teachers* section in the digital resources

Additional classroom materials: stiff paper or card, paints, slide presentation of local buildings

OPENING ACTIVITIES

- Give each pupil a sheet of A4 paper. Tell them to draw a big square in the centre to start off the house. Teach the word *chimney* if you haven't already, and draw a picture on the board. Do a dictation. Tell pupils you are going to 'build a house,' e.g. Say **This house has a big green door. There are two blue windows. The roof is red. The chimney is brown,** etc. Pupils should draw the parts of the house as you say them. Monitor carefully so that less confident pupils can keep up. Tell pupils to describe the house to their partner when they have finished.
- Ask pupils what they can see through their windows at home. Have them add what they can see to their pictures.
- If pupils made house collages or models in the previous class, ask them to talk about and describe their work.

MAIN ACTIVITIES

1 Listen and trace.

- Focus pupils' attention on the pictures of houses on the left and encourage pupils to follow with their finger as you read **Some people live in houses.** Ask the pupils **Do you live in a house?** Ask the pupils who live in houses to raise their hands. Encourage them to say *I live in a house.*
- Focus pupils' attention on the pictures of flats on the right. Encourage pupils to follow with their finger as you read **Some people live in flats.** Ask the pupils **Do you live in a flat?** Ask the pupils who live in flats to raise their hands. Encourage them to say *I live in a flat.*
- Draw a house on one side of the board and a flat on the other. Ask the pupils to line up in the correct place according to where they live. Encourage pupils by the house to say *I live in a house* and those by the flat to say *I live in a flat.*
- Draw a simple graph on the board and draw a flat at the bottom of one column and a house at the bottom of the other. Count the number of pupils who live in houses and flats and record the results in your graph.
- Comment on the results, e.g. **10 pupils live in a house and 15 pupils live in a flat.**
- Focus pupils' attention on the sentence under each of the photos. Play the audio and have pupils follow in their books and trace the words. Read each sentence together.

CD 1 • Track 22
Some people live in houses. Some people live in flats.

2 Number the pictures.

- Ask pupils to look at the pictures in activity 2. Ask **What are they doing?** *They are building a house.* Point to each picture and ask **What can you see?** Elicit vocabulary for *roof, house, wall, bricks.* Explain that cement is like glue, it holds the bricks together.
- Point to picture 1. Say **They are going to build a house. They have bricks and cement.** Say **Let's number the pictures together.** Ask **What picture is number 2?** When pupils respond correctly say **That's right. They build the walls first.** Ask pupils to write number 2 in the box. Ask pupils to now point to picture 3. Say **That's right. They build the roof next.** Ask pupils to write the number 3. Finally, ask **What picture is number 4?** Say **That's right, the house is finished.** *3, 4, 2, 1.*
- Go through the sequence again and encourage pupils to describe the sequence with you.

Reading. (CD 1. Track 23)

- Ask pupils to look at the reading box. Say **Let's listen and read.** Play the audio and encourage pupils to follow in their books. Elicit what Amy is doing. *She is painting a wall.*

CLOSING ACTIVITIES

- Tell pupils that you are going to build a house. Say **First, the walls.** Mime building the walls with bricks. Encourage the pupils to build the walls up around themselves. Say **Now, the roof.** Mime putting up the roof over your head. Continue building up on a small section of the roof and say **Don't forget the chimney!** Continue with the windows and door. Mime knocking at the door and say **Hello, welcome to my house!**
- Have pupils draw a window and a door in their notebooks. Ask them to count the number of windows and doors they have in their house or flat and write the numbers on their pictures. Ask pupils **How many doors / windows do you have in your house or flat?**

EXTRA IDEAS

- Give the pupils stiff paper or card and a selection of paints. Tell them to paint a picture of their house or flat.
- Go for a walk in your school neighbourhood and talk about the buildings pupils can see. Alternatively, show slides of photos you have taken. Describe and count windows and doors, etc.

PAGE 22 Rooms

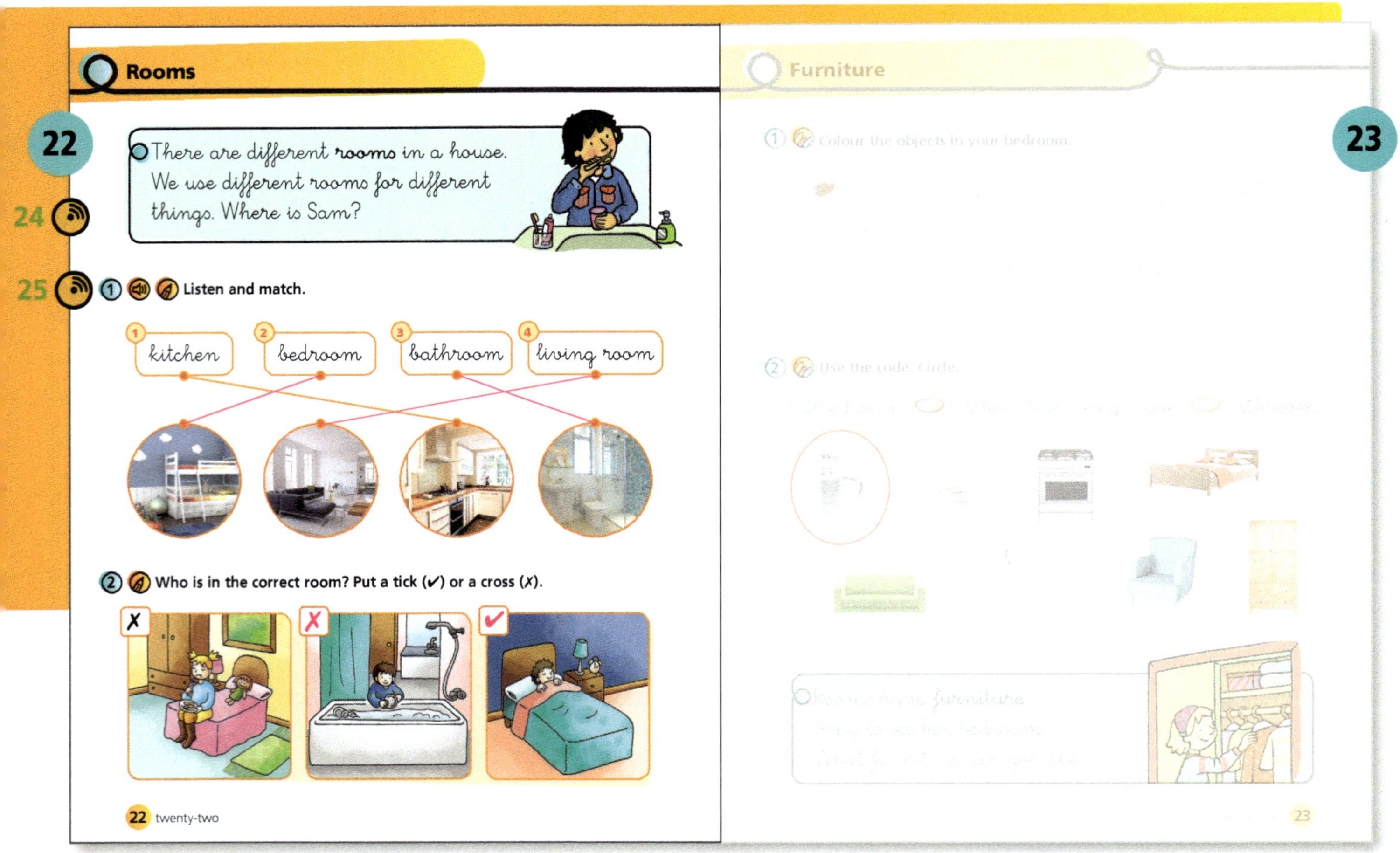

PAGE SUMMARY

Pupils will understand how we use different rooms for different activities. They will become familiar with the written form of the room names.

LANGUAGE

- House, flat
- Door, window, wall, roof
- Bedroom, bathroom, kitchen, living room
- There is one kitchen. There are two bathrooms.
- He/she is in the bedroom.

MATERIALS

Flashcards: (digital) see the *Teachers* section in the digital resources

Additional classroom materials: bean bag or ball, brick-sized sheets of paper

OPENING ACTIVITIES

- Have pupils sit down in a circle. Review where they live by asking the pupil to your left **House or flat?** Encourage the pupil to answer in a full sentence *I live in a house/flat*. Ask the pupil to their left the same question and continue around the circle. Focus the pupils' attention on the question by passing a bean bag, ball or soft toy around as the questions are being asked and answered. Extend by asking pupils questions about where they live and how many windows and doors there are.
- Do the *Building a house* mime from the previous lesson and review the materials for building a house.

MAIN ACTIVITIES

Reading. (CD 1. Track 24)

- Tell pupils you want to draw a house on the board. Encourage them to dictate what you should draw, e.g. *Draw a square. Draw a roof / a chimney / four windows / a door.* Thank pupils for their help. Rub out the windows and doors and divide the house into four (two rooms downstairs, two rooms upstairs). Write the names of the rooms slowly on the board, encouraging pupils to help you spell.
- Ask pupils to open their Pupil's Books on page 22 and look at the reading box. Say **Let's listen and read.** Play the audio, then ask pupils where Sam is and ask what he is doing. *In the bathroom, brushing his teeth.*

1 Listen and match.

- Ask pupils to look at the four photos in their books. Point to the first photo and ask **What can you see?** *A bedroom.* Point to each of the other photos in turn and ask the same question.
- Focus pupils' attention on the room names above the photos. Point to each word and encourage pupils to read with you.
- Say **Listen and match the words and the pictures.** Play the audio. Pause after the first word and point to the line matching *kitchen* and the photo. Pause after each word to allow pupils to match the words and pictures. *See answers opposite.*

CD 1 • Track 25

1. Kitchen. We cook food in the kitchen. Draw a line to the kitchen.
2. Bedroom. We sleep in the bedroom. Draw a line to the bedroom.
3. Bathroom. We have a shower in the bathroom. Draw a line to the bathroom.
4. Living room. We watch television in the living room. Draw a line to the living room.

2 Who is in the correct room? Put a tick (✔) or a cross (✗).

- Mime an activity and have pupils guess which room you are in, e.g. mime sleeping and say **I'm sleeping. Where am I?** *In the bedroom.* **I'm cooking. Where am I?** *In the kitchen,* etc.
- Focus pupils' attention on the pictures in activity 2. Point to the first picture and ask **Where is she?** *The bedroom.* **What is she doing?** *Eating.* Ask **Is that right?** *No.* Ask **Where do you eat?** *The kitchen or the dining room.* Point to the cross in the box, shake your head and say **She is not in the correct room.** Ask pupils what they do in their bedroom.
- Repeat the procedure with the other two pictures. Ask pupils if they need to put a tick or a cross. *See answers opposite.*

CLOSING ACTIVITIES

- Put a picture or flashcard of the living room on the board. Mime cooking. Ask **Is that right?** *No.* Ask pupils **Where do I cook?** *In the kitchen.* Put up a picture of the bathroom and mime having a shower. Ask **Is that right?** *Yes.* Say **That's right. I wash / have a shower in the bathroom.** Repeat with the other rooms.
- Hold up wordcards for each room and ask pupils to read each word. Write the name for each room on the board with the vowels missing. Ask pupils **What vowels are missing?** Have volunteers come up and stick the correct room picture next to its name.

EXTRA IDEAS

- Ask pupils **Which is your favourite room? Why?**
- Have pupils describe their own house. Encourage them by asking **How many rooms are there? How many bedrooms / bathrooms are there?**
- *Build a wall.* Give each pupil a brick-sized sheet of paper. Elicit what colour bricks are (*red or brown*) and ask pupils to colour their brick. Ask pupils to look back on the previous lessons of the unit and choose a word, associated with a house, to write on their brick. With pupils' help, use the bricks to build a wall display. Demonstrate how bricks are laid in a staggered fashion and elicit why this is. *It makes the wall stronger.*

PAGE 23 Furniture

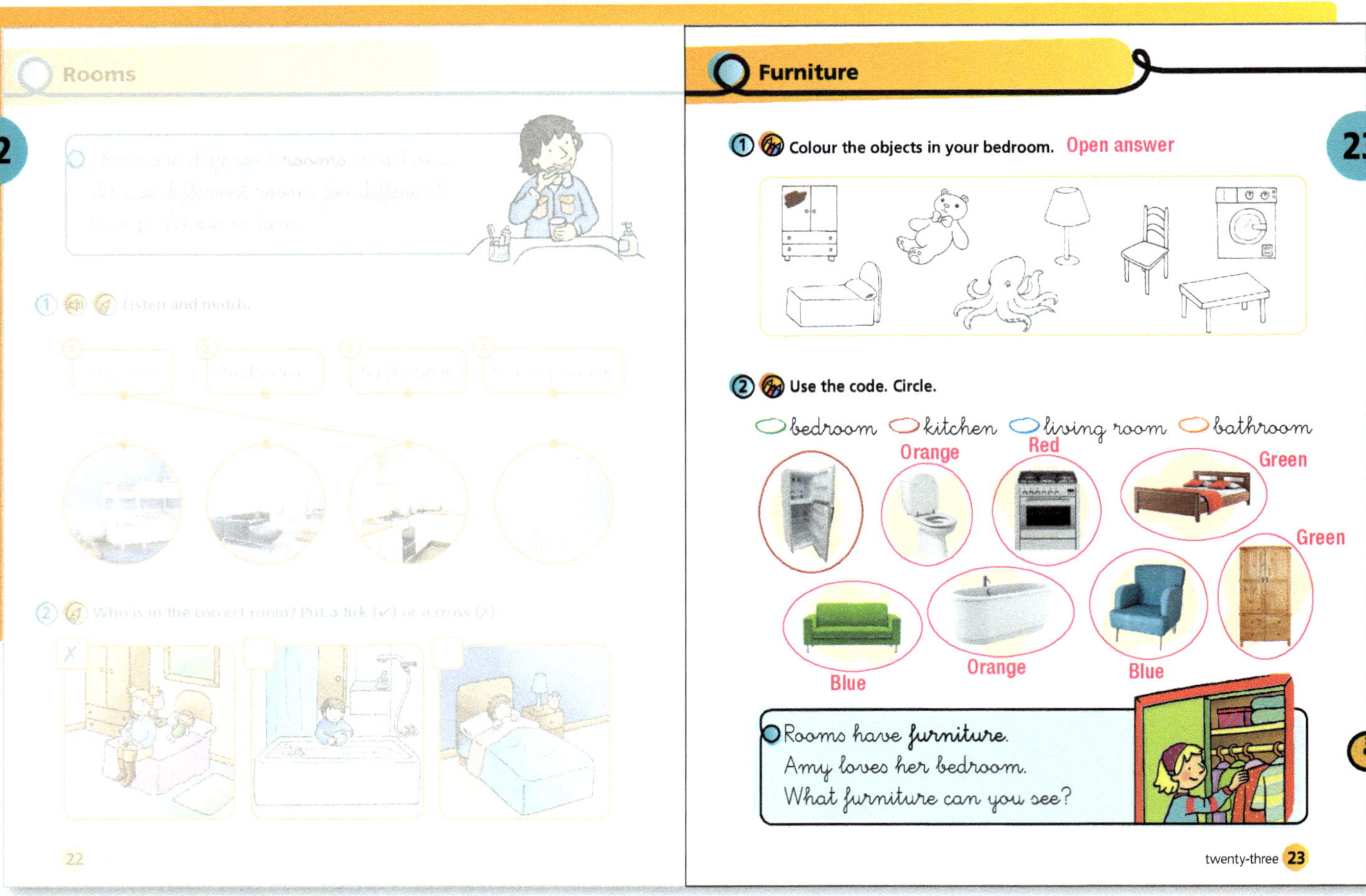

PAGE SUMMARY

Pupils will learn and/or review the names of different furniture items and identify in which room we normally find them.

LANGUAGE

- Bed, table, chair, wardrobe, lamp, television, sofa, toilet, shower, bath, fridge, washing machine, oven
- Bedroom, living room, bathroom, kitchen
- There is a bed. There are two chairs.
- He/she is in the bedroom.

MATERIALS

Flashcards: (digital) see the *Teachers* section in the digital resources

Additional classroom materials: magazines (with houses and furniture), A3 paper (one sheet per pupil)

OPENING ACTIVITIES

- Say **Let's build a house!** and do the *Build a house* mime from the previous lesson.
- Show volunteers a picture or flashcard of a room and have them mime an activity they do in that room for others to guess.
- Hand out mini whiteboards or recycled paper. Have pupils work in pairs. Say **Bedroom.** Have pupils spell the word with their partner and hold it up. Walk round and check spelling. Praise pupils and ask them to spell the word out for you as you write it the board. Each time you write the word on the board ask **What do we do in the (bedroom)?**

MAIN ACTIVITIES

1 Colour the objects in your bedroom.

- Play a friendly *Hangman* game with the word *furniture*. Explain that furniture is all the objects in our rooms that help us with our everyday living, e.g. tables and chairs.
- Put the picture or flashcard of the bedroom on the board. Elicit what furniture pupils have in their bedroom. *Bed, wardrobe, desk, chair, bookshelves,* etc. For every item pupils name, draw a picture on the board.
- Point to each item you have drawn on the board and elicit the name again. This time, write the name under the picture. Ask pupils what other things they have in their bedroom.
- Focus pupils' attention on the black and white pictures. Point to each one and ask **Do you have a (wardrobe) in your bedroom?** If pupils *say Yes,* ask further questions. **What colour is it? Is it big or small? What's inside it?** etc.
- Read the instruction and have pupils follow. Ask them to colour the objects in their bedroom.

2 Use the code. Circle.

- Put *bedroom, kitchen, bathroom, living room* pictures or flashcards spaced out along the top of the board. Leave a space underneath. Put furniture flashcards along the bottom half of the board. Ask two volunteers to come and take down the flashcards of furniture you can find in a bedroom. Place these under the *bedroom* flashcard at the top of the board, naming them as you do.
- Point to the *kitchen* flashcard and elicit the name. Ask **What furniture can you see in the kitchen?** Ask another two volunteers to take down the furniture for the kitchen and elicit the names of these. Place the furniture under the *kitchen* flashcard. Repeat the question for each room and gradually sort all the furniture into their rooms.
- Point to each room flashcard and say **In the (bedroom) I can see (a bed).** Have pupils name the furniture underneath.
- Focus pupils' attention on the instruction for activity 2 and read it out. Point to the first word and have pupils read *bedroom.* Ask **What colour are you going to circle the things in the bedroom?** *Green.* Repeat the question for the other rooms.
- Now point to each photo and ask **Where can you see a (fridge)? What colour circle?** Ask questions for the other photos and then have pupils use the code to circle the furniture. Walk round and check pupils are circling correctly. *See answers opposite.*

Reading. (CD 1. Track 26)

- Ask pupils to look at the reading box. Say **Let's listen and read.** Play the audio, then ask pupils what furniture they can see. *A wardrobe.* Ask what they can see inside Amy's wardrobe. *Clothes, a box.*
- Ask pupils to tell you what other things they have in their bedroom. *Toys, books,* etc.

+ CLOSING ACTIVITIES

- *Draw your bedroom.* Give each pupil a sheet of paper and ask them to draw their bedroom. Ask the pupils to show the finished pictures to the rest of the class or to a partner. Encourage them to name the items in their room and describe them together.
- Play *Memory chain.* One pupil begins: *In my bedroom there is a bed.* The next pupil must repeat the sentence and add another object: *In my bedroom there is a bed and a desk,* etc. Pupils continue in this way, adding an object until there are too many objects to remember or time is up. Once you have demonstrated the game, encourage pupils to play in small groups.

+ EXTRA IDEAS

- Give out an A3 sheet of paper to each pupil and have them fold it into four equal parts. Pupils should allocate a room per part: *bedroom, bathroom, living room* and *kitchen.* Write the words on the board for the pupils to copy. Give out magazines and have the pupils cut out furniture to stick in the correct room. Have pupils use the picture dictionary to label the furniture in their house.

PAGE 24 Family

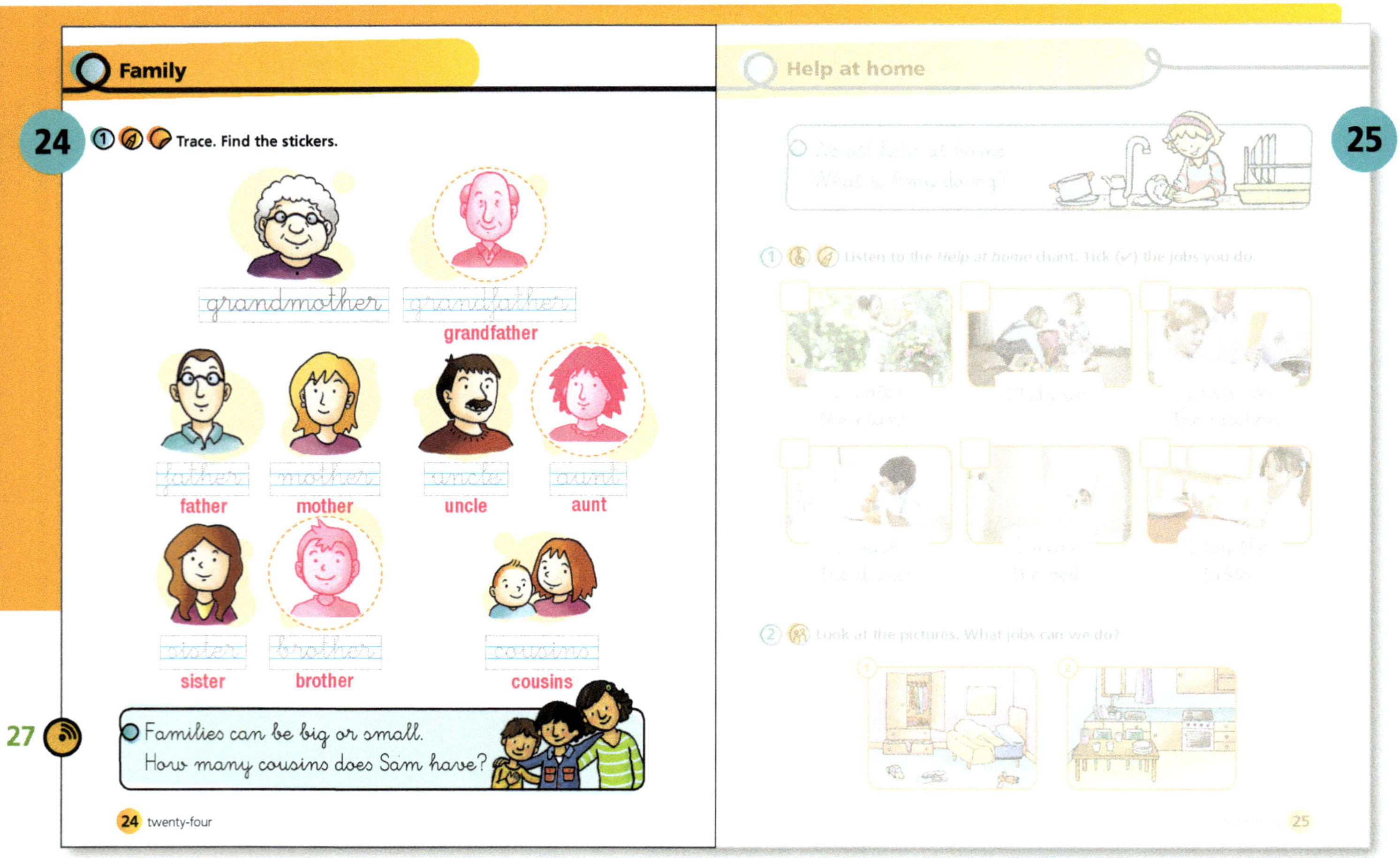

PAGE SUMMARY

Pupils will identify and talk about their family members and practise spelling family words. They will notice how some families are big and some are small.

Note: As family is potentially a very sensitive topic, consider beforehand if there are any delicate situations to be avoided, e.g. a parent who has died, parents recently divorced, etc.

LANGUAGE

- Grandmother, grandfather, father, mother, sister, brother, aunt, uncle, cousins
- Who is this? This is my brother.
- I have one brother. He/she has two sisters.

MATERIALS

Flashcards: (digital) see the *Teachers* section in the digital resources

Additional classroom materials: photos of your family. Ask pupils to bring in photos of their family to talk about

OPENING ACTIVITIES

- Play *Flash!* with furniture pictures or flashcards. Flash up a card very quickly and see if pupils can guess what they saw.
- Play *Board snap!* Stick a room flashcard on the board. Shuffle the furniture flashcards. Hold up the furniture flashcards one at a time. Pupils must look at the room flashcard on the board and look at the furniture flashcard in your hand. If the furniture matches the room they must shout *Snap!* When you have held up all the furniture cards, change the room on the board and repeat the activity.
- Play *Stop!* Call out random items of vocabulary, and when pupils hear a word related to home (*door, kitchen, bath*) they must shout *Stop!* e.g. **leg, pencil, green, library, fridge,** etc.

MAIN ACTIVITIES

1 Trace. Find the stickers.

- Hold up a flashcard or picture for *grandmother* and explain **This is my grandmother.** Do the same with the other family members: *grandfather, mother, father, sister, brother.* Each time you hold a flashcard up, place it on the board and gradually build up the family tree. Leave a space under each picture.
- Point to each family member on the board and this time ask **Who is this?** Elicit the name for each person. Explain **This is a family.** Write the word *family* as a heading on the board.
- Encourage pupils to use the word *mother (or mum).* If pupils ask why it is now *mother* and no longer *mummy,* say it is because they are now very big children and are learning the 'proper' words.
- Draw a branch off to one side of the family tree. Show the pupils flashcards for *aunt* and *uncle.* Add them to the family tree. Point to the aunt and ask the pupils **Who is this?** If a pupil answers correctly in their own language, reflect it back by saying **That's right! Aunt.** Repeat the process for *uncle* and *cousins.* Point to the *aunt, uncle* and *cousins* flashcards at random, naming them and encouraging pupils to repeat the vocabulary after you.
- Show the pupils a wordcard for one of the family members. Run your finger under the letters as you say the word, e.g. **Sister.** Encourage them to read the word together. Ask **Where is my sister?** and hold the word near different family members until the pupils say *Yes!* Stick the word under the appropriate flashcard. Repeat for another family member. This time choose a volunteer to place the word under the correct flashcard. Continue until the rest of the wordcards are in position under the corresponding flashcards. When they are all in position, point to each one again and read together.
- Say **Open your Pupil's Books on page 24.** Point to the name under each family member and encourage pupils to read the words together. Ask which family members are missing. *Grandfather, aunt, brother.*
- Say **Now we're going to write the words.** Pupils trace over the words and read them when they have finished. Then ask pupils to find the stickers. *See answers opposite.*
- Say **Stand up if you have sisters.** Ask random pupils how many sisters they have. Repeat with *brothers.*

Reading. (CD 1. Track 27)

- Ask pupils to look at the reading box. Say **Let's listen and read.** Play the audio. Ask pupils how many cousins Sam has. *Two.*
- Ask pupils to think about their families and how many cousins they have. Give pupils a moment to count. Tell them that when you say the word *cousins* they must hold up their fingers showing the number of cousins they have.

CLOSING ACTIVITIES

- Ask for the names of family members, e.g. **Do you have brothers? What is/are your brother(s) name(s)?** At this point you could also talk about the surnames of your family members.
- Play *Run and slap!* Write family vocabulary across the lower part of the board. Divide the class into two teams. Have a member from each team come and stand a metre from the board. Say **Sister.** Whoever is first to slap the word on the board gains a point for their team. Repeat with the other words.

EXTRA IDEAS

- Carry out a survey and complete a chart to show how many cousins each pupil has.
- Ask the pupils to bring in photos of their own family. Encourage them to show their photos to the rest of the class. They should point to the family members on the photo and name the people, e.g. *This is my sister. I have two cousins,* etc.

PAGE 25 Help at home

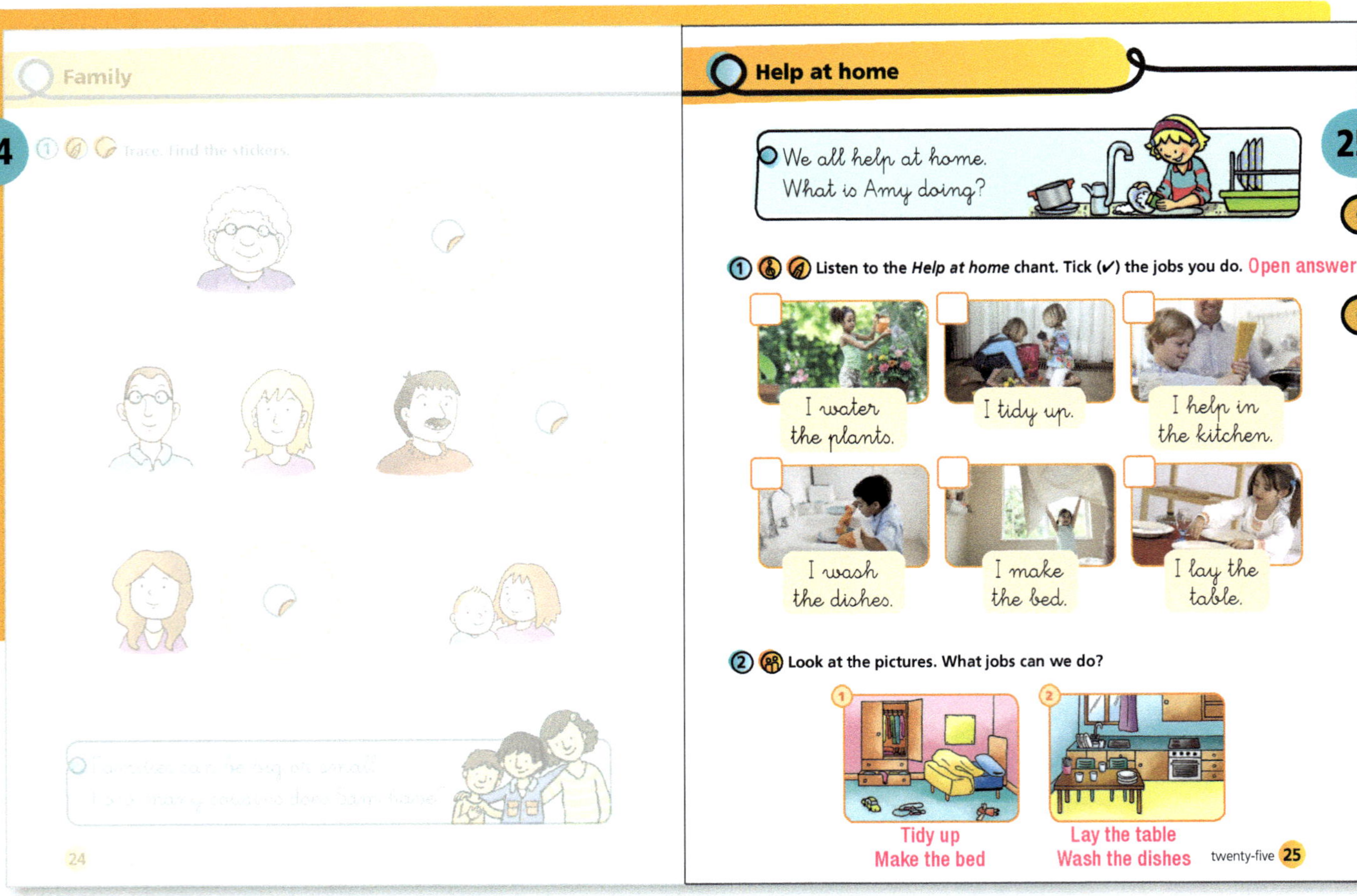

PAGE SUMMARY

In this lesson pupils will learn how to describe household jobs and consider what they do to help in the home.

LANGUAGE

- Water the plants, tidy up, help in the kitchen, wash the dishes, make the bed, lay the table
- Grandmother, grandfather, mother, father, sister, brother, aunt, uncle, cousins
- I have one brother. He/she has two sisters.

MATERIALS

Flashcards: (digital) see the *Teachers* section in the digital resources

Additional classroom materials: old or model camera, large sheet of card or paper

OPENING ACTIVITIES

- Play *Family photos*. Pretend to be a photographer. If possible, use a toy or old camera (or a rectangle of card with a circle and buttons to represent a camera for realism). Give family pictures or flashcards to some of the pupils. Tell them to form groups, e.g. **Mother, grandmother and sister** or **Aunt, uncle and cousins** and pretend to take their photograph.
- Show the *brother* picture or flashcard to the pupil on your left. Ask **How many brothers do you have?** Encourage them to answer in a sentence *I have (two) brothers*. Have the pupil pass the flashcard to the pupil sitting to their left. Repeat the question and help the pupil to answer in a sentence. If you have a confident class, pupils can begin to ask the question themselves. Once the *brother* flashcard is moving smoothly around the circle, start with the *sister* flashcard and then the *cousins* flashcard.

MAIN ACTIVITIES

Reading. (CD 1. Track 28)

- Review what pupils can do to help in the classroom (Unit 1). Ask **What do you do to help in the classroom?** *Put away materials, clean the board, put rubbish in the bin, help friends,* etc.
- Ask pupils **What do you do to help at home?** Let pupils come up with their own ideas. If they suggest a job in their own language, reflect it back in English, e.g. Say **Very good, you make the bed.**
- Tell pupils to open their Pupil's Books on page 25. Ask pupils to look at the reading box. Say **Let's listen and read.** Play the audio and ask what Amy is doing. *Washing the dishes.* Ask pupils to stand up if they wash the dishes at home.

1 Listen to the *Help at home* chant. Tick (✔) the jobs you do.

- Ask pupils to look at the photos. Point to the first one and ask **What is she doing?** *Watering plants.* Ask pupils to mime the action. Point to the sentence under the photo, read it and encourage pupils to follow with their finger. Repeat the procedure for the remaining photos.
- Focus pupils' attention on the musical note. Say **Let's listen to the *Help at home* chant.** Play the audio and ask pupils to listen and point to the jobs in the photos as they hear them. Play the audio again and pause after each job, encouraging pupils to mime it. Finally play the chant without stopping and have pupils join in with their mimes.

CD 1 • Track 29

What do you do to help at home? [x2]

I water the plants. I tidy up. I help in the kitchen.

What do you do to help at home? [x2]

I wash the dishes. I make the bed. I lay the table.

- Point to the first photo and say **Stand up if you water the plants at home.** Ask pupils to mime watering the plants.
- Point to the next photo and say **Stand up if you tidy up at home.** Ask pupils to mime tidying up. Continue in this way with the remaining photos of jobs.
- To those pupils who remain sitting ask **Who waters the plants / tidies up / washes the dishes at home?** Accept short answers, e.g. *father.*
- Tell pupils to now tick the boxes of the activities they do at home. As pupils do so, walk around and ask individual pupils **Do you help in the kitchen?** etc. Praise pupils for helping at home.

2 Look at the pictures. What jobs can we do?

- Ask pupils to look at the two pictures and name the furniture they see. Put up the corresponding flashcard as they name *bed, wardrobe, table, chair, oven.*
- Put pupils in groups of three. Tell pupils that they are going to look at the pictures and think about what jobs they can do to help.
- Give pupils time to make suggestions in their group and then ask for their ideas. Encourage pupils to mime the action as they name it. *See answers opposite.*

CLOSING ACTIVITIES

- Explain that it is important to help our mothers and fathers in the home (and also younger siblings). Encourage each pupil to say one job they do at home.
- Have volunteers stand up and mime a job for others to guess.

EXTRA IDEAS

- Make a *Helping hands* display. On a large sheet of card or paper, write the title *I help at home.* Tell pupils it is important to help around the house by doing as many jobs as possible. Write the names of some jobs on the board for the pupils to copy: *water the plants, wash the dishes, lay the table, tidy up,* etc. Pupils should trace around one of their hands and cut it out. On the hand they should write the job they do or draw a picture of themselves doing it. Stick the hands onto the display. Every time pupils help out with a new job, they can cut out a new hand for the display.

PAGES 26-27 Let's investigate and Make a difference

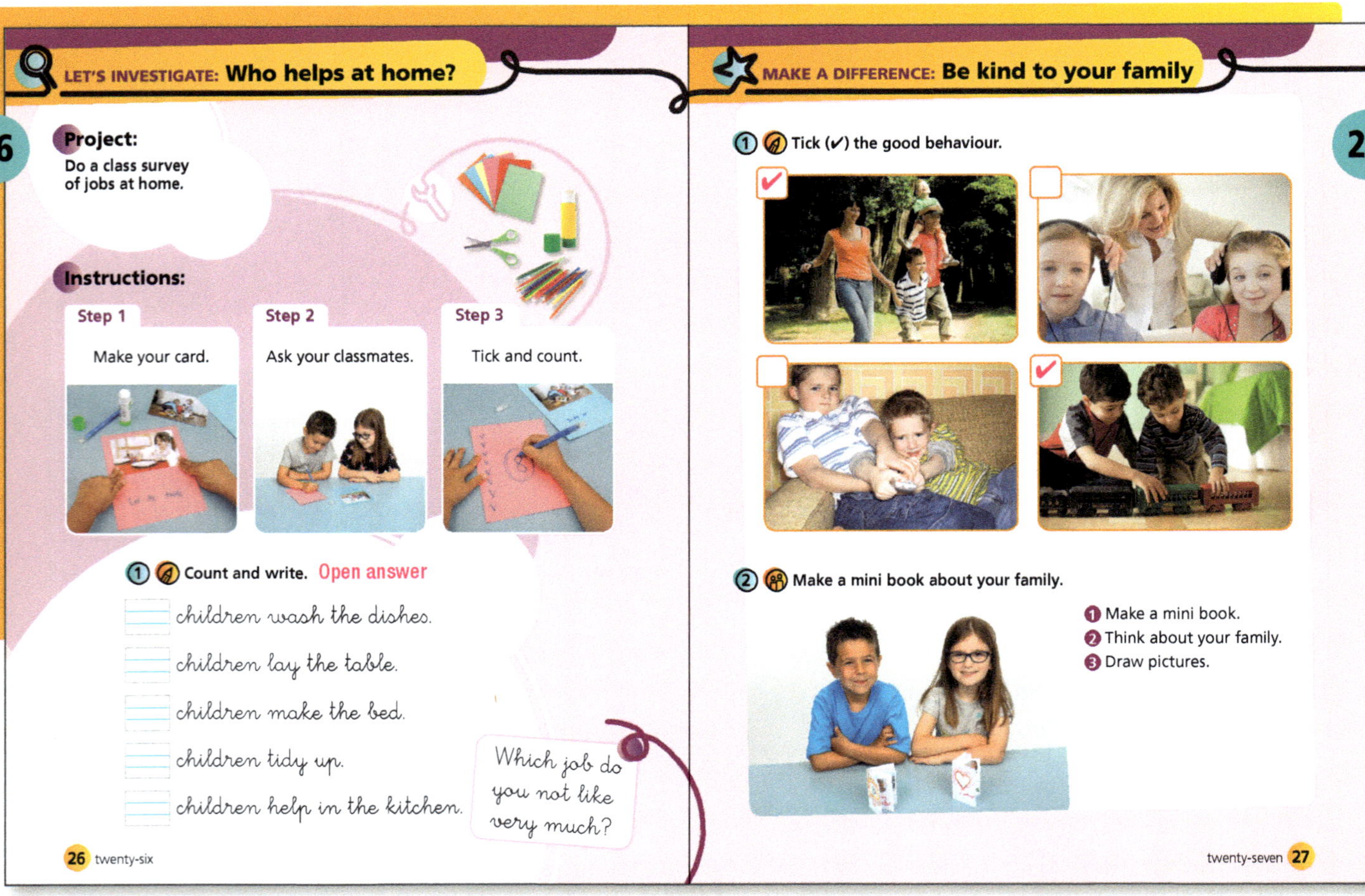

LET'S INVESTIGATE: **Who helps at home?**

26

Project:
Do a class survey of jobs at home.

Instructions:

Step 1 — Make your card.

Step 2 — Ask your classmates.

Step 3 — Tick and count.

① Count and write. Open answer

___ children wash the dishes.
___ children lay the table.
___ children make the bed.
___ children tidy up.
___ children help in the kitchen.

Which job do you not like very much?

26 twenty-six

MAKE A DIFFERENCE: **Be kind to your family**

27

① Tick (✓) the good behaviour.

② Make a mini book about your family.

1. Make a mini book.
2. Think about your family.
3. Draw pictures.

twenty-seven 27

PAGE SUMMARY

Pupils will carry out a simple survey to find out how many pupils do household jobs. They will also reflect on what is good behaviour in the home.

LANGUAGE

- Water the plants, tidy up, help in the kitchen, wash the dishes, make the bed, lay the table
- This is my grandmother / grandfather / mother / father / brother / sister / cousin.

MATERIALS

Flashcards: (digital) see the *Teachers* section in the digital resources

Additional classroom materials: A4 coloured card, magazines (with household jobs)

Pages 26 and 27 relate to household jobs and behaving thoughtfully towards your family. The ***Let's investigate*** page teaches pupils how to carry out a simple survey to see how many pupils in the class do a certain household job. Carrying out the survey makes pupils aware of the importance of helping at home and also provides a suitable context for using the language.

The ***Make a difference*** page develops the theme of the roles we play at home and makes pupils aware of the importance of behaving well and being kind to other family members in the home. Pupils make a small booklet to fill with drawings of family members to talk about with others. Make one yourself, before the class, to use as an example.

LET'S INVESTIGATE

⊕ OPENING ACTIVITIES

- Call out different household jobs and have pupils mime the action.
- Play the *Help at home* chant from the previous lesson and encourage pupils to join in.
- Ask individual pupils **Do you tidy up / lay the table?** etc.

MAIN ACTIVITIES

- Tell the pupils they are going to investigate how many of them help around the house and which jobs they do. Ask pupils to open their Pupil's Books on page 26. Point to and read out the task.
- Point to the photos and explain that each pupil is going to choose a household job and make a card. Divide the class into five groups and give each group a job to survey. Pupils will then make individual cards for that job by finding and sticking a picture and writing the job name.
- Pupils circulate and ask their classmates about the job on their card, e.g. *Do you make the bed / wash the dishes / tidy up?* etc. Make sure pupils know their question before they circulate.
- Demonstrate how pupils can collect answers by placing a tick on the other side of their card each time a classmate says *Yes* to their question.

1 Count and write.

- Focus pupils' attention on the sentences. Read each one out and encourage pupils to follow.
- Ask pupils to count up the ticks on their cards in their groups and write the number next to the job they investigated.
- Ask pupils for their results. Ask **How many children wash the dishes / lay the table?** Encourage pupils to listen to the results and write the number for the other sentences.

⊕ CLOSING ACTIVITIES

- Ask pupils which jobs they don't like doing.

MAKE A DIFFERENCE

⊕ OPENING ACTIVITIES

- Ask volunteers to mime good behaviour at school, e.g. *tidying up, putting rubbish in the bin, lining up correctly, sharing materials,* etc.
- Play the *Help at home* chant again from the previous lesson and encourage pupils to join in.

MAIN ACTIVITIES

1 Tick (✔) the good behaviour.

- Focus pupils' attention on the photos. Point to the first photo. With a more confident class ask **What are the family doing?** *Walking in the park.* Ask **Is this good behaviour?** *Yes.* With a less confident class, say **The family are walking in the park. Is this good behaviour?** Ask pupils to tick the box. Repeat the procedure for the other photos. *See answers opposite.*
- Ask pupils to work in pairs and mime bad or good behaviour at home (e.g. *throwing clothes on the floor, slamming doors, cleaning some spilt liquid,* etc.) for others to guess.

2 Make a mini book about your family.

- Make a mini book before the class to use as an example. Include drawings or photos of your family.
- Read the instructions and have pupils follow in their books.
- Demonstrate or show the video of how to fold the A4 paper to make a mini book. Show the class your example.
- Encourage pupils to talk about their family with classmates as they make their book.
- Encourage more confident pupils to look at the unit or their picture dictionary for the spelling of family words so they can label their pictures.

⊕ CLOSING ACTIVITIES

- Put pupils with a new partner and have them talk about their family using their booklets. *This is my grandmother. Her name is Berta,* etc.

PAGES 28-29 Let's remember

Let's remember

28

30

1 Listen and tick (✔).

2 Think about your home. Circle. Open answer

My home

My bedroom

My living room

My kitchen

28 twenty-eight

29

3 Trace.

brother

cousins

father

4 Match.

make the bed

wash the dishes

tidy up

Name three rooms in a house.

Name three objects in a bedroom.

Name three members of a family.

I know how to help at home every day!

Well done! Choose a sticker.

twenty-nine 29

PAGE SUMMARY

Pupils review unit content and undertake a simple self-assessment on the unit content.

LANGUAGE

- Grandfather, grandmother, father, mother, brother, sister, uncle, aunt, cousins
- Bedroom, living room, kitchen, bathroom, bed, sofa, fridge, toilet
- Make the bed, wash the dishes, tidy up
- I live in a house / flat.
- There is a bed. There are two tables.

MATERIALS

Flashcards: digital flashcards for the unit

Additional classroom materials: displays and posters made during the unit

MAIN ACTIVITIES

1 Listen and tick (✔).

- Shuffle pictures or flashcards for types of furniture and family members. Hold up the first flashcard, e.g. *fridge* and say **This is a bed.** Encourage pupils to correct you. *No, it's a fridge.* Hold up a flashcard of a family member, e.g. *grandmother.* Say **This is my cousin.** Pupils should say *No, it's your grandmother.* Continue holding up and making false statements about each of the flashcards. For each of the furniture items, ask **Which room is it in?**
- Ask pupils to open their Pupil's Books on page 28. Point to each photo and ask pupils what they can see.
- Tell pupils they are going to listen and tick the things they hear. Play the audio twice so that pupils have time to check their answers. *See answers above.*

CD 1 • Track 30

Window – window; grandfather – grandfather; bathroom – bathroom; chair – chair.

2 Think about your home. Circle.

- Draw a big picture of a house on the board and encourage pupils to tell you as much information as possible to build up the picture.
- Tell pupils to think about their homes. Draw their attention to the first row of pictures. Encourage pupils to read *My home* together. Point to each home in turn and ask **Is this your home?** When pupils say *Yes*, say **Circle your home.**
- Point to the second row of pictures. Read *My bedroom* together. Point to each picture in turn and ask **Is this in your bedroom?** When pupils say *Yes*, say **Circle it.** Repeat the procedure with the last two rows of pictures.
- Call a volunteer to come to the front and talk about the pictures they circled. Encourage them to say *I live in a house / flat. There is a bed in my bedroom*, etc.
- Have pupils work in pairs and tell each other what they have circled using full sentences.

3 Trace.

- Play *Hangman* with the word *family*.
- Play *Guess my word*. Have pupils guess the family words (*sister, aunt, grandmother*, etc.) that you write on the board before you finish spelling them.
- Have pupils look at page 29. Point to the word under the first picture. Encourage pupils to read the word with a partner before reading it to you. Repeat this step with the other two family words and have pupils trace them.
- With a partner, ask pupils to spell other family words and then to check them in their picture dictionary.

4 Match.

- Say **Show me what we can do to help in the home.** Appoint a volunteer to mime helping at home. Have the rest of the class guess. Nominate other volunteers to mime other activities.
- Focus the pupils' attention on the pictures and elicit what the children are doing.
- Focus attention on the phrases. Read them together one by one and have the pupils point to the corresponding picture below.
- Have pupils then read the phrases individually and draw a line to match the phrase with the corresponding picture. *See answers opposite.*

Self-assessment

- Focus pupils' attention on the self-assessment table. Read the first sentence together: *Name three rooms in a house.* Ask pupils to quickly draw a house with a partner, divide the house into rooms and name the rooms together.
- Now read the sentence: *Name three objects in a bedroom.* Ask partners to now draw three things in the bedroom of their picture and name them.
- Then read the sentence: *Name three members of a family.* Encourage pupils to count on their fingers as they name three family members to a partner.
- Finally, together read the sentence: *I know how to help at home every day!* Have pupils mime and guess activities they do to help at home with a partner.
- After reading each sentence, the pupils should tick the boxes according to whether they have learned a lot (*very happy face*), some things (*happy face*) or a little (*disappointed face*) about their home.
- Ask pupils to choose a sticker to show how they feel about their learning in the unit.
- Give individual attention to any pupils who choose the *disappointed* sticker.

+ EXTRA IDEAS

- If there is time, review and talk about any displays the class have done during the unit, such as paintings of their house, pictures of their bedrooms, the *Helping hands* display, the mini book about their family, etc.

UNIT 2

Activity book answers

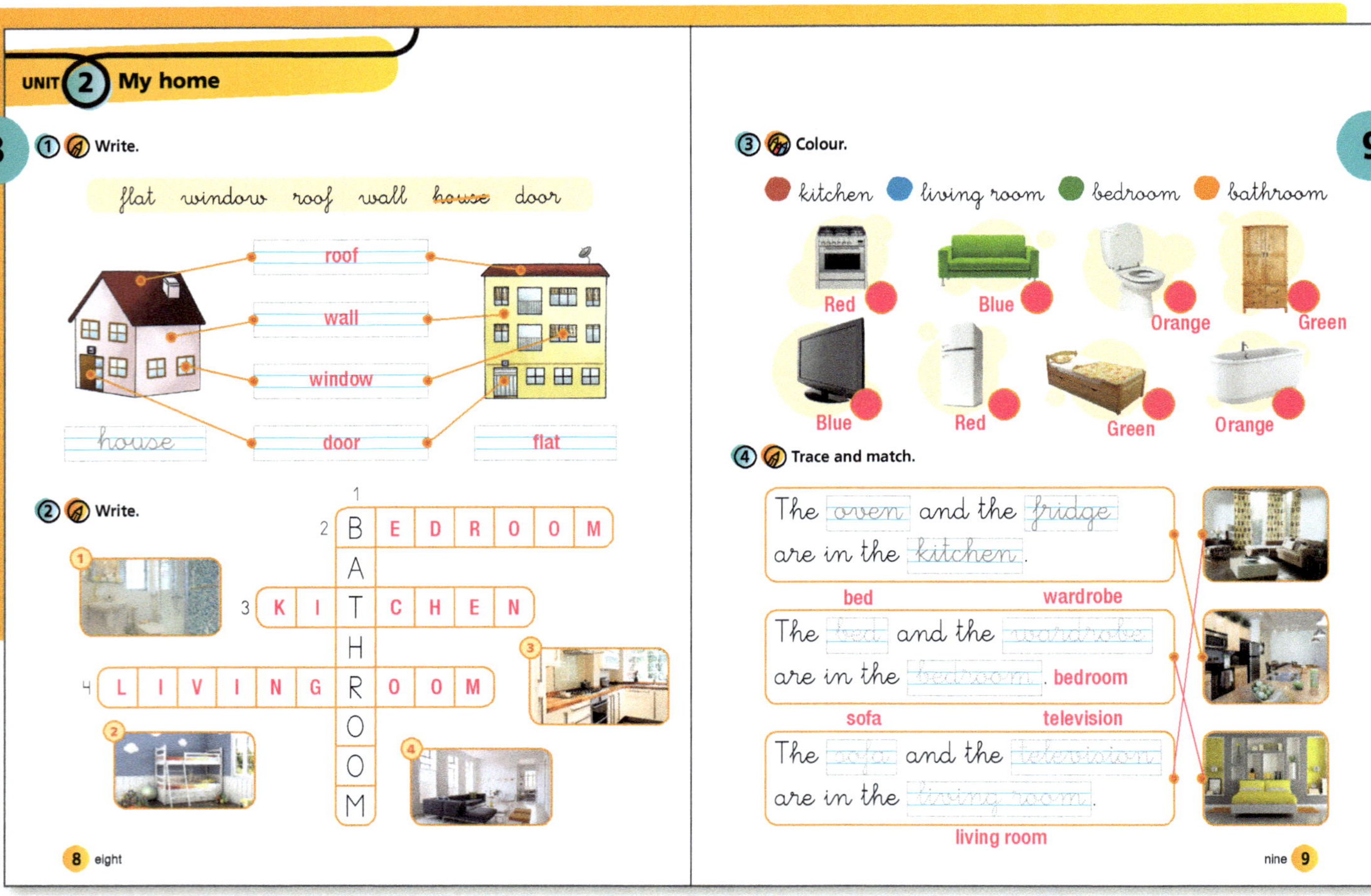

UNIT 2 My home

8

1 Write.

flat window roof wall ~~house~~ door

roof

wall

window

house

door

flat

2 Write.

1 BATHROOM

2 BEDROOM

3 KITCHEN

4 LIVING ROOM

8 eight

9

3 Colour.

kitchen living room bedroom bathroom

Red Blue Orange Green

Blue Red Green Orange

4 Trace and match.

The oven and the fridge are in the kitchen.

bed wardrobe

The bed and the wardrobe are in the bedroom. bedroom

sofa television

The sofa and the television are in the living room.

living room

nine 9

UNIT 2

10

5 Write.

cousins father grandmother sister uncle brother

grandmother

grandfather

father

mother

uncle

aunt

sister

brother

cousins

6 Circle the family members.

sisterkitchencousinsauntbedgrandfatherwardrobeunclemother

10 ten

11

7 Read and circle the correct word.

I wash/make the bed.

I lay/make the table.

I help in the kitchen/bedroom.

I water/wash the dishes.

I water/wash the plants.

I make the bed/tidy up.

8 Trace. Say who is doing each job.

wash the dishes

make the bed

make the bed

tidy up

tidy up

eleven 11

UNIT 2

Let's investigate at home!

Make a *Help at home* chart

1 

Design and colour your chart.

2 
Put it in the kitchen.

3 
Do the jobs on your chart every day.

4 

Put a sticker on your chart when you help at home.

1 Write. Open answer

Do you help at home every day? ______

What is your favourite job? ______

13

Skills check

1 Look at the pictures. Look at the letters. Write the words.

 f r i d g e — i / e f g / r d

1  h o u s e — h u / e s o

2  w a r d r o b e — b r e / r w / d a o

3  u n c l e — n e c / l u

4  w i n d o w — i w / w d / n o

5  c o u s i n s — s / o c i n / u s

TERM 1 Work together

CONTENT	EVALUATION CRITERIA
Conflict resolution strategies: use of rules and appreciation of peaceful and tolerant coexistence.	Recognise cooperation and dialogue as a way to avoid and resolve conflicts, encouraging democratic values.
Introduction to scientific knowledge and its application in the Social Sciences. Collect relevant information using different sources (direct and indirect).	Obtain specific and relevant information, using different sources.
Develop strategies to organise, memorise and remember information obtained through different methods and from different sources.	Develop a capacity for hard work and show perseverance while studying.
Team-building strategies.	Develop a cooperative and adaptive attitude, recognising merit in others' ideas and responding to situations with intuition, an open mind and flexibility.
Use of different text types and graphic languages.	Obtain, analyse and adapt the information received from a variety of different textual and graphic formats.
With help, plan and manage simple projects, showing independence and initiative in order to achieve objectives.	Develop creativity and initiative, improving their capacity to acquire information and ideas and present innovative conclusions.
Techniques for intellectual work. Elaboration of diagrams and summaries, memorising and structuring the information received. Reading techniques for Social Science publications.	Employ techniques appropriate to intellectual tasks; produce work and make presentations both individually and as a group, involving research, selection and organisation of texts of a social, geographical or historical nature, while showing autonomy and collaborative skills.
Rights and obligations.	Identify rights and obligations in the context of school and the classroom.

LEARNING STANDARDS	KEY COMPETENCES	PAGES
Values cooperation and dialogue as a way of avoiding and resolving conflicts.	SOC	30, 31
Appreciates the classroom assembly as an opportunity to air grievances and resolve conflicts.	SOC	30, 31
Looks for, selects and organises information, analysing it and drawing conclusions. Reflects on the process followed and reports on it orally.	MST, LIN, LTL	30, 31
Performs academic tasks in a responsible and effective manner.	LTL	30, 31
Uses vocabulary correctly in the presentation of their work.	LTL, LIN	30, 31
Develops a cooperative and adaptive attitude, recognising merit in others' ideas and responding to situations with intuition, an open mind and flexibility.	LTL, SOC	30, 31
Participates effectively and constructively in daily life and develops strategies for conflict resolution.	LTL, SOC	30, 31
Identifies and uses the correct code of conduct for their environment.	LTL, SOC	30, 31
Analyses information related to the subject area and handles images, tables, graphs, diagrams and summaries using both traditional supports and Information and Communication Technologies.	AUT, LTL	30, 31
Shows self-confidence, personal initiative, curiosity, interest and creativity in the learning process.	AUT, LTL	30, 31
Shows independence in the planning and carrying out of simple actions and shows initiative when taking decisions.	AUT, LTL	30, 31
Produces work and makes presentations both individually and as part of a group, participating in the research, selection and organisation of texts of a social, geographical or historical nature.	SOC, AUT	30, 31
Identifies their rights and obligations in the context of school and the classroom.	SOC	30, 31

PAGES 30-31 Work together: Conflict resolution

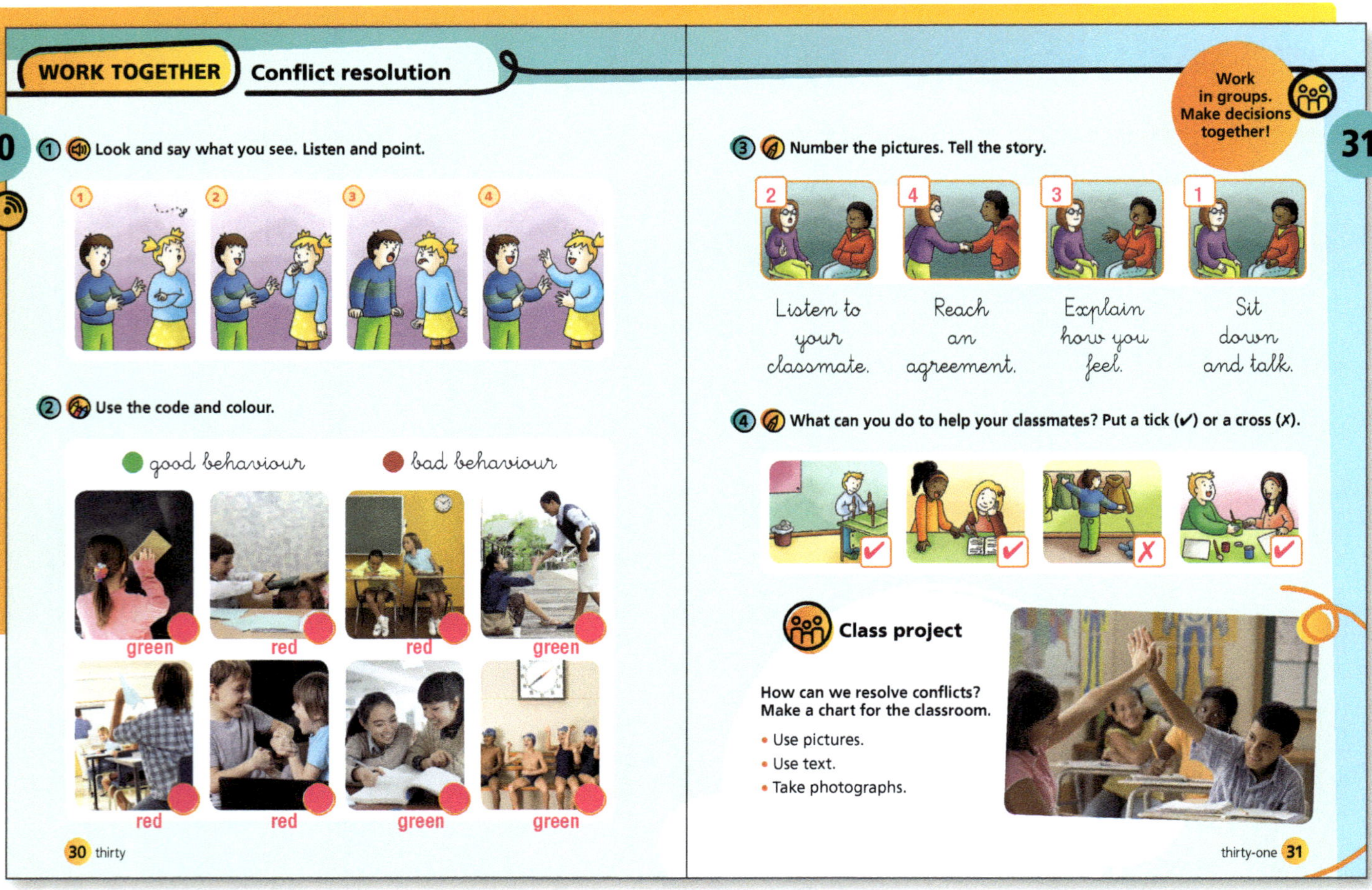

PAGE SUMMARY

On these pages pupils will revise what a conflict is, how to avoid them and different conflict resolution techniques. The different activities will be carried out following different cooperative learning structures that will provide the optimal learning experience for the pupil and guarantee the involvement of all the members of the group.

LANGUAGE

- Talk, listen, explain, reach an agreement, help, share
- Yes, it is / No, it isn't.
- I agree / I disagree. I think (…).

MATERIALS

Flashcards: (digital) see the *Teachers* section in the digital resources

Additional classroom materials: photos of different ways of resolving conflicts

OPENING ACTIVITIES

- Before doing these activities using different cooperative learning structures, you should form the groups. Teachers should form the groups rather than letting the pupils choose their own group members. Remember to form heterogeneous groups of three or four pupils.
- Tell the pupils what they will be doing in their groups, what procedures you will follow and what your expectations are. If during these activities any group is having problems, spend some time in class on the relevant team skills.

MAIN ACTIVITIES

1 Look and say what you see. Listen and point.

- This is a *Round robin* activity. Focus pupils' attention on the four pictures on page 30 and ask them to describe what they see.
- Ask pupils to take turns giving their opinions. Ensure that each pupil shares something with their group.
- Ask them to listen to the audio and point to the pictures described.

CD 1 • Track 31

1. Boy: **Hey, I'm talking to you. Why aren't you listening?** Girl: **La la la la ...**
2. Boy: **And that's what I did on my holidays!** Girl: **Mmm-hmm. Wow, that's really interesting!**
3. Boy: **It's your fault!** Girl: **No, it's your fault!**
4. Boy: **Haha, that's really funny!** Girl: **Haha, I know!**

2 Use the code and colour.

- This is a *Rally robin* activity. Focus your pupils' attention on the eight photos in activity 2.
- Ask pupils to decide whether the pictures show good or bad behaviour. Ensure that each pupil shares something with their group.
- Ask your pupils to take turns giving their opinions about the behaviour in the photos.
- Then ask them to colour the good behaviour green and the bad behaviour red. *See answers opposite.*

3 Number the pictures. Tell the story.

- This is a *Timed pair share* activity. Ask your pupils to work in pairs and look at the pictures. Tell them that they have to order the pictures to complete the story and find out how the two children resolved their conflict.
- Ask pupils to think independently about the pictures, choosing the correct answer for each of them. Then tell your pupils to discuss their answers in pairs, ensuring that pupils show their ideas and consider those of others.
- Ask the pairs to share their answers with the class and then number the pictures correctly. *2, 4, 3, 1.*

4 What can you do to help your classmates? Put a tick (✔) or a cross (✗).

- This is a *Stand up, hand up, pair up* activity. Before doing this activity, explain how this particular cooperative structure works:
  - The teacher says **Stand up, hand up, pair up as quickly as you can.**
  - Pupils stand up and keep one hand in the air until they find a partner. Pupils then high five their partner.
  - The teacher asks a question and provides thinking time.
  - Pupils share using the method the teacher gives.
- Say **Stand up, hand up, pair up as quickly as you can.** Using the zoom on the interactive whiteboard, show pupils the first picture. Ask them if we should do what the picture shows to help our classmates. Pupils discuss with their partner and share their ideas with the rest of the class.
- Repeat the process with the rest of the pictures. Pupils should work with a different partner for each picture and complete the boxes with a tick or a cross. *See answers opposite.*

CLASS PROJECT

- This is a *Rally coach* activity. Focus your pupils' attention on the class project. In their groups, they will make a conflict resolution chart for the classroom.
- Ask them to look for pictures and write short sentences on their chart.
- Tell them that when pupil A chooses a picture and writes a sentence, pupil B watches, listens, checks and praises.
- When pupil B chooses a picture and writes a sentence, pupil A watches, listens, checks and praises.
- Once they have finished, ask them to share their results with the class.

+ CLOSING ACTIVITIES

- Group assessment is essential in cooperative learning to ensure that there is analysis of interactions and promotion of teamwork. Pupils should learn that how they work together affects the quality and quantity of concepts that they learn and understand.
- Ask the pupils to reflect on how they felt in their cooperative groups.
- Then ask the pupils to discuss how the group worked together and identify ideas and actions that helped the group achieve its goals.
- Once they have shared their results, ask them to reflect on how could the project be made better next time.Invite your pupils to share their conclusions with the class.

PAGES 32-33 Review

32

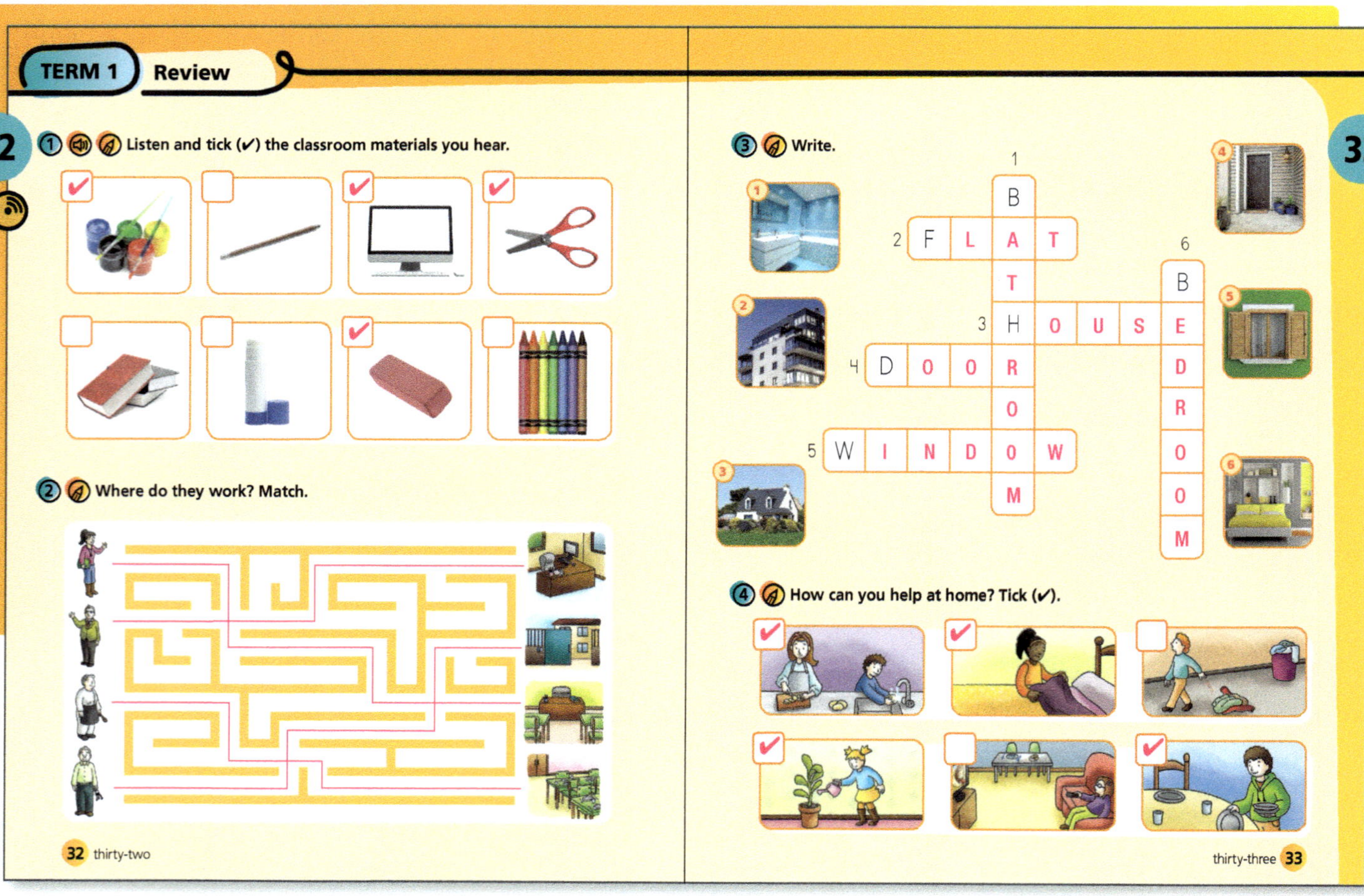

PAGE SUMMARY

Your pupils will use these pages to review content from Term 1 (Units 1 and 2).

LANGUAGE

- Paint, pencil, computer, scissors, books, glue, rubber, crayons
- Teacher, head teacher, cook, caretaker
- Playground, office, classroom, dining hall
- House, flat, window, door, wall
- Living room, kitchen, bedroom, bathroom
- Help in the kitchen, make the bed, water the plants, lay the table, wash the dishes, tidy up

MATERIALS

Flashcards: digital flashcards for Units 1 and 2

Additional classroom materials: origami paper or A4 paper cut into squares, posters and displays pupils have made during Units 1 and 2

OPENING ACTIVITIES

- Tell pupils that they are going to review things that they studied in Units 1 and 2. Divide the board into two. Ask pupils to help you spell the word *school* and write it at the top of one side of the board. Ask the pupils to help you spell the word *home* and write it on the other side. Divide the class into two teams and jumble all the flashcards or pictures from Units 1 and 2. Show a flashcard to one team, e.g. *crayons*. They must call out where it belongs: *Home!* or *School!* Put the flashcard on the board on the *school* side and continue with the other flashcards. This sorting game should be quite fast. No points are needed.
- Play *I Spy* with the flashcards on the board and review the names of the items. Ask pupils to help you spell the word on the board once it has been guessed.

MAIN ACTIVITIES

1 Listen and tick (✔) the classroom materials you hear.

- Ask pupils to open their Pupil's Books on page 32. Focus pupils' attention on activity 1 and ask them to look at the classroom items and name them together.
- Point to the instruction and read it out while they follow the words with their finger. Play the audio and have pupils tick the pictures they hear. Ask pupils which items have a tick. *See answers opposite.*

CD 1 • Track 32
Scissors – scissors; computer – computer; rubber – rubber; paints – paints.

- Put pupils in pairs and ask them to look in their picture dictionary and find the spelling for three of the items they see. Ask pupils to write the three words on a sheet of paper.
- Have pupils show their words to another pair and tick the words they have that are the same.

2 Where do they work? Match.

- Ask pupils to remember the names of people who help us in a school and elicit where they work.
- Say **Let's look at activity 2.** Read the question. Point to each person and ask **Who is this?** Ask pupils to name the places on the right. Ask **Who works in an office / playground?** etc.
- Ask pupils to match the person with the correct area in the school. *See answers opposite.*
- Review the activity by encouraging pupils to say *A teacher works in the classroom. The head teacher works in an office*, etc.

3 Write.

- Play *Guess my word.* Choose one of the words from the crossword and begin to spell it on the board. Ask pupils to guess your word before you finish spelling it. Repeat the game with other words from the crossword.
- Focus pupils' attention on the crossword on page 33 and point to picture 1. Ask **What room is it?** *Bathroom.* Using a whiteboard, a notebook or a sheet of paper, ask pupils to have a go at spelling the word *bathroom.* Tell pupils they can work or check with a partner.
- Help pupils by sounding out the word phonetically **B-a-th-r-oo-m**, and drawing the letter spaces on the board. Encourage pupils to check spellings in the unit or in the picture dictionary. Have a volunteer spell the word on the board. Ask the class **Is that right?** Point to the crossword and indicate where to write the word (in capitals).
- Repeat the procedure with the other words. *See answers opposite.*
- Ask pupils what furniture or objects they can find in a bathroom or bedroom. Ask pupils which rooms are not in the crossword. *Kitchen, living room, dining room.*

4 How can you help at home? Tick (✔).

- Say **This is how I help at home.** Mime some household jobs, e.g. laying the table, watering the plants, making the bed. Encourage pupils to guess the job.
- Read the question for activity 4 and focus pupils' attention on the pictures. Ask **What is he/she doing? Is he/she helping at home?** for each picture.
- Tell pupils to only tick the activities that help. *See answers opposite.* Ask pupils to tell you one thing they do to help at home.

CLOSING ACTIVITIES

- Encourage pupils to talk about or mime good behaviour at school or at home.
- Ask pupils how home and school are different or similar.
- Praise everyone for working well this term.

EXTRA IDEAS

- Play *Team mime.* Divide the class into two teams. One member of each team sits in a chair facing their team, but with their back to the board. Put a flashcard on the board from Unit 1 or 2. Both teams must mime what is on the flashcard for their team member to guess. The first to guess what their team is miming gains a point for their team. Repeat with new team members guessing each time. There should be no speaking, just miming!
- Teach pupils how to make an *Origami house.* Have pupils draw windows and a door on the front and choose two house words to write on the back.

UNIT 3 Where I live

CONTENT	EVALUATION CRITERIA
The street: characteristics and elements.	Understand the social organisation of their immediate surroundings: the street.
Correct behaviour in the street and road safety.	Respect the basic rules of pedestrians and users of public transport. Observe and recognise street elements essential for a pedestrian.
Cities, towns and villages.	Understand the social organisation of their immediate surroundings: cities, towns and villages.
Means of transport.	Identify the most common means of transport.
Introduction to scientific knowledge and its application in the Social Sciences. Collect relevant information using different sources (direct and indirect).	Obtain specific and relevant information, using different sources.
Develop strategies to organise, memorise and remember information obtained through different methods and from different sources.	Develop a capacity for hard work and show perseverance while studying.
Team-building strategies.	Develop a cooperative and adaptive attitude, recognising merit in others' ideas and responding to situations with intuition, an open mind and flexibility.
With help, plan and manage simple projects, showing independence and initiative in order to achieve objectives.	Develop creativity and initiative, improving their capacity to acquire information and ideas and present innovative conclusions.
Correct use of different materials.	Use the materials in a suitable way.
Techniques for intellectual work. Elaboration of diagrams and summaries, memorising and structuring the information received. Reading techniques for Social Science publications.	Employ techniques appropriate to intellectual tasks; produce work and make presentations both individually and as a group, involving research, selection and organisation of texts of a social, geographical or historical nature, while showing autonomy and collaborative skills.
Rights and obligations.	Identify some of their rights and obligations in the context of their city, town or village.

LEARNING STANDARDS	KEY COMPETENCES	PAGES
Identifies and names the different elements in the street.	SOC, LIN	34–38
Knows and respects the norms of road safety and uses them as a pedestrian and as a user of different means of transport.	SOC, LTL, AUT	34–37, 41, 45
Establishes routes on a simple plan of a town or city, and understands the concept of a safe route.	SOC, LTL, AUT	40, 41
Identifies and interprets the road signs necessary to ensure safety when walking in the street: traffic lights, pedestrian crossing, etc.	SOC, LTL, AUT	36, 37, 41
Lists certain characteristics of towns and villages.	SOC, LIN	39
Understands some differences between towns and villages, knows the elements of towns and cities and understands the idea of a neighbourhood and where they live.	SOC, AUT	38–40
Recognises the differences between different means of transport and values their usefulness.	SOC	42, 43
Classifies different means of transport that exist in their immediate surroundings and differentiates between transport of people and goods.	SOC	42, 43
Looks for, selects and organises information, analysing it and drawing conclusions. Reflects on the process followed and reports on it orally.	MST, LIN, LTL	44, 45
Performs academic tasks in a responsible and effective manner.	LTL	44, 45
Uses vocabulary correctly in the presentation of their work.	LTL, LIN	44, 45
Develops a cooperative and adaptive attitude, recognising merit in others' ideas and responding to situations with intuition, an open mind and flexibility.	LTL, SOC	35, 44, 45
Participates effectively and constructively in daily life and develops strategies for conflict resolution.	LTL, SOC	45
Identifies and uses the correct code of conduct for their environment.	LTL, SOC	45
Shows self-confidence, personal initiative, curiosity, interest and creativity in the learning process.	AUT, LTL	44, 45
Shows independence in the planning and carrying out of simple actions and shows initiative when taking decisions.	AUT, LTL	44, 45
Uses the materials in a suitable and careful way, thereby keeping them in good condition.	LTL, SOC	44
Produces work and makes presentations both individually and as part of a group, participating in the research, selection and organisation of texts of a social, geographical or historical nature.	SOC, AUT	34–45
Identifies some of their rights and obligations in the context of their city, town or village.	SOC	35, 36, 45

UNIT INFORMATION

UNIT SUMMARY

In this unit your pupils will look outside their home and into the wider community to notice the streets, facilities and features in the place that they live. They will study the differences between cities, towns and villages, and how maps and addresses can help us find our way around.

Pupils will also consider the different ways we travel on land, on water and in the air and how objects are transported.

Pupils will develop observation and map-reading skills. They will need continuous recycling of the wide range of vocabulary in the unit.

PROJECT

Let's investigate

In the *Let's investigate* activity on page 44, your pupils will investigate and make a map of their local area. You will need to prepare a simple street map of your local area on A3 card for each group.

The pupils need:

- A4 paper
- Pencil
- Coloured pencils, crayons or felt tips
- Glue
- Scissors

VALUES AND ATTITUDES

In this unit your pupils will learn the importance of observing basic safety rules in the street and how to behave responsibly when outside the home. Throughout the unit, try to encourage pupils to think about:

- How to be safe in the street.
- How to keep the streets clean.
- How to behave correctly in the place where they live.

Make a difference

The *Make a difference* page in this unit focuses on how to behave responsibly as citizens. Pupils will make a poster with advice on how to look after and keep clean the place where they live.

EVALUATION MATERIAL

These documents can be downloaded from the *Teachers* section of the digital resources and printed.

The materials include:

- **Unit diagnostic test:** provides an overview of the unit and allows you to assess the pupils' prior knowledge.
- **End-of-unit test:** in addition to the *Review* section at the end of each unit, this summative test can be used to evaluate pupils' progress after studying the unit content.
- **Unit evaluation grid:** based on the evaluation criteria and learning standards of the unit.

DIGITAL RESOURCES

Presentations

- **Unit summary**: a simple slide presentation with text, images and audio to review the main ideas of the unit. It can be used at the beginning of the unit to test pupils' prior knowledge of the unit content or at the end of the unit as a revision tool.
- **Let's investigate**: a slide presentation of the unit's *Let's investigate* page with text, photos and audio. The slide presentation is perfect for a heads-up class, showing the steps one by one. Use this tool to get the pupils to predict the next steps (with their books closed) or to focus their attention on each step as they carry out the project themselves.

Activities

- **Memory game**: useful activity for reviewing key vocabulary and modelling pronunciation.
- **Wordsearch**: use at the end of the unit as a revision activity. Turn it into a game by getting the pupils to work in teams.
- **Spelling**: get a volunteer to come to the board and carry out the activity, but with the help of the whole class.

Song lyrics

Listen to the song *Where I live* and follow the lyrics line by line.

Posters

Attractive and informative posters to display in class. You can use them to review key concepts and vocabulary.

Videos

Use the video links in this unit to present content in a dynamic, real-life context whilst reinforcing the pupils' listening skills.

Teachers

Digital flashcards: a bank of digital images which can be used in a variety of ways in class.

Downloadable pdfs: evaluation tests, evaluation grids, templates, useful links and further information.

PAGES 34-35 Where I live

PAGE SUMMARY

The aim of the unit opener is to encourage your pupils' observation skills and introduce them to the main activities and features of town life. You will be able to gauge and build on what vocabulary pupils already know and develop their confidence.

LANGUAGE

- Car, van, lorry, bicycle, bus, motorbike
- He/she is walking / driving / shopping / crossing the road / taking out money / riding a bicycle / reading / cleaning.

MATERIALS

Flashcards: (digital) see the *Teachers* section in the digital resources

WHAT CAN YOU SEE?

Before your pupils open their books, ask how they come to school and what they can see on their way. Write the names of transport on one side of the board and other things they can see on the other side. Draw simple pictures next to each word to help understanding.

Point to each word and picture on the board and say **Stand up if you can see (a bus) on the way to school.** Have pupils sit down between each statement.

Tell pupils to open their books on pages 34 and 35. Ask **Where is the chameleon?** *On the bus.* Ask pupils what transport they can see in the picture. Ask if they can add any more transport words to their list on the board.

Ask pupils to name things they can see in the picture that are not written on the board. Add this vocabulary. Read all the vocabulary on the board together and, at the same time, have pupils point to the things that are in the picture.

OPENING ACTIVITIES

- Play *I Spy* with things in the illustration.
- Tell pupils to close their books and remember what people are doing in the town, e.g. *shopping, riding a bicycle, walking, driving*, etc.

MAIN ACTIVITIES

1 What is Amy doing?

- Have pupils work in groups. Say **Count how many people you can see in the town**. Say **Where is Amy? What is she doing?** *Throwing rubbish in the bin.* Say **Find Sam. What is he doing?** *Waving to his mother.* Ask pupils to tell you where they think the two children are going. *To school.*

2 Count the different types of transport.

- Have the groups count the different types of transport. *Five.* Ask them to spell their names on a mini whiteboard or on a sheet of paper. Ask volunteers to spell a word on the board. Ask **What colour is the bus / van / car? What colour is your bicycle / car / school bus?**

3 Who is doing something wrong? Circle.

- Say **Amy is putting rubbish in the bin. This is good behaviour. Who is doing something wrong?** Again, encourage pupils to work together in groups to identify and circle the man dropping litter.
- Praise the class for working together and ask pupils to choose a sticker for their effort of working with a group.

4 Listen and colour the objects you hear.

- Have pupils look at the black and white pictures, point to the words and read them together.
- Focus pupils' attention on the musical note. Say **Let's listen to a song**. Tell the pupils that they are going to listen to the song twice and colour the pictures. Pause after each verse on the second listening to give pupils time to colour.

CD 1 • Track 33

See audio script below.

5 Sing the song and do the actions!

- Say **Now let's listen and do the actions**. Play the song, teach the actions and encourage pupils to copy. Repeat the song and do the actions together.

CD 1 • Track 34

There are lots of shops where I live *[jazz hands]*
Fantastic shops where I live *[wave hands over head]*
There are lots of shops where I live *[jazz hands]*
Fantastic shops where I live *[wave hands over head]*
Lots of people on a bus *[mime sitting on bus]*
On a yellow bus, going to the shops *[mime sitting on bus]*
See a man on his bike *[mime ringing bicycle bell]*
On his bicycle, going to the shops *[mime ringing bicycle bell]*
See a woman in a van *[mime driving a van]*
In her red van, going to the shops *[mime driving a van]*
There are lots of shops where I live *[jazz hands]*
Fantastic shops where I live *[wave hands over head]*
There are lots of shops where I live *[jazz hands]*
Fantastic shops where I live *[wave hands over head]*

CLOSING ACTIVITIES

- Have volunteers mime activities we do in a town, e.g. *walking, driving, shopping, riding a bicycle, talking, walking the dog, looking at a map.* For each mime ask **What is he/she doing?** Encourage the rest of the class to guess the activity.

EXTRA IDEAS

- *On the bus.* Where you have space, arrange chairs so that they resemble the inside of a bus (an aisle with two seats on either side). Choose a volunteer to be the driver. Encourage pupils to pretend that they are getting on the bus, saying good morning to the driver and pretending to pay. Once pupils are all seated on the bus, ask them where they want to go. Ask **What can you see through the windows?** Encourage pupils to use their imaginations to tell you what they can see.
- *Transport tally chart.* Explain how a tally chart helps us see the number of something in a given time. Draw a chart on the board and explain how to keep a record of the number of vehicles pupils see in 10 minutes from the playground or their bedroom window.

PAGE 36 Look left, look right

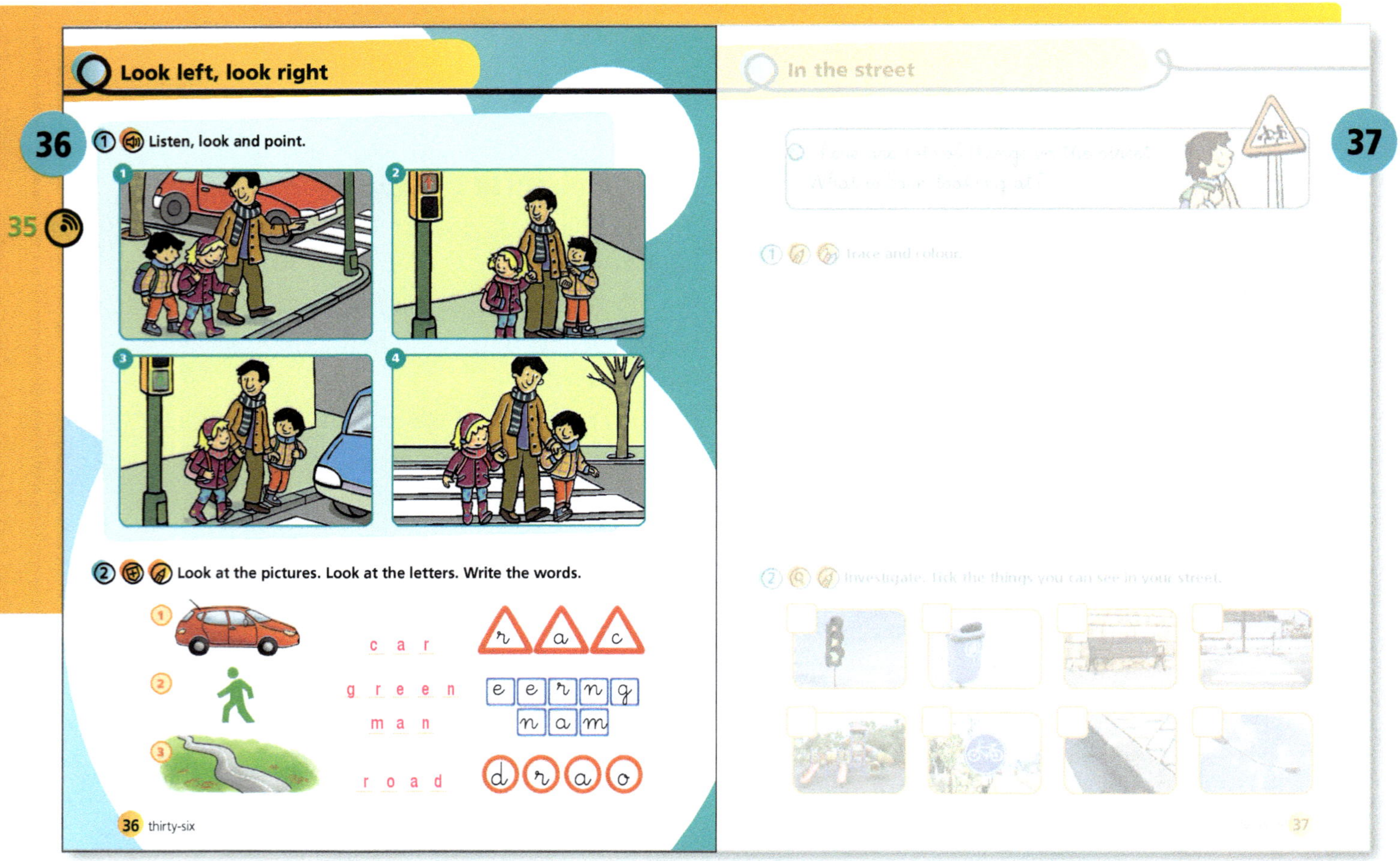

PAGE SUMMARY

Use the story to talk about road safety and how to cross a road using pedestrian crossings and traffic lights.

LANGUAGE

- Road, traffic lights, pedestrian crossing, red man, green man
- Car, bus, bicycle, van, motorbike, lorry
- Wait, look both ways, cross

MATERIALS

Flashcards: (digital) see the *Teachers* section in the digital resources

Additional classroom materials: hula hoops

OPENING ACTIVITIES

- Play the unit song and have pupils join in.
- Hand out an A5 sheet of paper to each pupil. Ask pupils to draw something they can see in their town or place that they live. Play *I Spy*. Say **I spy with my little eye something beginning with B**. If pupils have drawn something beginning with that letter (e.g. *bus, bicycle, bin*), they must stand up and show their picture.

MAIN ACTIVITIES

- Ask pupils **Who walks to school?** Encourage these pupils to talk about their journey: what they see on their way, who they walk with and how many roads they need to cross. Ask **How do you cross the roads?** *Holding a parent's hand, at a pedestrian crossing / traffic light.*

1 Listen, look and point.

- Ask pupils to open their Pupil's Books on page 36.
- Point to frame 1 and say **Look at the picture**. Ask **Who can you see?** Encourage pupils to say *Sam and Amy*. Explain that Sam's dad is with them. Ask pupils **Where are they? What are they doing? Where are they going?**
- Say **Let's listen to the story and find out**. Play the audio.

> CD 1 • Track 35
>
> **Look left, look right.**
>
> **The children are walking to school.**
>
> Frame 1
>
> Amy: **Come on, Sam. Let's cross the road.**
>
> Sam's dad: **No, Amy. We have to cross at the pedestrian crossing.**
>
> Frame 2
>
> Amy: **OK, we're at the crossing. Let's cross!**
>
> Sam: **No! We have to wait for the green man.**
>
> Frame 3
>
> Amy: **OK, I can see the green man.**
>
> Sam: **Yes, me too. Let's cross!**
>
> Sam's dad: **Be careful, children. We have to look both ways before we cross.**
>
> Frame 4
>
> Sam: **OK, look left, look right. Can we cross now?**
>
> Amy: **Yes, can we?**
>
> Sam's dad: **Yes, we can. Hurry up, we don't want to be late for school!**

- Now ask questions about the story. Point to frame 1 and ask **Where are the children going?** *To school.* Point to frame 2 and ask **What are they waiting for?** *The green man.* Point to frames 3 and 4 and ask **What are they doing now?** *Looking both ways, crossing the road.*
- Ask the class **Why do they wait for the green man?** *So they can cross the road safely.*

2 Look at the pictures. Look at the letters. Write the words.

- Focus pupils' attention on the first picture and ask **What can you see?** *A car.* Ask pupils to look at the letters and see if they can spell the word, one letter on each line.
- Repeat the question and procedure for the green man and the road. *See answers opposite.*
- Have volunteers come to the board and spell the words. Ask **Is that right?** for each word.

+ CLOSING ACTIVITIES

- Ask pupils to close their books. Ask them to spell *car, green man, road* on their mini whiteboards or on a sheet of paper. Have them hold up each word they spell. Have a quick look or walk round to check their spellings.
- Play *Green man, red man.* Hold up a *green man* sign and have pupils move around the classroom or playground. Suddenly, hold up a *red man* sign. Pupils must freeze and stop. When you show the *green man* sign again, they can continue to move. Encourage pupils to do a different movement each time, e.g. *run, skip, hop, jump, twirl.*

+ EXTRA IDEAS

- Play the audio for the story again. Encourage pupils to work in groups of three to act out the story.
- Go out to the playground or gym. Have pupils work in pairs. Give each pair a hula hoop. One pupil must stand in the hula hoop. They are the 'car'. Their partner is the 'driver', and must hold the hula hoop around their partner's waist. Explain that pupils must 'drive around' without bumping into each other. Tell pupils that when you shout **Traffic lights red!** they must stop and when you shout **Traffic lights green!** they can move again.

PAGE 37 In the street

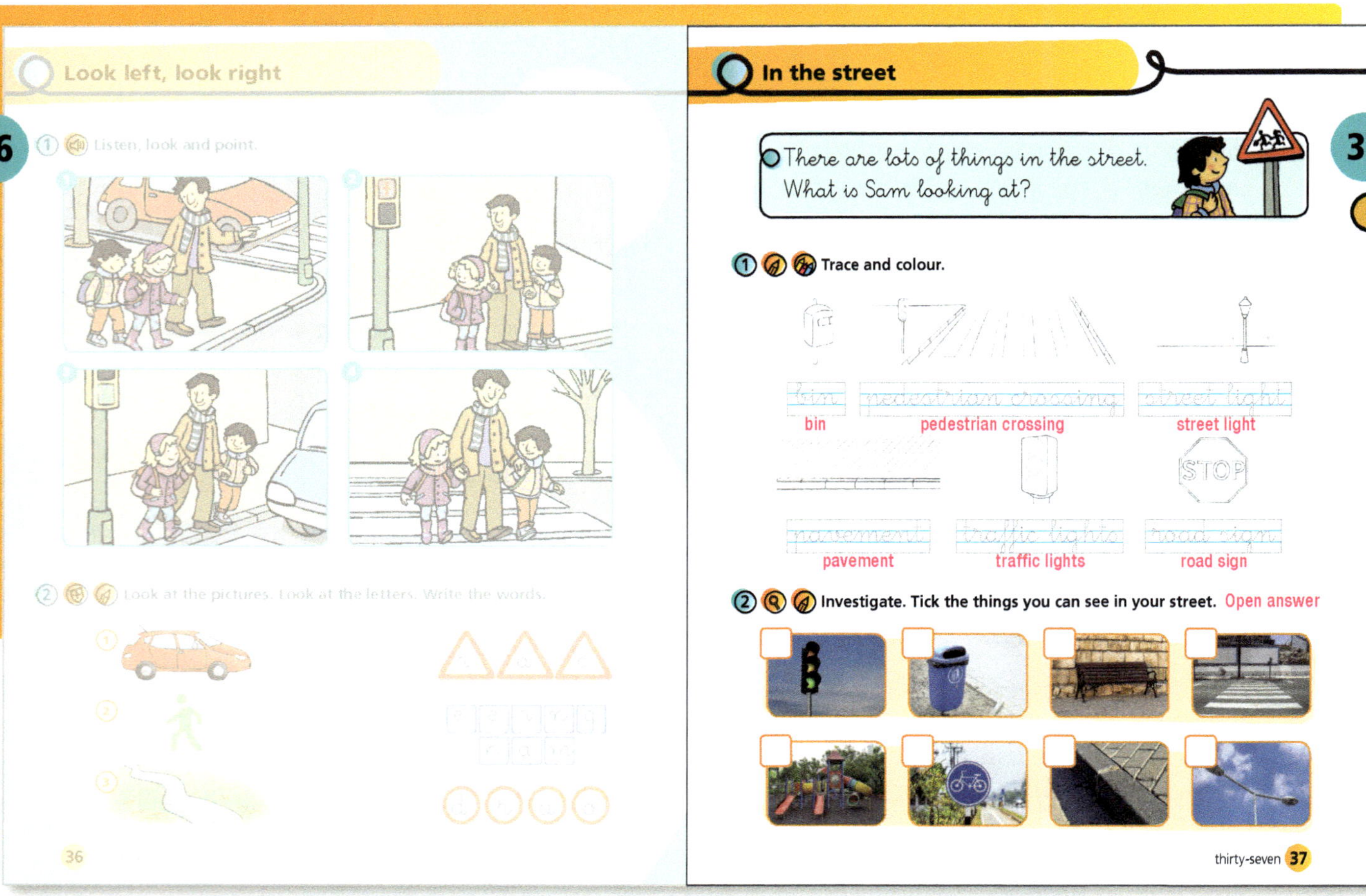

PAGE SUMMARY

Your pupils will take a closer look at and identify the things we can see in street.

LANGUAGE

- Bin, pedestrian crossing, street light, pavement, traffic lights, road sign, bench, playground
- What can you see?
- In my street, I can see a bench.

MATERIALS

Flashcards: (digital) see the *Teachers* section in the digital resources

Additional classroom materials: pictures of different street scenes

OPENING ACTIVITIES

- Play *Green man, red man*. Hold up the *green man* sign and say **Stamp your feet**. Have pupils stamp their feet. Hold up the *red man* sign. Pupils must freeze and stop. Hold up the green man and say **Clap your hands**. Have pupils do the action and stop when you hold up the red man. Repeat with other actions, e.g. **Wiggle your hips, bend your arms, hop, click your fingers**, etc.
- Draw a pedestrian crossing on the board. Encourage pupils to tell you what they must do when they want to cross a road.

MAIN ACTIVITIES

Reading (CD 1. Track 36)

- Ask pupils to open their books on page 37 and look at the reading box. Say **Let's listen and read**. Play the audio and encourage the pupils to follow in their books.
- Ask pupils to tell you what Sam is looking at. *A road sign.* Ask pupils if they know what the sign means. *School or school crossing.*
- Ask pupils what other road signs they see in the streets. *Speed signs, stop signs, parking signs,* etc.

1 Trace and colour.

- Ask pupils what other things they can see in the street.
- Focus pupils' attention on the black and white pictures. Point to the word or words under each picture and have pupils read them with you. Have pupils repeat the words several times to practise pronunciation. Have them pronounce the words slowly, then quickly, quietly, angrily, etc.
- Tell pupils to trace the words and then read them to a partner.
- Point to each picture and ask **What colour is the bin / pedestrian crossing?** etc. Encourage pupils to colour the pictures realistically.

1 Investigate. Tick the things you can see in your street.

- Point to each picture and have pupils tell you what they can see.
- Ask pupils to think about the street where they live and tick the things they can see.
- Encourage pupils to say *In my street I can see (traffic lights)* to a partner. Have volunteers share their sentences with the rest of the class.
- Ask pupils if there is anything else in their street that isn't in the photos, e.g. *trees, newspaper stand, plant pots, post box, telephone box, steps,* etc.

+ CLOSING ACTIVITIES

- Tell pupils to close their books. Draw a street on the board. Draw the road and the pavement and ask pupils to help you build up the scene. Elicit from them the features that help us in the street. *Traffic lights, pedestrian crossing, street light, post box, telephone box, bin,* etc.
- Write some of the vocabulary from the lesson on the board but with the vowels missing. Have pupils fill in the missing vowels with a partner on a mini whiteboard or in a notebook.

+ EXTRA IDEAS

- Have pupils work in groups. Give each group pictures of different street scenes and have them talk about what they see.
- Ask pupils to draw their house or flat and the street where they live. Encourage them to label the different features in their pictures.

PAGE 38 What is your address?

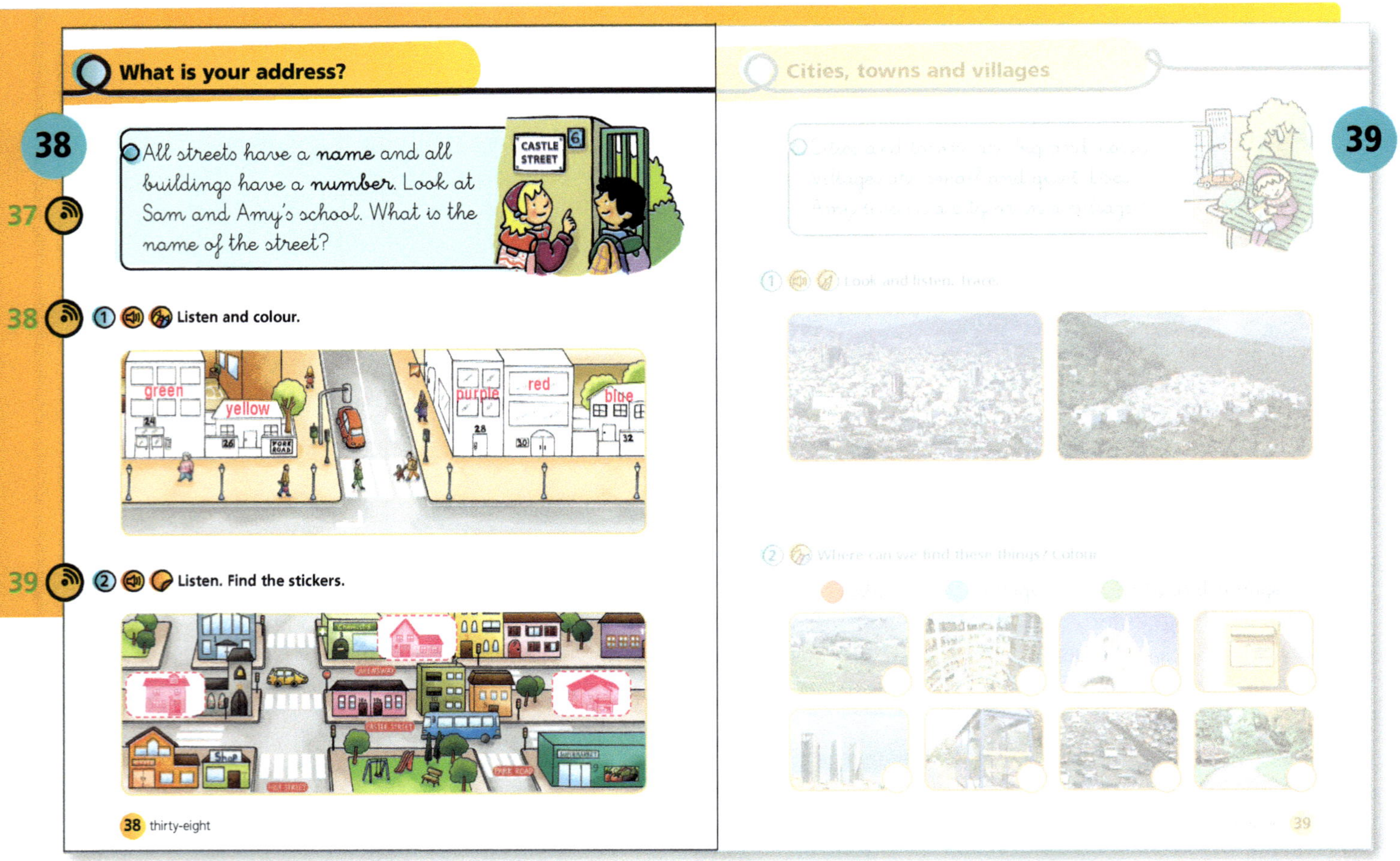

PAGE SUMMARY

Your pupils will understand that all streets have a name and that all buildings have a number.

LANGUAGE

- Where do you live? What is your address?
- Street, road, building, pavement, traffic lights, pedestrian crossing
- Numbers 1-100
- Red, green, yellow, blue, purple, pink
- Next to, opposite, on the corner

MATERIALS

Flashcards: (digital) see the *Teachers* section in the digital resources

OPENING ACTIVITIES

- *Stand in line*. Hand out a slip of paper to each pupil with a random number on it between 20 and 100. Tell pupils that when you clap your hands they must stand in a line in the order of their numbers. Indicate that the lowest number will be on the left and the highest on the right. Have pupils stand in order and read out their numbers to check. Ask pupils along the line which number comes directly before or after their number.
- Play *Pictionary*. Begin to draw a picture of something you can see on a street (*road sign, bench, traffic lights, bin,* etc.). Ask pupils to guess your picture before you finish drawing it. Repeat the game with one or two more street features.
- Ask pupils to close their eyes and imagine they are walking along the street. Ask them to think about what sounds they can hear as they walk along. Have pupils share their ideas.

MAIN ACTIVITIES

Reading. (CD 1. Track 37)

- Ask pupils to tell you where they can see numbers in a town. *On houses, buses, car number plates,* etc.
- Ask pupils to open their Pupil's Books on page 38 and look at the reading box. Say **Let's listen and read.** Play the audio and encourage pupils to follow in their books.
- Ask pupils **What is the name of the street where Sam and Amy's school is?** *Castle Street.* Explain that a number and the name of a street is called our *address*. Ask pupils what their school address is. Tell them if they don't know.

1 Listen and colour

- Ask pupils to look at the buildings in the picture and tell you what numbers they can see. Ask them what the name of the road is. *York Road.*
- Explain that pupils are going to listen to different children talking about where they live and colour the houses. Play the audio and have pupils listen. Play again and pause the recording after each instruction to allow pupils time to colour. When pupils have finished, ask **What colour is house number 30 / 26 / 24?** etc. *See answers opposite.*

CD 1 • Track 38

Boy: **I live at number 26 York Road. Colour my house yellow.**

Girl: **I live at number 30 York Road. Colour my house red.**

Woman: **I live at number 24 York Road. Colour my house green.**

Boy: **My best friend Tom lives at number 32 York Road. Colour his house blue.**

Girl: **And my best friend Maria lives on the corner at number 28 York Road. Colour her house purple.**

2 Listen. Find the stickers.

- Ask pupils what places they can see in the town. Encourage pupils to name the supermarket, church, library, chemist's, baker's and park. If pupils don't know the word in English, accept it in their own language and say **That's right. We can see a (park).** Establish what we do in each place, e.g. *We buy food at the supermarket.*
- Say **Point to the chemist's / church,** etc. Ask **What is the chemist's address?** *3 Queensway.* **What is the church's address?** *14 Castle Street,* etc.
- Tell pupils to listen to the descriptions and find the sticker. Play the audio and pause after each description. Elicit the first address and the colour of the house. *16 Castle Street. Yellow.* Ask pupils where they are going to put the sticker. *Next to the church.* Play the rest of the audio and pause after each description to elicit where pupils will put the sticker. *Next to the chemist's. Opposite the supermarket.*

CD 1 • Track 39

Amy: **I live at number 16 Castle Street, next to the church. My house is yellow. Can you find the sticker?**

Sam: **I live at number 5 Queensway, next to the chemist's. My house is pink with a pointed roof. Can you find the sticker?**

Amy: **We walk to school together. Our school is at number 6 Castle Street.**

Sam: **Our school is big and yellow. It's opposite the supermarket! Can you find the sticker?**

- Ask questions about the completed picture. Encourage pupils to use *next to* and *opposite* to describe the places in the picture along with the address.

CLOSING ACTIVITIES

- Point out how buildings on one side of the road have even numbers and on the other they are odd. Read the numbers in each street.
- Ask pupils why we need an address. *To help us find buildings / to know where we live.*

EXTRA IDEAS

- Play *Repeat if true.* Make true or false statements about the picture in activity 2. If your statement is true, pupils must repeat it, e.g. **The shop is next to the library.**
- Draw a quick picture of your house or flat on the board and say **I live in a house / flat.** Write the number 10 on the door and *Long Street* on a sign outside. Say **I live at number 10 Long Street.** Choose a confident volunteer to come out and repeat the process, drawing their flat and saying their address. Write the model sentences on the board and encourage pupils to say or write their information.

PAGE 39 Cities, towns and villages

PAGE SUMMARY

Your pupils will learn how cities and towns are different from villages. They will be able to name features they can find in a town or city and not in a village.

LANGUAGE

- City, town, village
- Field, shopping centre, cathedral, post box, skyscraper, bus stop, motorway, park

MATERIALS

Flashcards: (digital) see the *Teachers* section in the digital resources

Additional classroom materials: envelopes or slips of paper (one per pupil) each with a pupil's address on (number and street), pictures of cities or villages (these can be photocopied), atlases

OPENING ACTIVITIES

- Play *BuzzFizz*. Have pupils count to 30. Each pupil must say a number but if their number is an even number they must say *buzz* instead of the number, e.g. *1, buzz, 3, buzz, 5, buzz,* etc. Repeat the activity, but this time have pupils replace the odd numbers with the word *fizz*, e.g. *fizz, 2, fizz, 4, fizz, 6,* etc.
- Write pupils' addresses on envelopes or slips of paper before the class. Shuffle all the addresses and give one out to each pupil. Tell pupils that they are going to walk around and ask classmates *What is your address?* to find the owner of the address just like a postman or postwoman.
- Discuss the use of each of the things you can find in the street. Ask the pupils **What is a bin for?** Encourage them to answer *A bin is for rubbish*. Ask **What is a post box for?** *A post box is for letters*. Ask questions for *traffic lights, street lamp, pedestrian crossing* and *phone box*, encouraging pupils to suggest uses for each one. Accept answers in their own language and help rephrase in English.

MAIN ACTIVITIES

- Write *city and town* on one side of the board and *village* on the other. Read the headings together and ask pupils what they know about these places. Elicit any information pupils can tell you.

Reading. (CD 1. Track 40)

- Ask pupils to look at the reading box. Say **Let's listen and read**. Play the audio and have pupils follow in their books.
- Ask pupils to find the words that describe cities and towns. *Big and noisy.* Write these words on the board under the heading *city and town*. Ask pupils to find the words that describe villages. *Small and quiet.* Write them on the board.
- Ask pupils where Amy lives. *In a city or town.* Ask pupils why they think this. *Big road and building.*
- Ask pupils **Where do you live: a city, town or village?**

1 Look and listen. Trace.

- Focus pupils' attention on the first photo. Ask them what they can see. Have pupils read the word under the photo. Repeat the procedure with the second photo.
- Play the audio for the first photo. Ask pupils to tell you about a city. Explain that services means things that help us live in a city like buses, trains, hospitals, post offices, shops, etc.
- Play the audio for the second photo. Ask pupils to tell you about a village.
- Ask **Which has more services and people, a city or a village?** *A city.*

CD 1 • Track 41

City. A city has lots of buildings and services. Lots of people live there. It is big and noisy.

Village. A village has only a few buildings and services. Not many people live there. It is small and quiet.

- Ask pupils to trace the words *city* and *village*. Have them close their books and write the words again on a sheet of paper or in their notebooks. Then have them check the spelling in their Pupil's Books.

2 Where can we find these things? Colour.

- Look at each of the photos and have pupils tell you what they can see. Help pupils with new vocabulary. Talk about the photos a second time so that pupils have an opportunity to use any new vocabulary.
- Read the words above the photos and draw pupils' attention to the colour code.
- Point to each photo and ask **City, village or city and village?**
- Finally, have pupils colour the circles on the photos according to the code. *See answers opposite.*

CLOSING ACTIVITIES

- Look back at the two sections on the board. Point to the heading *city and town* and ask pupils what other words you can add to this section. *Traffic, lots of services, shopping centres, skyscrapers,* etc. Point to the heading *village* and ask what you can add to this section. *Fields, small roads, small shops, fewer services,* etc. Ask what you can find in both places. *Bus stop, post box,* etc.
- Ask pupils to talk about the place where they live. Encourage them to use vocabulary from the lesson. Ask pupils if they like where they live and why.

EXTRA IDEAS

- Give each pupil a picture or a photocopy of part of a city or village. Have them stick the picture in the centre of an A4 sheet of paper. Ask pupils to add to the picture by drawing in features (like skyscrapers, shops, an airport, etc.) and continuing roads, adding fields or a river, etc.
- Hand out atlases and look at a map of Spain. Have pupils name cities in the country.

PAGE 40 Maps

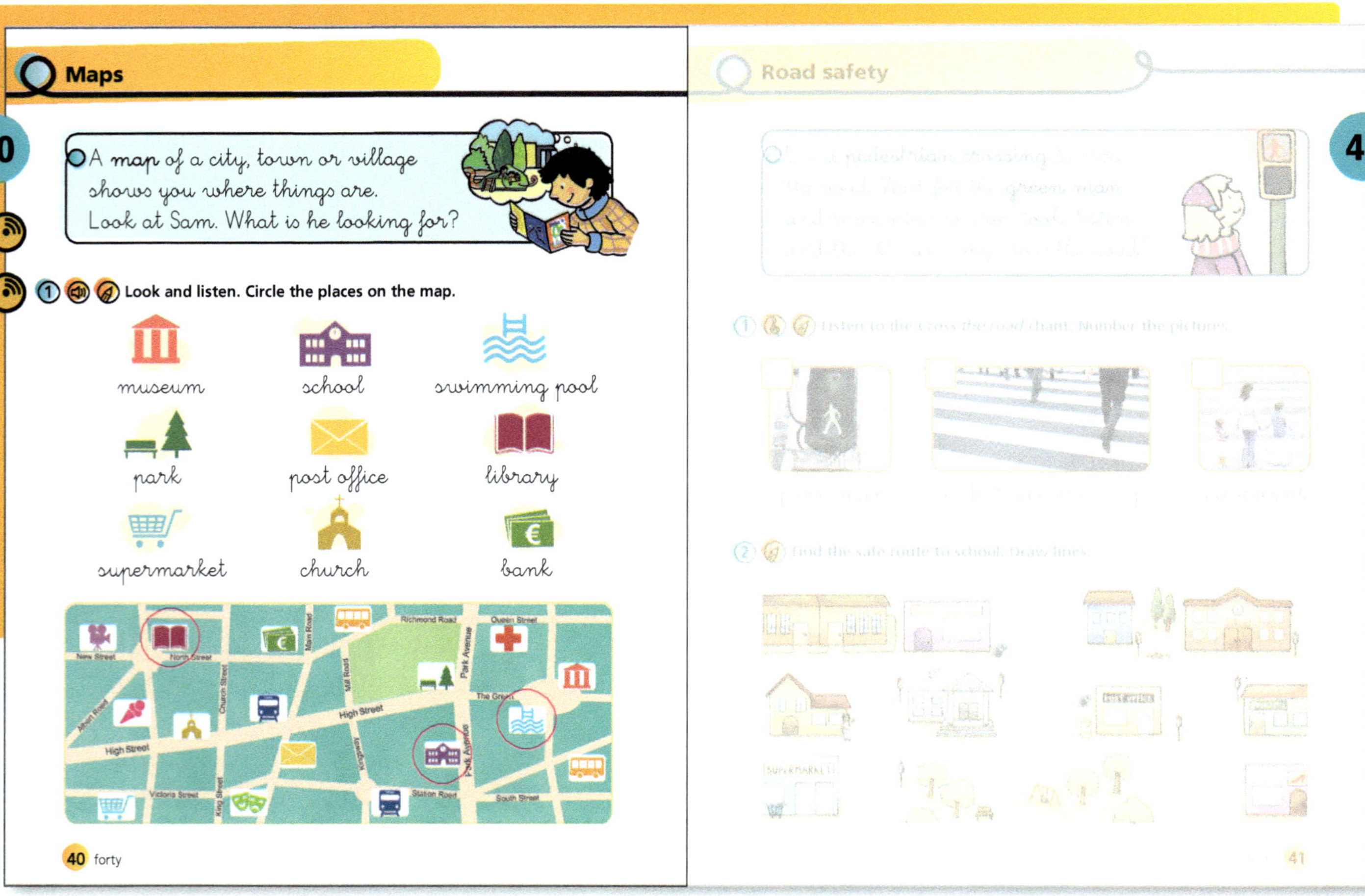

PAGE SUMMARY

Your pupils will understand how maps can help us locate buildings and guide us through a city. Pupils will start to develop simple map-reading skills and see how we use symbols to represent buildings and areas.

LANGUAGE

- Museum, school, swimming pool, park, post office, library, supermarket, church, bank
- Where is the post office? It's near/on Station Road.
- There is a library. There are two swimming pools.

MATERIALS

Flashcards: (digital) see the *Teachers* section in the digital resources

Additional classroom materials: map of the local area, photos of different places in your city, town or village for a slide presentation

OPENING ACTIVITIES

- Ask pupils **What is your address?** Have them tell a partner. Encourage pupils to say *My address is (...).* Then pick pupils at random and ask them to tell you their address.
- Write the name of the city, town or village where your school is located on the board. Ask pupils to describe it. *In my city / town / village there is / there are two parks,* etc.
- Play *In my town.* Say *In my town (or city or village) there is a road.* The next pupil in the chain must repeat the sentence and add another place, e.g. *In my town there is a road and a park,* etc. After an initial practice, encourage pupils to play in groups of five or six.

MAIN ACTIVITIES

Reading. (CD 1. Track 42)

- If possible, take in a map of your city, town or area. Open the map and pretend to be examining it in front of the class. Ask pupils to explain what you are doing. Put the map up on the board and ask pupils why we use maps and what things we can see on maps.
- Tell pupils to open their Pupil's Books on page 40 and look at the reading box. Say **Let's listen and read**. Play the audio and have pupils follow in their books.
- Ask pupils what Sam is looking for. *A park*. Ask pupils if there is a park near where they live. Ask pupils how they go to the park and how they know where it is.

1 Look and listen. Circle the places on the map.

- Show pupils pictures or flashcards of the different symbols, one by one, and ask if they can guess what each one represents. Show the symbol of the park. Say **What is this?** *It's a park*. Repeat with the other symbol flashcards and put them up on the board.
- Turn the flashcards over. Ask pupils if they can remember which symbol was where. Point to the first card and say **What is this?** Turn over the card once the pupils have made a guess and see if they guessed correctly.
- Hold up a wordcard for each symbol. Read the word together and encourage volunteers to label each symbol.
- Ask pupils to look at activity 1. Read the name under each symbol together.
- Point to or zoom in on each symbol on the map. Ask **What is this?** and elicit the name of the place. Ask pupils to look at the street names and ask **Where is it?** Encourage pupils to answer in full sentences, e.g. *It's on Park Avenue.*
- Once pupils are familiar with the map say **Now let's listen**. The first time you play the audio have pupils listen and point to each of the places they hear. Play the audio a second time and this time have them circle each of the places they hear. *See answers opposite.*

CD 1 • Track 43

Museum – museum; school – school; swimming pool – swimming pool; park – park; post office – post office; library – library; supermarket – supermarket; church – church; bank – bank.

Now look at the map.

Boy: **Where is the school?**

Girl: **The school is on Park Avenue, near the park. Circle it.**

Boy: **Where is the library?**

Girl: **The library is on North Street, on the roundabout. Circle it.**

Boy: **Where is the swimming pool?**

Girl: **The swimming pool is on The Green, opposite the museum. Circle it.**

Boy: **Thank you!**

CLOSING ACTIVITIES

- Flash up each of the symbols again. Ask pupils to name the place and what you do in each place. Ask **What do you do at a swimming pool / supermarket / cinema?** etc.
- Play *Repeat if true*. Make true or false statements about the places on the map. Explain that if your statement is true, pupils must repeat it, e.g. **The supermarket is on Victoria Street. The hospital is on South Street.** Give pupils time to look at the places on the map to decide if the statement is true or false.

EXTRA IDEAS

- *Design a street*. Draw a small neighbourhood with two or three streets on the board and write names on the streets. Put pictures or flashcards of the symbols face up on the floor. Name a place and have a volunteer pick up the correct flashcard and stick it on your map, e.g. **There is a swimming pool on Queen Street.** Once all the flashcards are in position, ask the pupils what else we see in the street, e.g. *bin, post box, traffic lights, phone box,* etc. Elicit suitable places on the map for these items and encourage the pupils to come out and draw them on the board.
- Show a slide presentation of places in your city, town or village and encourage pupils to talk about them.

PAGE 41 Road safety

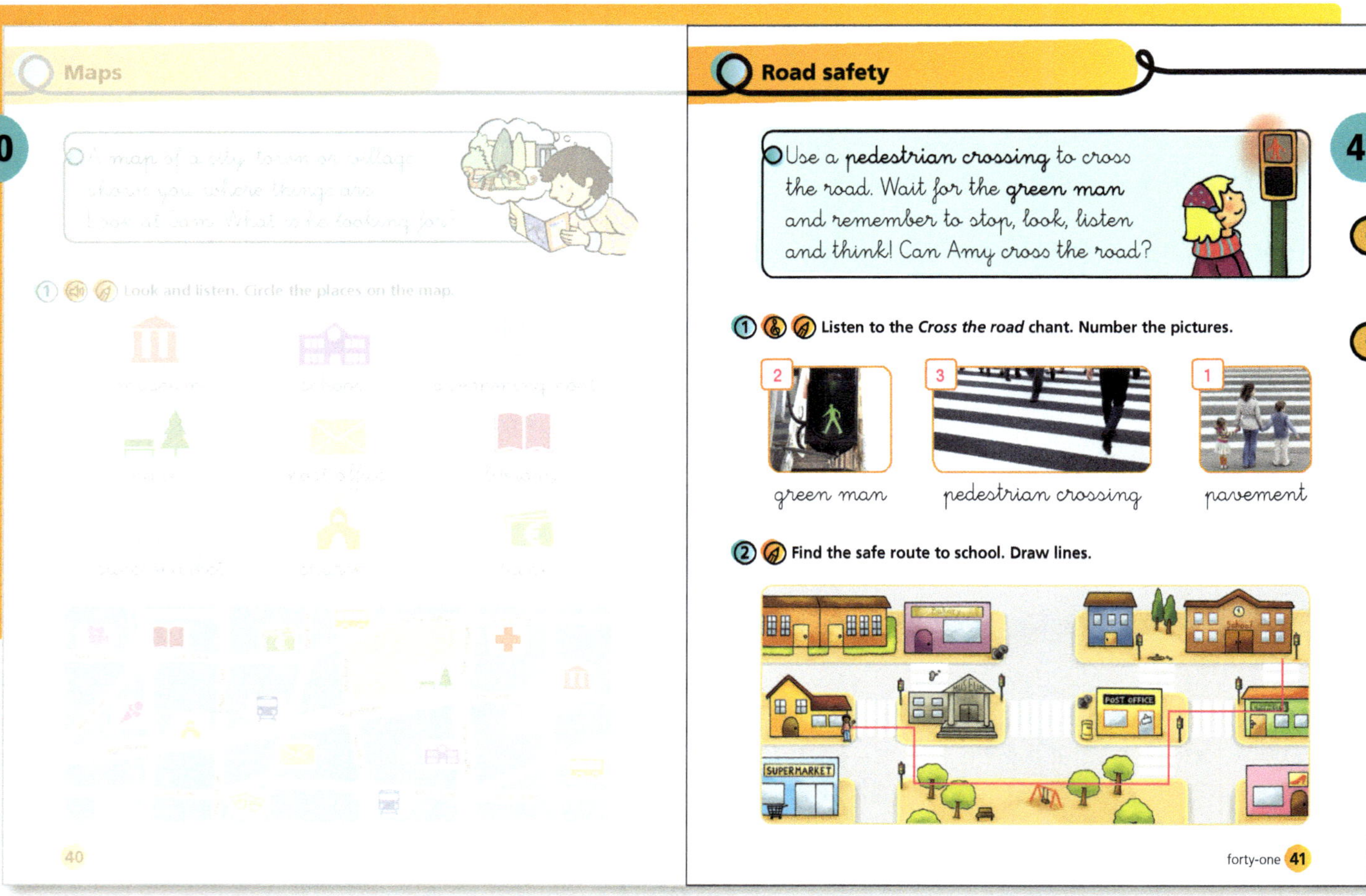

PAGE SUMMARY

Pupils will review road safety and what we need to remember when crossing a road.

LANGUAGE

- Pedestrian crossing, green man, pavement
- Stop, look, listen, think, stand, wait, cross

MATERIALS

Flashcards: (digital) see the *Teachers* section in the digital resources

Additional classroom materials: A4 black card (one sheet per pupil)

OPENING ACTIVITIES

- Play *Quick flash*. Hold flashcards of the map symbols in a pile facing you. Quickly turn the pile around to face the pupils, then turn it back again. Pupils say which symbol they saw. If they are correct, say **Yes, that's right. It's a (library)** and stick the flashcard up on the board. If pupils guess incorrectly, say **No, try again** and flash the card again.
- Carry out a vocabulary review. Tell the pupils that you are going to draw two streets on the board. Write a name on each street. Draw the roads and the pavement. Say **I want to buy some food**. Encourage pupils to tell you to draw a supermarket. Say **I want to get a book / see a film / go swimming** and encourage pupils to tell you what you need to add to the drawing. Elicit what else we see in the street, e.g. *traffic lights, pedestrian crossing, street light, post box, bin*. When you have finished, ask pupils to describe the town you have drawn and/or ask them questions about where things are.

MAIN ACTIVITIES

Reading. (CD 1. Track 44)

- Draw two parallel lines to create a road in the playground. Demonstrate crossing the road badly, in different ways. Exaggerate your actions to show pupils that they must not run, they must cross in a straight line, they must concentrate and not turn around in the middle, etc. Cross from one side to the other first by running, then by crossing diagonally, then by starting to cross and changing your mind halfway. Encourage pupils to point out what you are doing wrong each time. Ask for a volunteer to demonstrate how to cross the road properly. Say **Remember to stop, look, listen and think!** Encourage the pupil to mime stopping, looking, listening and thinking in order to cross the road safely. Ask pupils to cross the road one by one, praising them if they do a good job. Finally, have pupils cross the road at the same time, encouraging them not to push or rush.
- Ask pupils to open their Pupil's Books on page 41. Say **Let's listen and read**. Play the audio and encourage pupils to follow in their books. Ask pupils if Amy can cross the road. *No.* Ask **Why not?** *The man is red.*

1 Listen to *Cross the road* chant. Number the pictures.

- Focus pupils' attention on the musical note. Say **Let's listen to the *Cross the road* chant**. Play the audio.

CD 1 • Track 45

Cross the road, cross the road
How do we cross the road?
Stand on the pavement [x2]
Wait for the green man [x2]
Cross on the pedestrian crossing [x2]
That's how we cross the road!

- Ask pupils what instructions they heard in the song. *Stand, wait, cross.* Ask pupils to look at the photos, point to the first photo and ask **What can you see?** Point to the word under the photo and have pupils read together. Repeat the steps with the other two photos and words.
- Say **Let's listen to the chant again and number the pictures**. Play the audio and pause after each instruction (if necessary) to give pupils time to number the photos.
- Ask **Which is photo 1 / 2 / 3?** Check answers. *2, 3, 1.*
- Play the chant one more time and encourage pupils to join in.

2 Find the safe route to school. Draw lines.

- Tell the pupils again that they have to be careful when crossing the road. Ask them where they should cross. *On a pedestrian crossing.* Ask them when they should cross. *When the green man is showing.* Ask them what else they should do. *Stop, look, listen and think.*
- Focus pupils' attention on the map. Say **Point to the school**. Ask them how they can get from the post office to the school. Encourage them to run their finger along and over the pedestrian crossing. Ask pupils to go from the park / bakery / museum to the school. Finally, ask pupils how to get from the house where the boy lives to the school. Ask them to draw the safe route using a pencil. *See answer opposite.*

CLOSING ACTIVITIES

- Make sure pupils know their left from their right. Have pupils listen and follow your instructions. **Walk, walk, turn left, walk, walk, turn right,** etc.

EXTRA IDEAS

- Make a *Stripes* display. Give each pupil an A4 sheet of black card. Have pupils paint white lines on the black card. Tell them they can paint vertical, horizontal or diagonal lines. Make a black and white display.
- Pupils work individually or in groups to make a poster to increase road safety awareness. Ask them to write the slogan *Stop! Look! Listen! Think!* and decorate the poster as they wish. Display the posters around the school.

PAGE 42 We travel on land, water and in the air

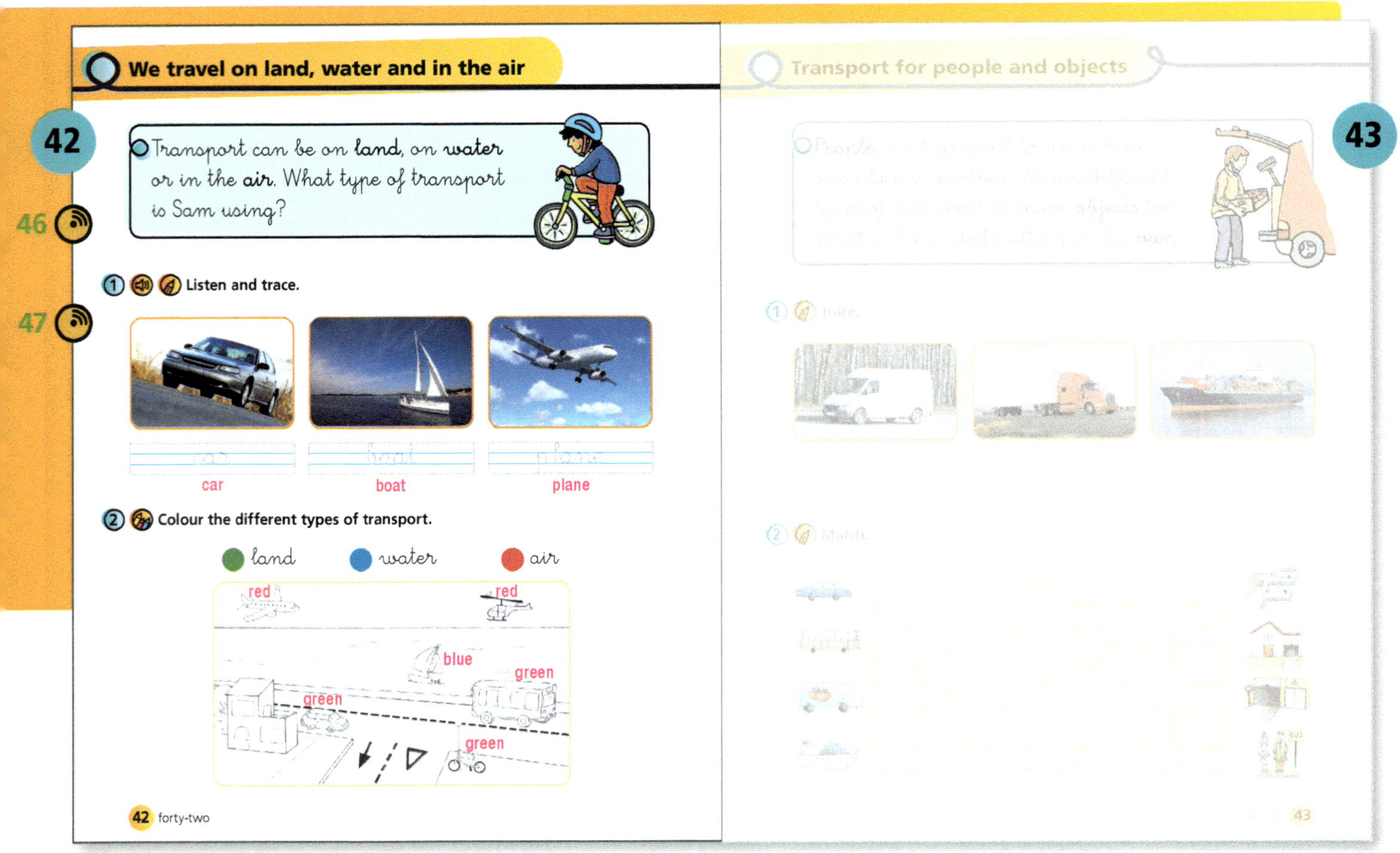

PAGE SUMMARY

Pupils will identify different types of transport and classify them according to whether they travel on land, on water or in the air.

LANGUAGE

- Car, boat, plane, helicopter, bus, bicycle, train
- On land, on water, in the air

MATERIALS

Flashcards: (digital) see the *Teachers* section in the digital resources

Additional classroom materials: A3 card (two blue sheets, one green or brown sheet), magazines (with vehicles)

OPENING ACTIVITIES

- Play the *Pedestrian crossing race*. Divide the pupils into two teams. Draw a pedestrian crossing on the board with five or six stripes. Show the pupils two small action figures (the tutor may have toys in the classroom for wet break times) and ask the pupils to give them names. Allocate one figure per team and stick up the two figures with Blu-tack on one side of the pedestrian crossing. Tell the pupils that the first action figure to reach the other side safely is the winner. Ask questions to the teams in turn, e.g. **What are the colours on a traffic light? Name something you can see on a street. What do you do at a library / bank?** etc. Move the figures across the crossing when the pupils answer correctly.

Note: If you do not have action figures, you can use flashcards of Sam and Amy or simply ask the questions as revision.

MAIN ACTIVITIES

Reading. (CD 1. Track 46)

- Play *Hangman* with the word *transport*.
- Ask pupils what transport they remember from the opening illustration. As they name the transport, have a pupil draw a simple picture on the board. Hold up wordcards and have pupils read the word, then choose a volunteer to come and stick the wordcard next to the correct drawing on the board.
- Ask pupils to open their books on page 42 and look at the reading box. Say **Let's listen and read**. Play the audio and encourage the pupils to follow in their books.
- Draw three big squares on the board. Support pupils' understanding of land by drawing some hills and trees in the first square and write *on land* underneath. In the second square draw waves to represent water. Write *on water* underneath. Finally, draw clouds in the last square and write *in the air* underneath. Encourage pupils to read the words with you.
- Ask pupils what type of transport Sam is using. *A bicycle*. Ask whether you use a bicycle on land, on water or in the air. *On land.*
- Draw a bicycle or add a picture or flashcard to your *land* square. Ask pupils **Do you have a bicycle? Where do you travel to on your bicycle?**

1 Listen and trace.

- Focus pupils' attention on the photos. Point to each one and ask pupils to name the transport. Say **Let's listen and trace**. Play the audio and pause after each word so pupils can trace. Read the words together.

> CD 1 • Track 47
> Car – car; boat – boat; plane – plane.

- Point to the picture of the car or hold up a picture and ask **Does it travel on land, on water or in the air?** Encourage pupils to say *It travels on land*. Choose a volunteer to come and place the car in the correct square on the board. Repeat the question for *boat* and *plane* and have pupils place them in the correct squares. Point to each picture and have pupils repeat together *A car travels on land. A boat travels on water. A plane travels in the air.*

2 Colour the different types of transport.

- Ask pupils to look at the picture and name all the types of transport they can see. Focus their attention on the words above the picture and read each one together. After each word ask **What colour is it?**
- Ask **What types of transport travel on land?** Encourage pupils to say *A car / bicycle / bus travels on land.* Ask **What types of transport travel on water?** *A boat travels on water.* Finally, ask **What transport travels in the air?** *A plane / helicopter travels in the air.*
- Have pupils colour in the transport according to the code. Check their work by asking **What colour is the car / plane / boat?** etc. *See answers opposite.*

CLOSING ACTIVITIES

- Ask pupils which types of transport they use. Point to each one in turn and ask **Have you travelled by bus / car / plane / bicycle / boat / helicopter?** Ask pupils to raise their hands if they have travelled on one of these types of transport and write the figure next to each picture. Comment on the most popular and more unusual types of transport.
- Ask the pupils **How do you go to school?** Encourage them to say *By car*, etc. Ask them how they go to other places, such as the museum or the supermarket.

EXTRA IDEAS

- Have pupils work in pairs and ask them to spell *bicycle, car, plane, boat* and *bus* on a mini whiteboard or in their notebooks. Encourage pupils to talk about where the transport travels: on land, on water or in the air.
- Make transport collages. Have three groups each paint an A3 sheet of coloured card to represent travel by land, water or air. Have group members prepare the headings *Travel on land / on water / in the air*. Have other members cut out different types of transport to stick on the posters.

PAGE 43 Transport for people and objects

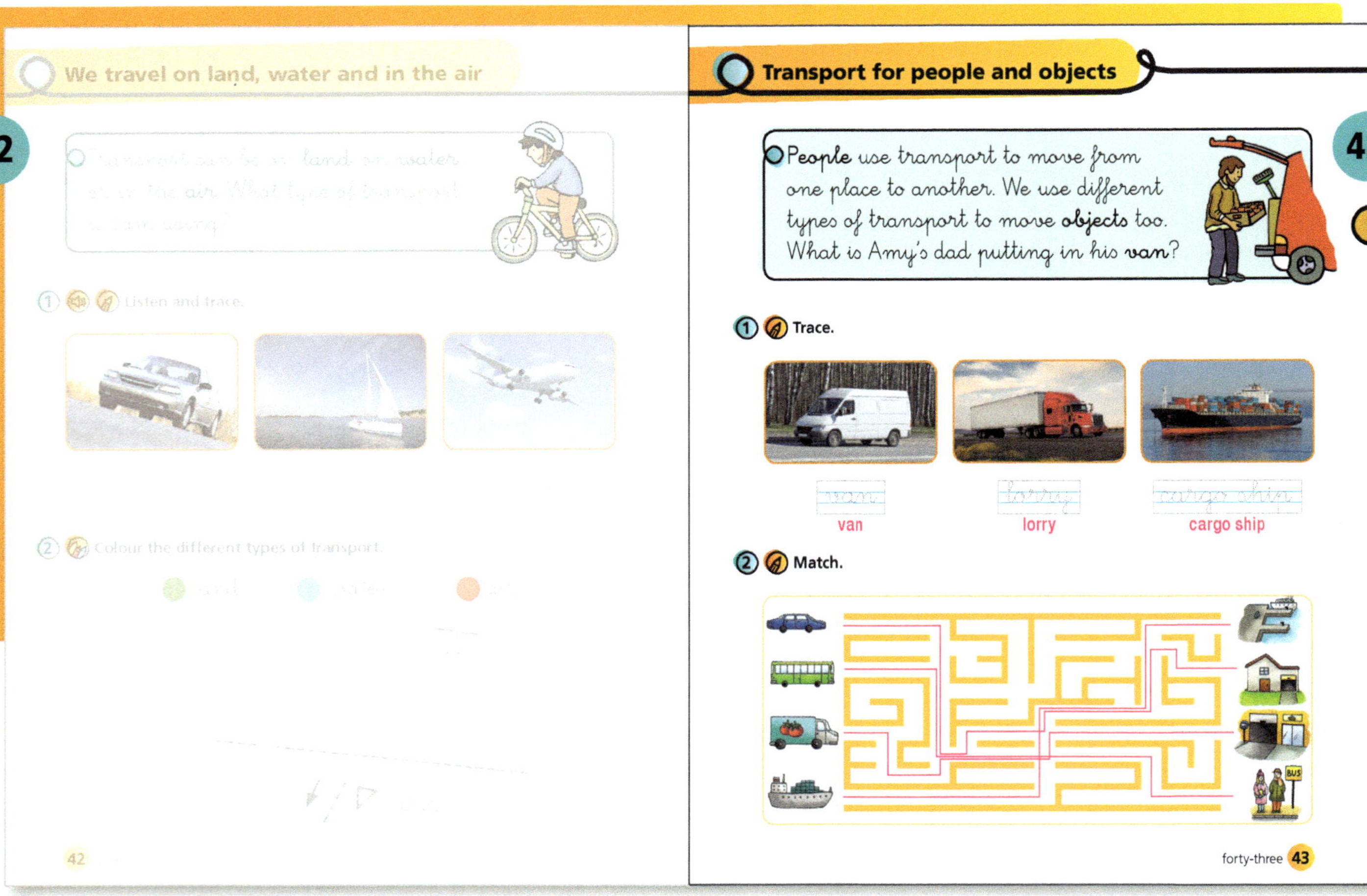
We travel on land, water and in the air

42

Transport for people and objects

43

People use transport to move from one place to another. We use different types of transport to move **objects** too. What is Amy's dad putting in his **van**?

① Trace.

van | lorry | cargo ship

② Match.

forty-three 43

PAGE SUMMARY

Your pupils will learn how we also use transport to move things from one place to another.

LANGUAGE

- Van, lorry, cargo ship, car, boat, plane, helicopter, bus, bicycle, train
- On land, on water, in the air
- Port, garage, airport, bus stop
- Put in, transport, travel, carry, move

MATERIALS

Flashcards: (digital) see the *Teachers* section in the digital resources

Additional classroom materials: small toy vehicles (cars, lorries, planes, helicopters, buses, etc.), bean bags, small boxes, balls, globe, recycled materials to make a model car, container of water

OPENING ACTIVITIES

- Ask pupils to choose one of the toy vehicles and describe it together, e.g. *A bus. It has four wheels. It's big. It travels on land.* Describe one of the vehicles and ask the pupils to guess which one you are describing. Use the following model: *It has (two) wheels. It's (big / small / medium-sized). It travels (on the road / on the water / in the air).*
- Give groups some toy vehicles and have them talk about them in groups, describing the number of wheels, colour, how it travels, etc.
- Give each pupil a bean bag, ball or box. Encourage pupils to move around the classroom demonstrating the different ways they can transport these objects.

MAIN ACTIVITIES

Reading. (CD 1. Track 48)

- Have pupils stand in a line facing you. Give one pupil at the end of a line a box. Have the pupils pass the box down the line to the last pupil at the other end. As pupils pass the box along, encourage them to say a word related to cities, villages, streets or transport.
- Show pupils a globe. Ask them how we can carry or transport things from one side of the world to another, across countries and oceans. Encourage pupils to suggest boats, planes, lorries, etc.
- Ask pupils to open their books on page 43 and look at the reading box. Say **Let's listen and read**. Play the audio and encourage the pupils to follow in their books.
- Ask pupils what Amy's dad is putting in his van. *Apples.* Ask pupils what other things we can transport in vans and lorries. *Food, furniture, petrol, animals, wood,* etc.

1 Trace.

- Focus pupils' attention on the photos. Point to each one and ask pupils to read the name of the transport. Ask **How does it travel: on land, on water or in the air?** Have pupils trace the word after reading it.
- Explain how cargo ships carry heavy things (like cars and machines) from one country to another on the sea. Explain that lorries and vans carry things on land.

2 Match.

- Focus pupils' attention on the types of transport in the picture and ask pupils to name each one. Ask **What can we transport in a car / bus / lorry / cargo ship?**
- Point to the pictures on the right of the picture. Ask **What transport travels to a port?** *A ship.* **What transport goes in a garage?** *A car.* **What transport travels to a supermarket?** *A lorry.* **What transport travels to a bus stop?** *A bus.*
- Say **Match the transport with the place**. Encourage pupils to draw lines to match up the transport and places. *Car – garage; bus – bus stop; lorry – supermarket; cargo ship – port.*

CLOSING ACTIVITIES

- Hold up a toy vehicle or a transport flashcard and elicit as much information as you can for each vehicle (size, wheels, where it travels, what it transports, etc.).
- Ask pupils what they do when they go on a long journey in a car, e.g. **Do you play games / sleep / look out the window?**

EXTRA IDEAS

- Make a model car. Have pupils work in groups to create a model car or lorry. Give each group recycled materials (cereal boxes, plastic bottles, lids, kitchen paper rolls, etc.) and encourage them to work together to build a car or lorry.
- Make a paper plane. Have pupils follow simple instructions to make a paper plane that they can then test out in the playground.
- Make an origami boat. Have pupils follow simple instructions to make a paper boat that they can sail in a container full of water. Encourage pupils to blow their boats from one side of the container to the other.

PAGES 44-45 Let's investigate and Make a difference

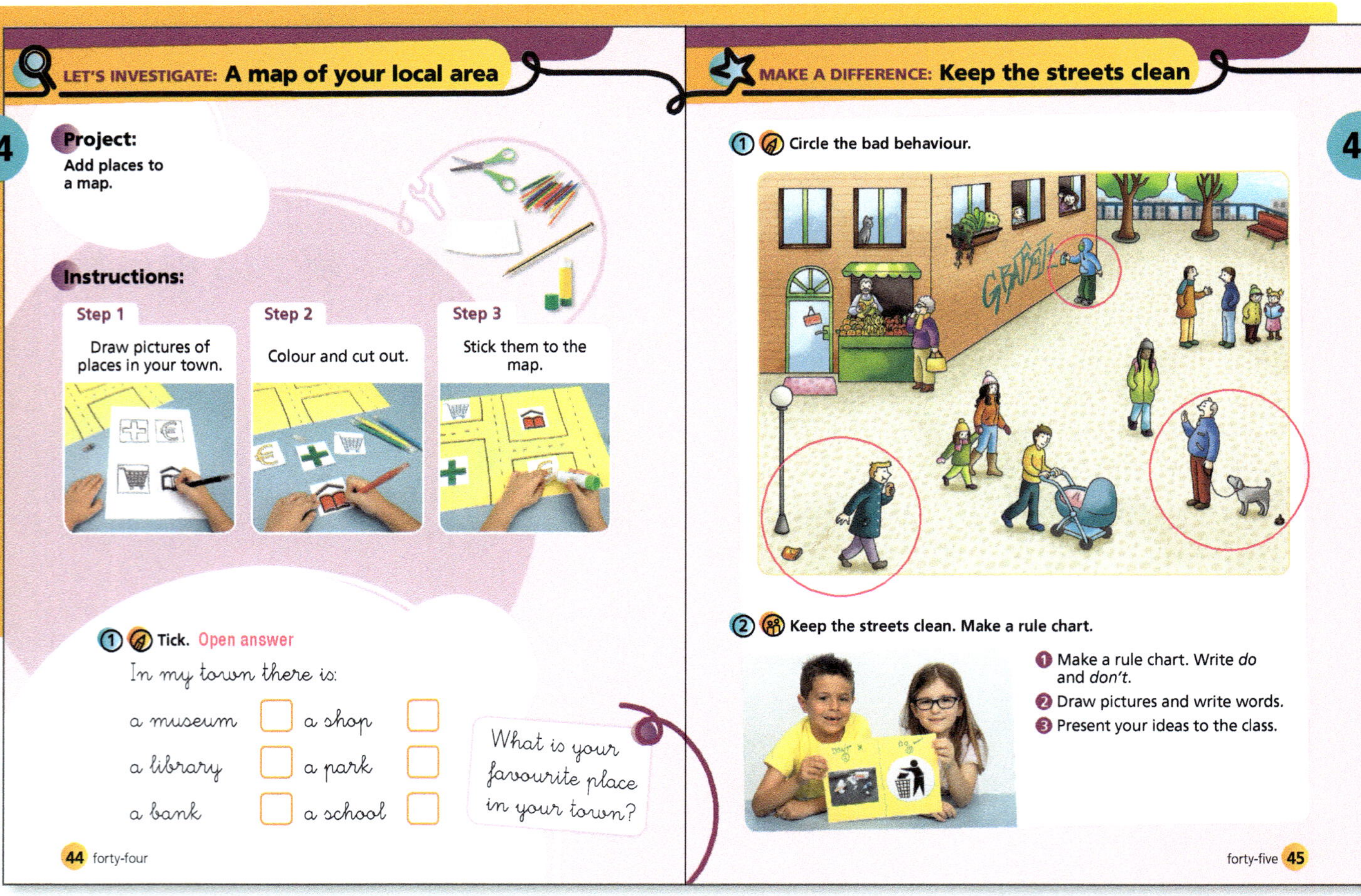

LET'S INVESTIGATE: **A map of your local area**

44

Project:
Add places to a map.

Instructions:

Step 1
Draw pictures of places in your town.

Step 2
Colour and cut out.

Step 3
Stick them to the map.

1 Tick. Open answer

In my town there is:

a museum ☐ a shop ☐
a library ☐ a park ☐
a bank ☐ a school ☐

What is your favourite place in your town?

44 forty-four

MAKE A DIFFERENCE: **Keep the streets clean**

45

1 Circle the bad behaviour.

2 Keep the streets clean. Make a rule chart.

1 Make a rule chart. Write *do* and *don't*.
2 Draw pictures and write words.
3 Present your ideas to the class.

forty-five 45

PAGE SUMMARY

Pupils will consolidate their knowledge of their local area and the facilities in their area by making their own map. They will also consider how they can look after the place where they live.

LANGUAGE

- Museum, school, swimming pool, park, post office, library, supermarket, church, bank, shop
- Rubbish, graffiti
- Throw, pick up, clean, paint

MATERIALS

Flashcards: (digital) see the *Teachers* section in the digital resources

Additional classroom materials: photos of your local area or the area around the school (include street names and some shops)

Pages 44 and 45 allow pupils to reflect on their local area. The ***Let's investigate*** page allows pupils to consolidate their knowledge and vocabulary of facilities and services in a town as they make their own maps of the local area.

The ***Make a difference*** page encourages pupils to observe people's behaviour in a town. They will share ideas about how they can keep their streets clean so that everyone can enjoy being out in the town. Pupils will work together to make a rule chart to promote responsible behaviour in a town.

- Put pictures or flashcards of the different places around the classroom, playground or gym. Elicit the name of each place as you do so, e.g. *library*, *supermarket*, etc. Divide the class into groups: *lorries, vans, cargo ships, planes* and *buses*. Say **Lorries go to the supermarket. Planes go to the museum. Vans go to the bank**, etc. Encourage pupils to move to the different areas in different ways, such as hopping, jumping, twirling, etc.

LET'S INVESTIGATE

⊕ OPENING ACTIVITIES

- Show photos or create a slide presentation of your own local area or the area around the school. Encourage pupils to talk about what they see and review some of the unit vocabulary (include street names and numbers, street details and shops).

MAIN ACTIVITIES

- Ask pupils to open their books on page 44. Say **Let's investigate how we can make a map of our local area**. Read the instructions for step 1 and elicit places in their local area that they want to draw. Read the instructions for step 2 and ask pupils to tell you what materials they are going to need. *Scissors and coloured pencils or felt tips.*
- Focus pupils' attention on step 3 and read the instruction. Ask pupils what they will need to stick their pictures. *Glue.*
- Put pupils in groups and give out a simple street map you prepared (see the unit introduction) to each group. As pupils are working, walk round and ask questions about what they are drawing and cutting. Ask **What place is that? What can you do there? What is next to / opposite it?**

1 Tick.

- Point to activity 1. Encourage pupils to read each sentence with you. Ask them to look at their maps and tick the box if there is a museum, library, bank, etc. on their map.

⊕ CLOSING ACTIVITIES

- Ask pupils what their favourite place is in their town and why.
- Have volunteers stand up and describe their maps.

MAKE A DIFFERENCE

⊕ OPENING ACTIVITIES

- Ask pupils to work in groups and tell each other what they know about good behaviour at school and at home.
- Have each group mime an example of good behaviour for another group to guess, e.g. *tidying up, washing dishes, throwing rubbish in the bin, sharing, making their bed,* etc.

MAIN ACTIVITIES

1 Circle the bad behaviour.

- Ask pupils to open their books on page 45 and look at the picture. Tell pupils they have 30 seconds to look at the picture and then they must close their books again.
- Ask pupils to tell you what they remember about the scene and describe what people were doing. Have them start their sentences with *A man / woman / girl / boy is (talking).*
- Have pupils open their books again and see if they managed to describe everybody.
- Ask pupils **Who is behaving badly?** Have them describe the people who are not behaving well and circle them. *See answers opposite.*

2 Keep the streets clean. Make a rule chart.

- Read the instruction and have pupils follow in their books.
- Elicit important rules for keeping the streets clean.
- Focus pupils' attention on the photo so they can see how to make their chart.

⊕ CLOSING ACTIVITIES

- Have pupils hold up and read their rules to the rest of the class.

PAGES 46-47 Let's remember

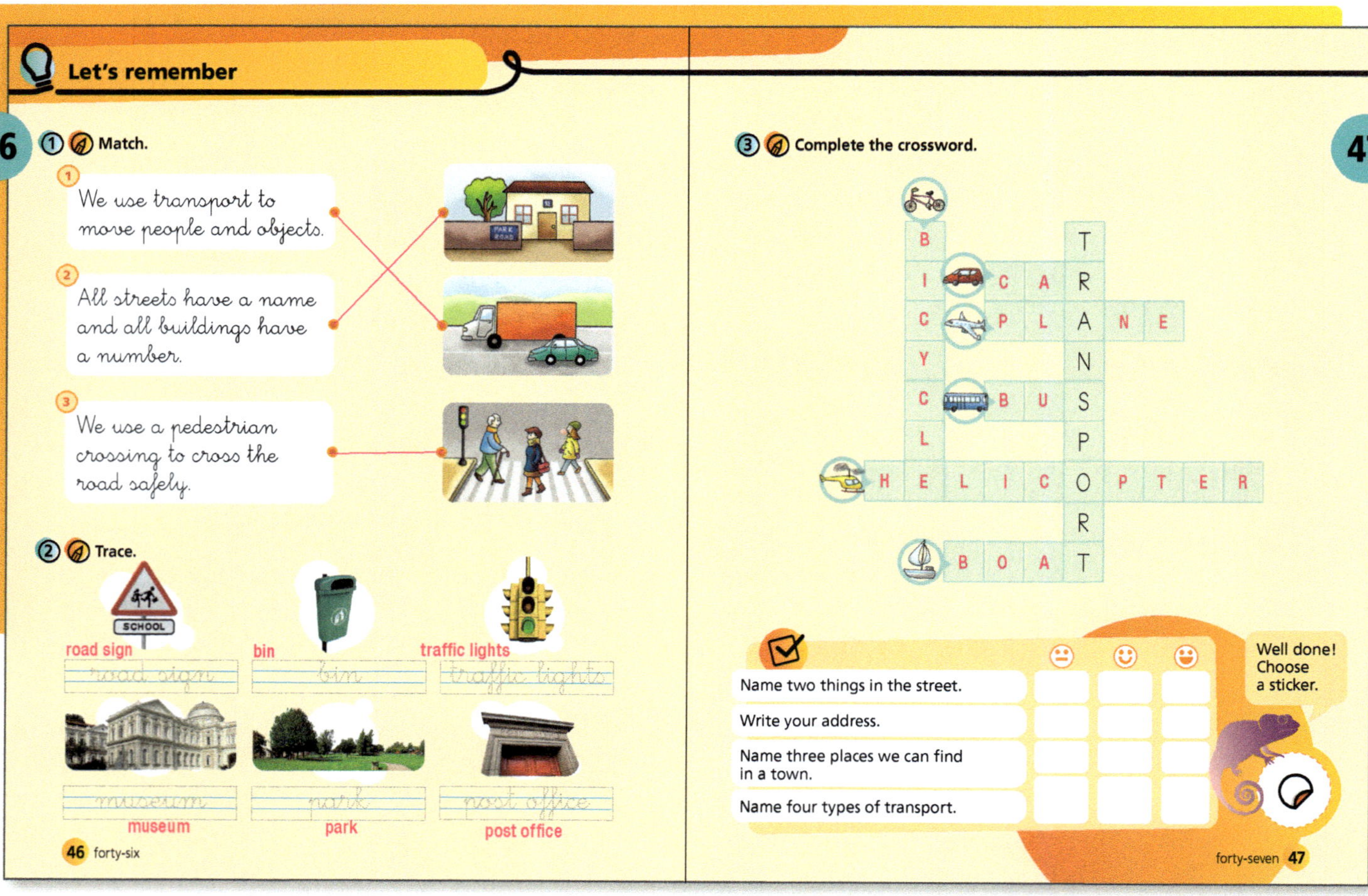

PAGE SUMMARY

Pupils review unit content and undertake a simple self-assessment on the unit content.

LANGUAGE

- Pedestrian crossing, green man, road sign, bin, traffic lights, pavement
- Museum, park, post office
- Car, bus, plane, boat, cargo ship, lorry, van, bicycle, motorbike, helicopter, train

MATERIALS

Flashcards: digital flashcards for the unit

OPENING ACTIVITIES

- Take the pictures or flashcards you've used in the unit and put them on the board. Describe an object and have pupils guess which one you are describing, e.g. **It has three colours: red, amber, and green. It tells cars to stop and cars to go.** *Traffic lights.* **It's big. It travels on water and transports objects across the world.** *Cargo ship.*
- Create a *Revision map*. Write *where I live* inside a box near the top of the board. Draw three more boxes branching off below and write *places*, *transport* and *things*. Ask pupils to name as many places, types of transport and street elements as they can remember and write them under the correct heading. Start them off with an example for each category and encourage them to recall all the information and vocabulary they have learned during the unit.

Note: If you have a weak class, show them pictures or flashcards, or name items and then have pupils classify them under the correct heading.

MAIN ACTIVITIES

1 Match.

- Tell pupils to open their Pupil's Books on page 46. Tell them that they are going to remember the things that they have learned about towns and transport in the unit.
- Point to each picture and have pupils tell you what they can see.
- Point to the first text box and say **Let's read together.** Make sure pupils are pointing to the words as they read them. Ask pupils to tell you which picture it describes and to draw a line. *The second picture.* Point to the car and lorry and ask **Which one carries people? Which one carries objects?**
- Repeat the procedure with the other two texts. *See answers opposite.*
- Ask pupils how we can cross the road safely. *Using the pedestrian crossing, waiting for the green man, waiting and looking.*

2 Trace.

- Point to each photo and ask pupils what they can see. Ask pupils **What do you do in a museum / park / post office?**
- Focus pupils' attention on the words below each photo and read them together. Ask pupils to trace them and then read them to a partner.
- Play *Guess my word.* Start to write a word on the board from the unit. Ask pupils to guess the word before you finish writing it.

3 Complete the crossword.

- Review different types of transport, their characteristics and where they go.
- Focus the pupils' attention on the pictures of the vehicles in the crossword. Point out which direction they need to write the words (*bicycle* goes down, *car* goes across). Have pupils write the words in the crossword. Encourage pupils to check their spelling by using the Picture dictionary in their books or looking back at the unit.
- When pupils have finished, ask them to spell the words out to you as you write them on the board.
- Have pupils check that their spelling is correct in the crossword. *See answers opposite.*

Self-assessment

- Focus pupils' attention on the self-assessment table. Read the first sentence together: *Name two things in the street.* Ask pupils if they can name two things in the street. Have them tell their partner.
- Read the next sentence: *Write your address*. Ask pupils to write their address in their notebook or on a mini whiteboard.
- Together read: *Name three places we can find in a town*. Again have pupils think of three places and then whisper them to a classmate. Ask pupils how many places they can name together.
- Finally, read the last sentence: *Name four types of transport*. Ask pupils to use their fingers to name four types. Ask pupils if they can also spell the names of four types of transport.
- After reading each sentence, the pupils should tick the boxes according to whether they have learned a lot (*very happy face*), some things (*happy face*) or a little (*disappointed face*) about the area where they live.
- Ask pupils to choose a sticker to show how they feel about their learning in the unit.
- Give individual attention to any pupils who choose the *disappointed* sticker.

Activity book answers

UNIT 3 Where I live

14

① Trace and match.

road sign

pavement

traffic lights

② Colour. Find the words.

road – green man – red man – car

q	g	a	d	z	b
s	r	c	k	l	h
h	e	r	j	i	w
r	e	d	m	a	n
o	n	w	a	p	c
a	m	e	m	a	t
d	a	a	c	a	r
e	n	s	d	o	f

14 fourteen

15

③ Look and write.

The supermarket is at 9 Park Road.

I live at 10 Castle Street.

My best friend lives at 5 Queensway.

The chemist's is at 3 Queensway.

The church is at 14 Castle Street.

fifteen 15

UNIT 3

16

④ Where do we find these things? Write *yes* or *no*.

	in a city	in a village	city and village
(village)	no	yes	no
(city)	yes	no	no

⑤ Circle and write.

museum – swimming pool
I swim in the swimming pool.

park – post office
I play in the park.

school – supermarket
I study at school.

library – bank
I read in the library.

16 sixteen

17

⑥ Write and match.

pedestrian crossing – ~~bin~~ – green man

Throw your rubbish in the bin.

Use a pedestrian crossing to cross the road.

Wait for the green man before you cross the road.

⑦ Do they travel on land, on water or in the air? Write.

boat – lorry – helicopter – plane – bicycle – cargo ship

land	water	air
lorry	boat	helicopter
bicycle	cargo ship	plane

seventeen 17

UNIT 3

Let's investigate at home!

Invent a new type of transport

1. Draw the body of your new type of transport.

2. Add wheels and windows.

3. Add more details.

4. Colour and cut out your picture.

1 Write. Open answer

My new type of transport has ______ wheels.
It has ______ windows.

Skills check

19

1 Look at the pictures. Look at the letters. Write the words.

s c h o o l — **school** / scohol

1 

c h u r c h — cuhrch / **church**

2 

p a v e m e n t — pevament / **pavement**

3 

l i b r a r y — **library** / libarry

4 

v i l l a g e — **village** / villaeg

5 

t r a f f i c l i g h t s — **traffic lights** / triffac litghs

UNIT 4 The world around us

CONTENT	EVALUATION CRITERIA
The natural environment: observation of its principal characteristics. Elements of the landscape.	Identify the principal elements of the natural environment, both near and far, based on observation.
Air and its characteristics: essential for living things. Wind.	Understand what air is, its basic characteristics and the fact that it is essential for life. Understand what wind is.
Weather.	Describe the basic aspects of weather: cold, heat, wet, dry. Differentiate between them.
Water: essential for life. Characteristics, states, uses and responsible use of.	Recognise water as an essential ingredient of life on Earth and value it is an essential and scarce resource that needs to be used responsibly.
Natural and human elements of landscapes.	Differentiate between natural and man-made elements of their surroundings, beginning to understand the human impact on the natural environment.
Human use of the natural environment.	Identify the elements and fundamental resources of the natural environment and how they are used by human beings.
Pollution and caring for the natural environment.	Develop positive attitudes towards environmental problems, valuing and caring for their natural environment.
Introduction to scientific knowledge and its application in the Social Sciences. Collect relevant information using different sources (direct and indirect).	Obtain specific and relevant information, using different sources.
Develop strategies to organise, memorise and remember information obtained through different methods and from different sources.	Develop a capacity for hard work and show perseverance while studying.
Team-building strategies.	Develop a cooperative and adaptive attitude, recognising merit in others' ideas and responding to situations with intuition, an open mind and flexibility.
With help, plan and manage simple projects, showing independence and initiative in order to achieve objectives.	Develop creativity and initiative, improving their capacity to acquire information and ideas and present innovative conclusions.
Correct use of different materials.	Use the materials in a suitable way.

LEARNING STANDARDS	KEY COMPETENCES	PAGES
Describes orally the basic elements of the natural environment.	MST, SOC	48–59
Carries out observations of some elements following advice from an adult.	MST, SOC, LTL	48–59
Collects and elaborates information about certain aspects of their natural environment, using images, drawings, oral and written sources.	MST, LTL, LIN, AUT	48–59
Observes and identifies specific elements of the landscape: mountain, plain, valley, etc.	MST	49, 51
Describes, simply, certain characteristics of air and identifies it as essential for life.	MST, LIN	53
Explains what wind is.	MST, LIN	53
Identifies and describes meteorological phenomena such as rain, snow, wind, etc.	MST, LIN	56–58
Observes certain atmospheric phenomena and presents the information simply.	MST, LIN, LTL, AUT	57, 58
Collects weather information.	MST, LTL, AUT	58
Identifies water as an essential element for life on Earth.	MST, SOC	54, 55
Values water as a scarce resource that needs to be consumed responsibly.	MST, SOC, LTL	55, 59
Understands some of the places water is found on Earth: seas, lakes, rivers, etc.	MST	51, 54
Differentiates between natural and man-made elements of landscapes and describes them orally.	MST, LIN	48–52
Identifies examples of obvious human activity in the nearby environment and describes them orally.	MST, LIN, SOC	52
Explains how human beings use natural resources.	MST, SOC, LIN	53, 55
Develops a positive attitude towards environmental problems.	SOC, LTL, AUT	59
Understands the positive and negative effects humans have on the natural environment and expresses their opinion in simple terms.	MST, SOC, LTL, AUT, LIN	52, 59
Identifies possible causes of air and water pollution and understands the importance of conserving these resources for future generations.	MST, SOC, LTL	59
Looks for, selects and organises information, analysing it and drawing conclusions. Reflects on the process followed and reports on it orally.	MST, LIN, LTL	58, 59
Performs academic tasks in a responsible and effective manner.	LTL	58, 59
Uses vocabulary correctly in the presentation of their work.	LTL, LIN	58, 59
Develops a cooperative and adaptive attitude, recognising merit in others' ideas and responding to situations with intuition, an open mind and flexibility.	LTL, SOC	49, 59
Identifies and uses the correct code of conduct for their environment.	LTL, SOC	59
Shows self-confidence, personal initiative, curiosity, interest and creativity in the learning process.	AUT, LTL	58, 59
Shows independence in the planning and carrying out of simple actions and shows initiative when taking decisions.	AUT, LTL	58, 59
Uses the materials in a suitable and careful way, thereby keeping them in good condition.	LTL, SOC	58

UNIT INFORMATION

UNIT SUMMARY

In this unit your pupils will look further afield to what lies beyond the place where they live. They will observe the different types of landscapes that surround them and what features can be found in each.

Pupils will consider the differences between natural and made-made elements in their environment, and how natural elements such as water are essential to our daily lives.

Finally, pupils will go on to observe and understand the different types of weather and how to interpret weather maps and symbols.

There is a lot of new vocabulary and concepts in this unit. Make sure you review, recycle and concept check as you progress through the unit, and continually provide visual support and encouragement.

PROJECT

Let's investigate

In the *Let's investigate* activity on page 58, your pupils will keep a record of the weather for a week.

You do not need to prepare anything beforehand.

The pupils need:

– Their notebooks

– A pencil

– Coloured pencils, crayons or felt tips

– A4 paper (one sheet per pupil)

Remind pupils to record the weather every day and at the end of the week, use their records to answer the questions in their books.

VALUES AND ATTITUDES

In this unit pupils will consider the impact the natural world has on our lives and how we must make sure we look after the environment and its natural resources. Throughout the unit, try to encourage pupils to think about:

- What we can do to look after the environment.
- How we can be careful with water.
- How to behave when we are out and about.

Make a difference

The *Make a difference* page in this unit focuses on understanding the simple things we can do in our immediate surroundings to look after the environment. The survey encourages pupils to be aware of their own environmental behaviour, as well as teaching them how to collect simple data.

EVALUATION MATERIAL

These documents can be downloaded from the *Teachers* section of the digital resources and printed.

The materials include:

- **Unit diagnostic test:** provides an overview of the unit and allows you to assess the pupils' prior knowledge.
- **End-of-unit test:** in addition to the *Review* section at the end of each unit, this summative test can be used to evaluate pupils' progress after studying the unit content.
- **Unit evaluation grid:** based on the evaluation criteria and learning standards of the unit.

DIGITAL RESOURCES

Presentations

- **Unit summary**: a simple slide presentation with text, images and audio to review the main ideas of the unit. It can be used at the beginning of the unit to test pupils' prior knowledge of the unit content or at the end of the unit as a revision tool.
- **Let's investigate**: a slide presentation of the unit's *Let's investigate* page with text, photos and audio. The slide presentation is perfect for a heads-up class, showing the steps one by one. Use this tool to get the pupils to predict the next steps (with their books closed) or to focus their attention on each step as they carry out the project themselves.

Activities

- **Memory game**: useful activity for reviewing key vocabulary and modelling pronunciation.
- **Wordsearch**: use at the end of the unit as a revision activity. Turn it into a game by getting the pupils to work in teams.
- **Spelling**: get a volunteer to come to the board and carry out the activity, but with the help of the whole class.

Song lyrics

Listen to the song *The world around us* and follow the lyrics line by line.

Posters

Attractive and informative posters to display in class. You can use them to review key concepts and vocabulary.

Videos

Use the video links in this unit to present content in a dynamic, real-life context whilst reinforcing the pupils' listening skills.

Teachers

Digital flashcards: a bank of digital images which can be used in a variety of ways in class.

Downloadable pdfs: evaluation tests, evaluation grids, templates, useful links and further information.

PAGES 48-49 The world around us

PAGE SUMMARY

The aim of the unit opener is to encourage your pupils' observation skills and invite them to take a look at the world around them through the illustration. Find out what your pupils can already tell you about the countryside and coast to help you build on that knowledge. Pupils answer the questions in groups then learn the actions to the song.

LANGUAGE

- House, mountain, sea, forest, beach, road, river, farm, fields, windmills, village, bridge
- Boat, car, road sign
- Coast, inland
- What is he/she doing? He/she is washing the car / hanging out the washing / picking flowers.

MATERIALS

Flashcards: (digital) see the *Teachers* section in the digital resources

WHAT CAN YOU SEE?

Put up pictures or flashcards of *coast* and *inland*. Point to each one in turn and ask the pupils where they go for their summer holidays. **Do you go to the coast? Or do you go inland for your holidays?** Encourage discussion, then ask pupils to draw a picture of their summer holidays. Tell them they can include family members and show any activities they do. Set a time limit and when pupils have finished, encourage them to talk about their picture with a partner or in a small group.

Say **Open your Pupil's Books on page 48** and read the title of the unit. Explain that they are going to study landscapes, which is everything that they can see around them outside, and the weather. Give pupils a few moments to look at the illustration. Ask pupils to name things they can see in the illustration that are also in the summer holiday pictures they drew. Ask pupils **What animals / transport / food can you see?** *Cows, dog, chameleon, car, boat, bread.* Ask pupils to name two living and two non-living things. *Tree, flowers, animals, car, boat, windmills,* etc. Ask **Where is the chameleon?** *On the water fountain.*

OPENING ACTIVITIES

- Use the zoom to focus on different areas of the illustration and highlight any possible new vocabulary. *Mountain, field, windmill, river, bridge,* etc.
- Ask pupils **Where is Sam? Where is Amy?** Encourage them to point to them in the picture.
- Say **Point to someone who is happy / thirsty / picking flowers / hanging out washing / washing the car,** etc. With a more confident class, elicit the information by pointing to the different people in the illustration and asking **What is he/she doing?**

MAIN ACTIVITIES

1 Can you see any water in the picture? Point.

- Ask pupils to close their books for a moment and, working in a group, think about what water they can see in the picture. Have pupils open their books and check if they remembered all the places. Talk about the use of water and places we see water. *River, sea, water fountain, hose, sprinklers.*
- Ask pupils **Why is the man using water?** *He is washing his car because it's dirty.* **Why is the girl using water?** *She is thirsty.* **Why is there water in the field?** *Plants need water to grow.* You could also point out that the woman is hanging wet clothes out to dry and that cows need water to drink.

2 What is the weather like?

- Look out of the classroom window and ask pupils what the weather is like. They will probably be used to talking about the weather as part of their daily routine in their English class. If not, ask **Is it sunny / cloudy / rainy / windy?** and draw simple illustrations on the board.
- Read the question and have pupils look at the illustration. Elicit that it is *cloudy* and *windy*. Pupils should notice the hat flying off the woman's head. Ask groups to look and tell you things that need the wind. *Sailing boat, windmills.*

3 Who is doing something wrong? Circle.

- Read the question and have groups look to find the answers. *Sam is opening the gate where the cows are, Amy's sister is picking flowers.* Have pupils circle them and talk about why this is not good behaviour. Pupils then choose a sticker for their effort of working with a group.

4 Listen and tick the things you hear.

- Ask pupils to look at the photos. Read the words under each picture together and help with pronunciation.
- Focus pupils' attention on the musical note. Say **Let's listen to a song.** Tell the pupils that they are going to listen to the song twice and tick the things that they hear.

CD 1 • Track 49
See audio script below.

5 Sing the song and do the actions!

- Say **Now let's listen and do the actions.** Play the song, teach the actions and encourage pupils to copy. Repeat the song and do the actions together.

CD 1 • Track 50

A big mountain, I can see *[mime a mountain]*
It's natural [x2] *[wave hands in air]*
A little house, I can see *[draw house in air]*
It's man-made [x2] *[march on spot]*
Natural or man-made, do you know? *[shrug]*
Mountain, beach, house or road *[spin around]*
A sandy beach, I can see *[mime sunbathing/relaxing]*
It's natural [x2] *[wave hands in air]*
A big grey road, I can see *[mime driving]*
It's man-made [x2] *[march on spot]*
Natural or man-made, do you know? *[shrug]*
Mountain, beach, house or road *[spin around]*

CLOSING ACTIVITIES

- Ask pupils to close their books and, in groups, remember all the things they can from the illustration.
- Ask pupils what they like to do when they are on holiday.

EXTRA IDEAS

- Have pupils label some of the elements in the pictures they drew, using vocabulary from page 49.
- Have pupils look at their drawings and play *Stand up if.* **Stand up if there is a road / an animal / the sea in your picture,** etc.

PAGE 50 Where are we going for our picnic?

PAGE SUMMARY

Use the story to talk about and compare the things we can do at the beach with the things we can do in the country. Pupils will consider the different elements we can find in each place.

LANGUAGE

- Picnic, mountain, sea, beach, country, river
- By the river, near the mountains, in the sea, at the beach
- Cloudy, rainy
- Go for a walk, have a picnic, swim

MATERIALS

Flashcards: (digital) see the *Teachers* section in the digital resources

Additional classroom materials: picnic basket, food pictures or real picnic food, ask pupils to bring in one item for a class picnic

OPENING ACTIVITIES

- Play *I Spy* with the opening illustration on pages 48 and 49.
- Give pupils a simple picture dictation to review some of the previous lesson's vocabulary, e.g. Say **Draw two mountains, a river between the mountains, a windmill on one mountain, a forest on the other mountain, three cows near the windmill, a house next to the river, a boat on the river, a cloudy sky**. When you have finished, ask pupils to describe the picture with a partner.

MAIN ACTIVITIES

- Tell pupils they are going to listen to a story about a picnic. Take in a basket or draw one on the board. Ask pupils to tell you what things you could put in your basket for a picnic.
- If you wanted you could put some food items (or food pictures or flashcards) in the basket for pupils to guess. Ask pupils what their favourite picnic food is.

1 Listen, look and point.

- Ask pupils to open their Pupil's Books on page 50.
- Point to frame 1 and say **Look at the picture**. Ask **Who can you see?** Encourage pupils to say *Sam and Amy (and their mums and dads).*
- Write the word *landscape* on the board and remind pupils that this is everything they can see around them outside. Point to each frame and ask what landscape pupils can see.
- Say **Let's listen to the story.** Play the audio.

CD 1 • Track 51

Where are we going for our picnic?

The children are going for a walk in the country.

Frame 1

Sam: What a beautiful place for a walk!

Amy: Yes, but I'm hungry! Let's have our picnic!

Frame 2

Penny (Amy's sister): Let's have our picnic here by the river. It's near the mountains so it's nice and cool.

Sam: That's a good idea!

Frame 3

Amy: No, let's go to the coast. We can have our picnic at the beach!

Sam: Oooh yes. And we can swim in the sea too!

Frame 4

Sam's mum: But look at the sky over there. It looks cloudy at the beach. It might even be rainy!

Amy: Oh dear!

Sam: You're right. Let's have our picnic here.

- Play the story again, this time pausing after each frame and asking further questions. Ask **Where are they? Why does Amy want the picnic now? Where is the river? What can they do at the beach? What is the weather like at the beach? Where do they have their picnic in the end?**

2 Read and put a tick or a cross.

- Point to the first photo and encourage pupils to read the sentence together. Ask pupils **Is that right?** *Yes.* **Tick or cross?** *Tick.*
- Repeat the procedure for the other two photos. *See answers opposite.*
- Explain that when the land is very flat, with no mountains, we call this a *plain*. Tell pupils that they can see a plain in the second photo (as well as the windmills).

CLOSING ACTIVITIES

- Ask pupils to describe their picnic experiences. Ask them where they like to go for their picnics and what activities they do.
- Have pupils listen to the story again and in groups of three or four, act out each scene.

EXTRA IDEAS

- Play *In my picnic basket there is / are*. Say **In my picnic basket, there are some strawberries.** Choose a volunteer to repeat your sentence and add something else to the basket, e.g. *In my picnic basket there are some strawberries and a sandwich.* Continue to add more items with new volunteers until someone makes a mistake. Start again with a new volunteer.
- Have a class picnic. Make a list of food for a picnic and have each pupil agree to bring one thing on the list to share at the picnic. Talk about healthy food they can bring, such as carrots, apples, grapes, etc. On the day, put all the food into a big basket and go out to the playground (or local park). Discuss what games pupils can play out in the country. *I Spy, hide-and-seek, games with a ball, kite flying*, etc. Remind pupils of the importance of good behaviour when they are out. They should throw rubbish in bins, or take it back home to a bin, respect animal habitats, etc.

PAGE 51 Different landscapes

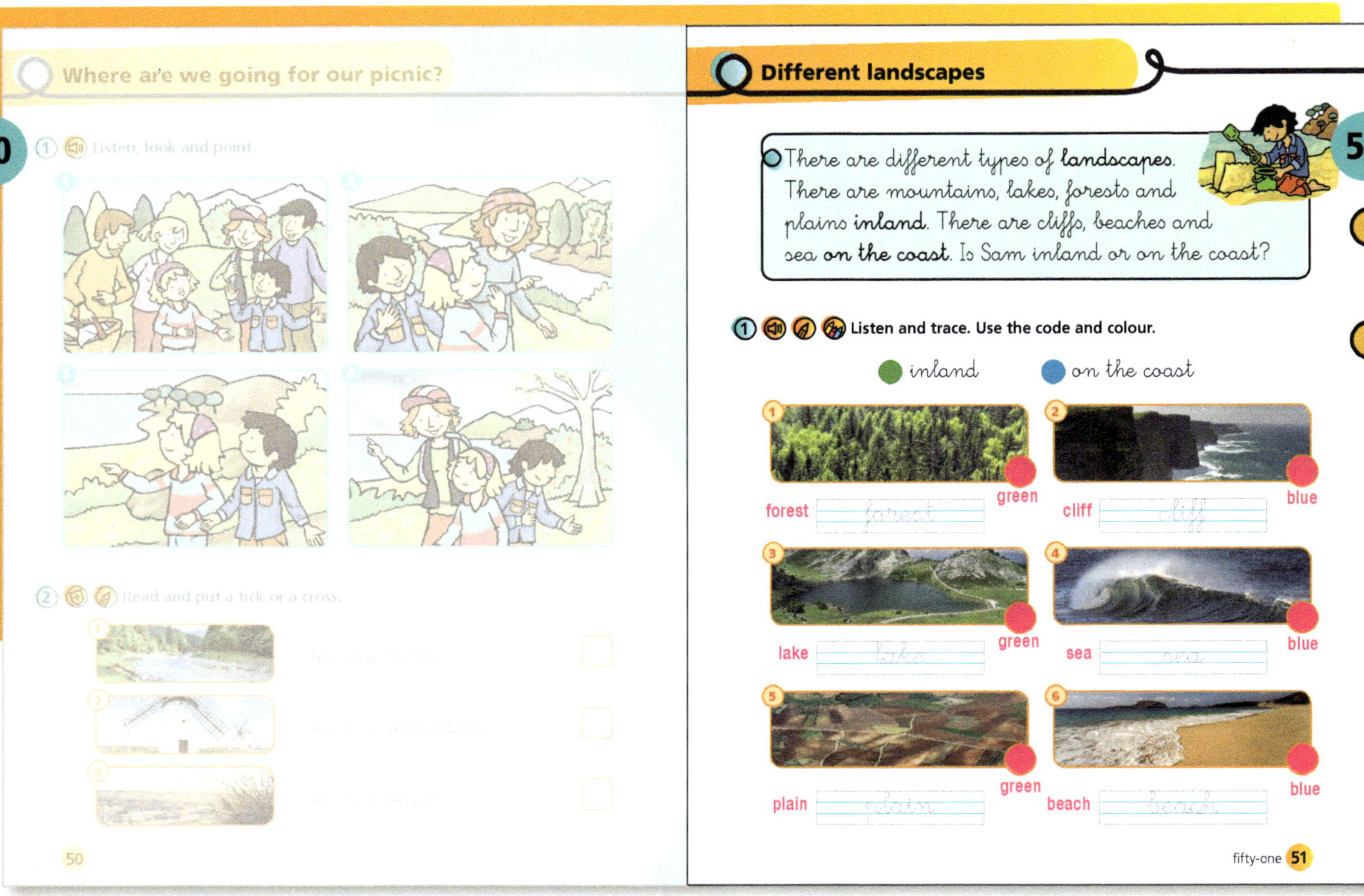

PAGE SUMMARY

Your pupils will look at landscapes in more detail and identify the differences between inland and coastal areas.

LANGUAGE

- Landscape
- Inland, mountain, lake, forest, plain
- Coast, cliff, beach, sea
- There is a lake inland. There are cliffs on the coast.

MATERIALS

Flashcards: (digital) see the *Teachers* section in the digital resources

OPENING ACTIVITIES

- Have volunteers mime a summer activity for the rest of the class to guess, e.g. *swimming in the sea, flying a kite, building sandcastles, walking in the mountains, having a picnic, taking photos,* etc.
- *Picture dictation.* This time have pupils dictate to you what inland or coastal scene you should draw, e.g. *Draw a mountain. Draw a forest on the mountain. Draw a house in the forest,* etc. Describe the finished scene together and encourage pupils to begin their sentences with *There is / There are.*

MAIN ACTIVITIES

Reading (CD 1. Track 52)

- Tell pupils that they will be looking at different types of landscapes in this lesson. Remind pupils that a landscape is everything you can see around you outside. Draw a Venn diagram on the board incorporating two landscape pictures or flashcards. Place a picture of *countryside* (inland landscape) in one circle and say **inland**. Place a picture of *beach* (coastal landscape) in the other circle and say **the coast**. Ask pupils for their ideas of what items could go could go in the sections. Don't write anything down for the moment.
- Ask pupils to open their books on page 51 and look at the reading box. Say **Let's listen and read about different types of landscapes**. Play the audio and encourage the pupils to follow in their books.
- Show pupils pictures or flashcards of *mountain*, *lake*, *forest* and *plain*. Repeat the name for each item and encourage pupils to repeat the words. Ask **Inland or on the coast?** *Inland*. Place the pictures in the *inland* section of the Venn diagram.
- Show pupils pictures of *cliff*, *beach* and *sea*. Ask **Inland or on the coast?** *On the coast.* Place the pictures in the *coast* section of the Venn diagram.
- Ask pupils to look at Sam and tell you where he is, inland or on the coast. *On the coast*. Ask pupils what he is doing. *Building a sandcastle.*

1 Listen and trace. Use the code and colour.

- Remove all the pictures from the board.
- Focus pupils' attention on the photos in the book. Point to number 1 and ask pupils to tell you what they see. Point to each photo in turn and name each item together.
- Play the audio and have pupils listen and follow in their books. Play the audio a second time and this time pause after each description and give pupils time to trace the words in their books. When they have finished, encourage pupils to read the words with a partner.

CD 1 • Track 53

1. Forest. We find forests inland.
2. Cliff. We find cliffs on the coast.
3. Lake. We find lakes inland.
4. Sea. We find sea on the coast.
5. Plain. We find plains inland.
6. Beach. We find beaches on the coast.

- Draw pupils' attention to the colour code. Read the word *inland* and ask **What colour is inland?** *Green.*
- Read the words *on the coast* and ask **What colour is on the coast?** *Blue.* Point to picture 1 and ask **What colour?** *Green.* Have pupils colour the circle green. Encourage pupils to say *We find forests inland.*
- Repeat the procedure for each photo and encourage pupils to say the full sentence after colouring, e.g. *We find cliffs on the coast.*

CLOSING ACTIVITIES

- Shuffle the pictures or flashcards of landscapes. Hold up the flashcard of *beach* and ask pupils **Can you find beaches inland or on the coast?** *On the coast*. Have a volunteer place the flashcard in the correct section of the Venn diagram. Repeat the procedure until all the flashcards have been placed on the board. With a more confident class, you include a feature that we find both inland and on the coast, such as a river. This goes in the centre of the Venn diagram.
- Show the pupils a landscape wordcard. Run your finger under the letters and encourage them to read the word together, e.g. *cliff.* Choose a pupil to place the wordcard under the *cliff* flashcard. Repeat the step with other wordcards. When you are finished, point to each one and have pupils read each word again.

EXTRA IDEAS

- Describe and draw. Give the pupils an A4 sheet of paper and ask them to fold it in half. Tell them to write *inland* on one side and *on the coast* on the other. Dictate, e.g. **Draw the sea. Draw a mountain. Draw cliffs**, etc. Pupils should draw the items in the correct scene.

UNIT 4

PAGE 52 Natural and man-made features

PAGE SUMMARY

Your pupils will take a closer look at the features of a landscape and decide if they are natural or man-made.

LANGUAGE

- Landscape, mountain, river, house, road, park, windmill
- Natural, man-made

MATERIALS

Flashcards: (digital) see the *Teachers* section in the digital resources

Additional classroom materials: A3 coloured card, magazines (with landscapes)

OPENING ACTIVITIES

- Give each pupil two slips of paper and tell them to write the word *coast* in big letters in blue crayon on one slip and *inland* in big letters in green crayon on the other. Show landscape flashcards one by one. Pupils hold up the blue sign if they can normally find this item on the coast and hold up the green sign if it is found inland. If pupils think the item can be found on the coast and inland, they hold up both signs.
- Draw a vertical line on the board and write *inland* on one side and *on the coast* on the other. Hold up the flashcards one by one and have a volunteer place the flashcard in the correct column on the board. Encourage pupils to say *We find (mountains) inland,* etc. Once all the flashcards have been placed on the board, write the name under each one with vowels missing e.g. *cl_ff, l_k_,* etc. Have pupils work with a partner and spell the words on a mini whiteboard or in their notebooks.

MAIN ACTIVITIES

Reading. (CD 1. Track 54)

- Ask pupils to open their books on page 52 and look at the reading box. Say **Let's listen and read more information about landscapes.** Play the audio and encourage the pupils to follow in their books.
- Explain to pupils that natural features are plants, animals and things that are part of the Earth, like rocks, soil and water. Tell them that man-made features are things that have been made or changed by people.
- Write *natural features* on one side of the board and *man-made features* on the other. Ask pupils to look back at the reading box and find the examples of natural features. *Mountains and rivers.* Ask pupils if they can give you any more examples of natural features. Ask pupils to now find the examples of man-made features in the reading box. *Houses and roads.*

1 Use the code. Circle.

- Focus the pupils' attention on the pictures. Say *Point to the mountains.* Make sure all the pupils are pointing to the mountains and ask **Is a mountain natural or man-made?** Encourage them to say *A mountain is natural.* Focus pupils' attention on the green and red circles. Say **Green for natural, red for man-made.** Ask pupils what colour they will circle the mountains. *Green.* Say **Point to the house.** Make sure all the pupils are pointing to the house and ask **Is a house natural or man-made?** Encourage them to say *A house is man-made.* Ask pupils what colour they will circle the house. *Red.* Repeat for the other features and have pupils circle in the correct colour. *See answers opposite.*
- Draw pupils' attention back to the board and ask them to tell you another feature you can add to each section, e.g. *flowers – natural, bridges – man-made.*

2 Investigate your environment. Put a tick and circle.

- Have pupils look through their classroom window. Ask them what natural features they can see, and then what man-made features they can see in their school environment.
- Focus pupils' attention on the picture of the school / house. Say **Can you see a school / house from the window?** Tell them that if their answer is *yes*, then they can put a tick in the box and if their answer is *no*, then they must put a cross.
- Point to the words under the picture and have pupils read them with you. Ask **Is a school / house natural or man-made?** *Man-made.* Tell them to circle their answer.
- Point to the picture of the mountains and ask if they can see mountains from the classroom window. Tell them to put a tick if their answer is *yes* and a cross if their answer is *no*. Read the words under the picture and decide if mountains are natural or man-made. Have them circle the correct answer. *Natural.* Repeat for the remaining two pictures.

CLOSING ACTIVITIES

- Remind pupils that the world is made up of natural and man-made features. Ask them to suggest more examples of natural and man-made features that they can see outside.
- Hold up wordcards with natural and man-made features written on them. Encourage pupils to read them together and then have volunteers put the wordcard in the correct column on the board. When all the wordcards have been classified, read through the words again together.

EXTRA IDEAS

- Take the class out into the area around the school and investigate numbers of natural and man-made features.
- Make a natural and man-made mural with objects and features cut out from magazines.

PAGE 53 Air

PAGE SUMMARY

Your pupils will learn and understand how air is important to life.

LANGUAGE

- Air, wind
- Living things, non-living things
- Wind moves things.

MATERIALS

Flashcards: (digital) see the *Teachers* section in the digital resources

Additional classroom materials: scenic photos from magazines or old calendars or the internet, electric fan, balloons, drinking straws

OPENING ACTIVITIES

- Play a reading classification game. Draw a large tree on the board to represent natural features and a large house for man-made features. Shuffle and give out photocopied wordcards and ask pupils to form a line down the centre of the classroom. Pupils should read their wordcard and stick it inside either the tree or the house according to whether it is natural or man-made. Once all the words are in position, allow pupils time to read them and comment if any have been placed incorrectly. Once the words have been checked, read through each set as a class.
- Describe pictures. Show the pupils some scenic photos from old calendars, magazines or the internet. Encourage pupils to describe the scenes by first saying if they are inland or on the coast, and then going on to describe the features they can see. Pupils can then classify all the features according to whether they are natural or man-made.

MAIN ACTIVITIES

- Breathe in and out and say **Air**. Encourage pupils to breathe in and out with you. Ask **What needs air?** Encourage the pupils to say *People need air. Plants need air. Animals need air.* Ask **Can you see air?** *No.* **Can you feel air?** *Yes.* Blow on your hand to demonstrate that when air moves, we can feel it. Encourage pupils to blow on their own hands to feel the air. Finally, ask **Does air move?** *Yes.* Say **Air that moves is called wind.**
- Turn on a fan and tell pupils they must be very careful not to come too near it. Ask a volunteer to sit at a safe distance from the fan, but near enough for the rest of the pupils to see the effect when the fan blows the pupil's hair. If you do not have access to an electric fan, you can use a paper fan or blow on a pupil's hair yourself to make it move.

Reading. (CD 1. Track 55)

- Ask pupils to look at the reading box. Say **Let's listen and read**. Play audio and have pupils follow in their books.
- Ask pupils to hold up a sheet of paper and blow it. Say **We can also blow the air and move things**. Ask what Sam is playing with. *A kite*. Ask pupils if they have a kite and where they go to fly it.

1 Do these things need air? Put a tick or a cross.

- Ask **Do plants need air?** *Yes*. Write *Plants need air* on the board. Ask **Do animals need air?** *Yes*. Write *Animals need air* on the board. Encourage pupils to make sentences about different animals, e.g. *Ducks need air. Elephants need air. Cats need air,* etc. Finally, ask **Do children need air? Do teachers need air?** *Yes.* Write the sentence on the board. Read all the sentences together and tell the pupils **All living things need air**. Ask them to repeat the sentences after you.
- Read the instruction and have pupils follow in their books. Point to the first photo and ask **Are they living things?** *Yes*. **Do they need air?** *Yes*. **Tick or cross?** *Tick*. Have pupils put a tick in the box. Repeat the questions with the other photos. *See answers opposite.*
- Review the activity by pointing to each photo again and encouraging pupils to say together *Children / stones / flowers do / don't need air.* Ask pupils to think of more things that need air.

2 Listen and colour the things that move in the wind.

- Ask pupils what we call air that moves. *Wind.* Ask them if they can think of things that move in the wind. Accept any sensible suggestions and reflect any suggestions given in their own language back in English. Possible suggestions include: *leaves, clouds, hair, trees, water,* etc. Encourage the pupils to make sentences: *The wind moves leaves. The wind moves hair,* etc.
- Ask pupils to look at the black and white picture. Ask **What can you see in the picture?** Encourage pupils to name some of the things they already know, e.g. *boat, tree, leaves, kite,* etc.
- Tell pupils to listen and point to the things as they hear them. Play the audio.

> **CD 1 • Track 56**
>
> Girl: **The leaves move in the wind. The clothes move in the wind. The smoke moves in the wind. The girl's hair moves in the wind.**
>
> Boy: **The boat moves in the wind. The kite moves in the wind. The windmills move in the wind. The flag moves in the wind.**

- Now tell pupils to colour all the things that are moving in the wind. *See answers opposite.*

CLOSING ACTIVITIES

- Write *All living things need* … on the board and have pupils finish the sentence with the word *air*.
- Ask pupils to crouch down on the floor and grow taller as they take in a deep breath of air. Shout **Pop!** and have pupils imitate a deflating balloon.
- With books closed, ask pupils to name as many things as possible that move in the wind.

EXTRA IDEAS

- *Air in balloons*. Give out balloons to the pupils. Ask them to blow into the balloons several times and then hold the end with one hand so that no air escapes. Show them how to let out the air slowly. Encourage them to feel the air as it leaves the balloons.
- Make flags with paper and drinking straws. Have pupils go out on a windy day to observe the flags blowing in the wind.

PAGE 54 Water

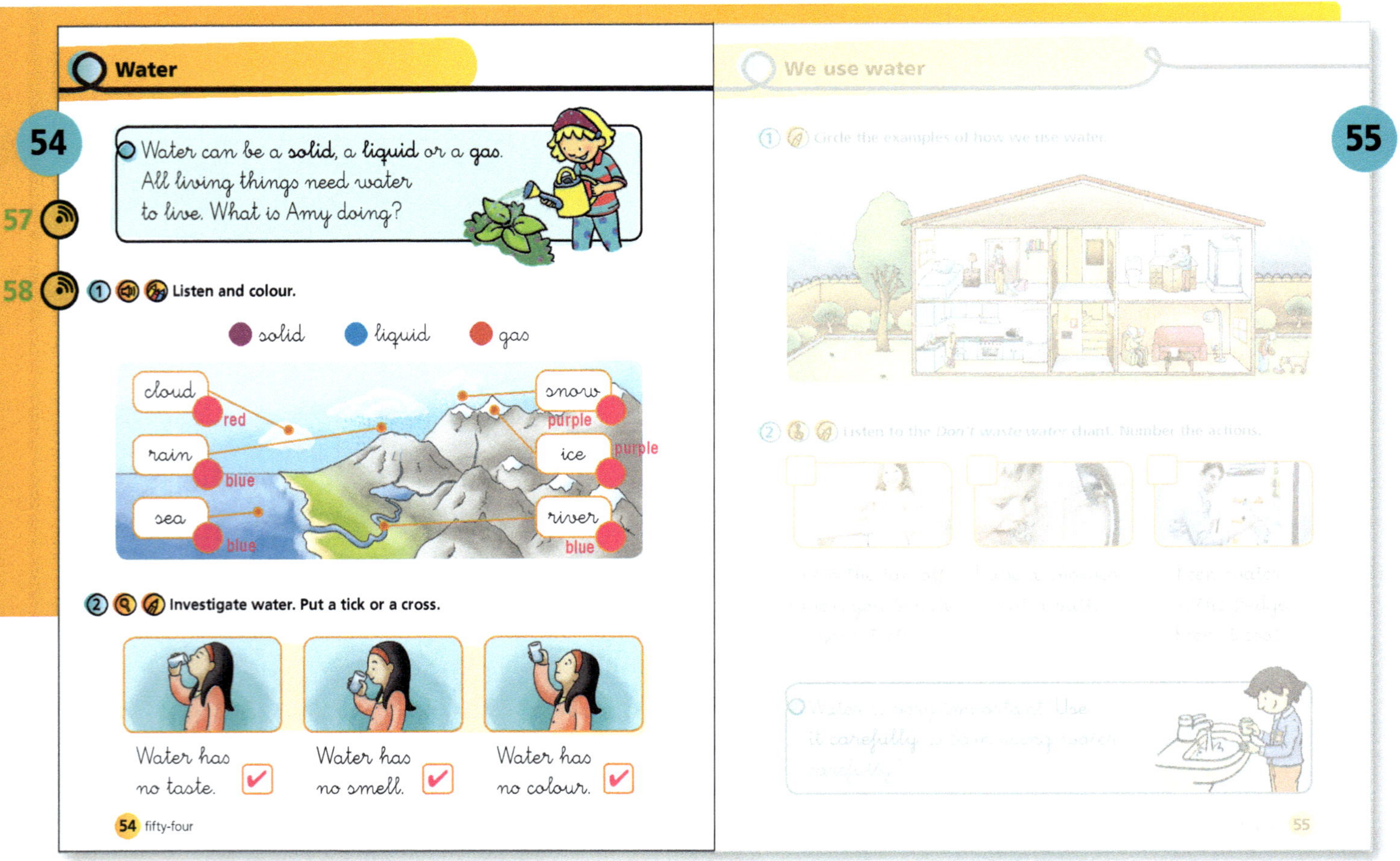

PAGE SUMMARY

Pupils will study the characteristics of water. They will learn that water is a natural substance that can be found in three forms: solid, liquid and gas. It has no taste, no smell and no colour.

LANGUAGE

- Water, solid, liquid, gas
- Cloud, snow, rain, ice, sea, river, lake
- Water has no taste / no smell / no colour.

MATERIALS

Flashcards: (digital) see the *Teachers* section in the digital resources

Additional classroom materials: plastic letters or plasticine, ice cubes, glass of water, kettle with water, clear plastic cups of water (one per group or per pupil)

OPENING ACTIVITIES

- Play *What needs air?* Mix together eight to ten pictures or flashcards of people, plants, animals and non-living things from previous units. Make sure that the top card is something that needs air (e.g. *flowers*) and the second is something that does not (e.g. *pencils*). Show the flashcards to pupils one by one and ask questions about each one, e.g. **Do flowers need air?** *Yes.* **Do pencils need air?** *No*, etc.
- Play *Blowing in the wind.* Mime flying a kite and have pupils guess what you are doing. Ask **What else moves in the wind?** Elicit *leaves, clouds, windmills, hair, washing*, etc. Go out to the playground or an area where pupils have space to move around. Tell pupils that when you clap your hands they must imagine that the wind is blowing them all over the place. They must move around but not bump into each other. If they do they must stop and stand still.
- Hand out plastic letters or plasticine to small groups. Have them spell *air, wind* and *water.*

MAIN ACTIVITIES

- Tell pupils that they are going to learn about water in the next two lessons.
- Hold up a glass or bottle of water and ask pupils if they know where we can see water. Accept any sensible suggestions and reflect any suggestions given in their own language back into English. *The rain, in a bottle, in the bathroom / kitchen, in the tap, in the sea,* etc.

Reading. (CD 1. Track 57)

- Ask pupils to look at the reading box on page 54. Say **Let's listen and read**. Play the audio and have pupils follow in their books.
- Ask pupils what Amy is doing. *Watering the plants.* Ask pupils what other things need water. Show a mix of pictures or flashcards of people, plants, animals and non-living things from previous units. Ask questions as you show each picture, e.g. **Do flowers need water?** *Yes.* **Do pencils need air?** *No.* At the end, remind pupils that all living things need both air and water.
- Draw three columns on the board. Write *solid, liquid* and *gas* at the top of each column. Explain that water has three forms. Knock on your desk and say **Solid**. Ask pupils if they know when water is solid and see if pupils can suggest snow or ice. Take in some ice cubes and have pupils pass them round in a container. Point to the word *liquid* on the board and pour a glass of water or turn on a tap, say **Liquid** (elicit or show other examples of liquids: milk, juice, a fizzy drink, oil). Finally, point to the word *gas*. Say **Gas** and explain that gas is in the air all around us but we can only see it in special situations. Boil a kettle so pupils can see steam and explain that this is water as a gas.

1 Listen and colour.

- Show pupils flashcards or pictures of water in its different forms, one by one, and ask **Is this water?** Introduce the vocabulary by saying **That's right! There's water in the sea / a river / a cloud / snow / ice / rain**. Hold up each flashcard again and have pupils remember and repeat the name.
- Focus pupils' attention on the picture. Point to each word and encourage pupils to read them with you. Read the words *solid, liquid, gas* together and elicit the colour code for each.
- Play the audio and have pupils listen and point to each element. Play the audio a second time and this time pause after each sentence. Ask **What colour is cloud?** Say **That's right, red. Cloud is a gas.** Have pupils colour the circle. Repeat for the other elements in the picture. *See answers opposite.*

> **CD 1 • Track 58**
> We can see water in many places.
> Cloud. The water in the clouds is a gas.
> Rain. The water in the rain is a liquid.
> Sea. The water in the sea is a liquid.
> Snow. The water in the snow is a solid.
> Ice. The water in the ice is a solid.
> River. The water in the river is a liquid.

- Hold up the *cloud* flashcard and elicit its name. Ask **Is a cloud a solid, liquid or gas?** *A gas.* Choose a volunteer to place the flashcard in the correct column on the board. Repeat with other flashcards.

2 Investigate water. Put a tick or a a cross.

- Focus the pupils' attention on the photos. Explain that the girl is doing an experiment with water. Pour water into several clear plastic cups and hand them to small groups of pupils. Say **Look at the water**. Encourage pupils to hold up their water and look at it carefully. Say **What colour is water? Is it blue? Is it green?** Go through all the colours until pupils reach the conclusion that *Water has no colour.* Say **Smell the water. What does water smell like? Does it smell like chocolate / flowers?** Help pupils reach the conclusion that *Water has no smell.* Say **Taste the water. What does water taste like? Is it sweet / sour / salty / bitter?** Help pupils conclude that *Water has no taste.*
- Read the sentences together and have pupils put a tick or cross. *See answers opposite.*

CLOSING ACTIVITIES

- Ask pupils to tell you everything they have learned about water.

EXTRA IDEAS

- Have pupils keep a record of how many glasses of water they drink in a day.

UNIT 4

PAGE 55 We use water

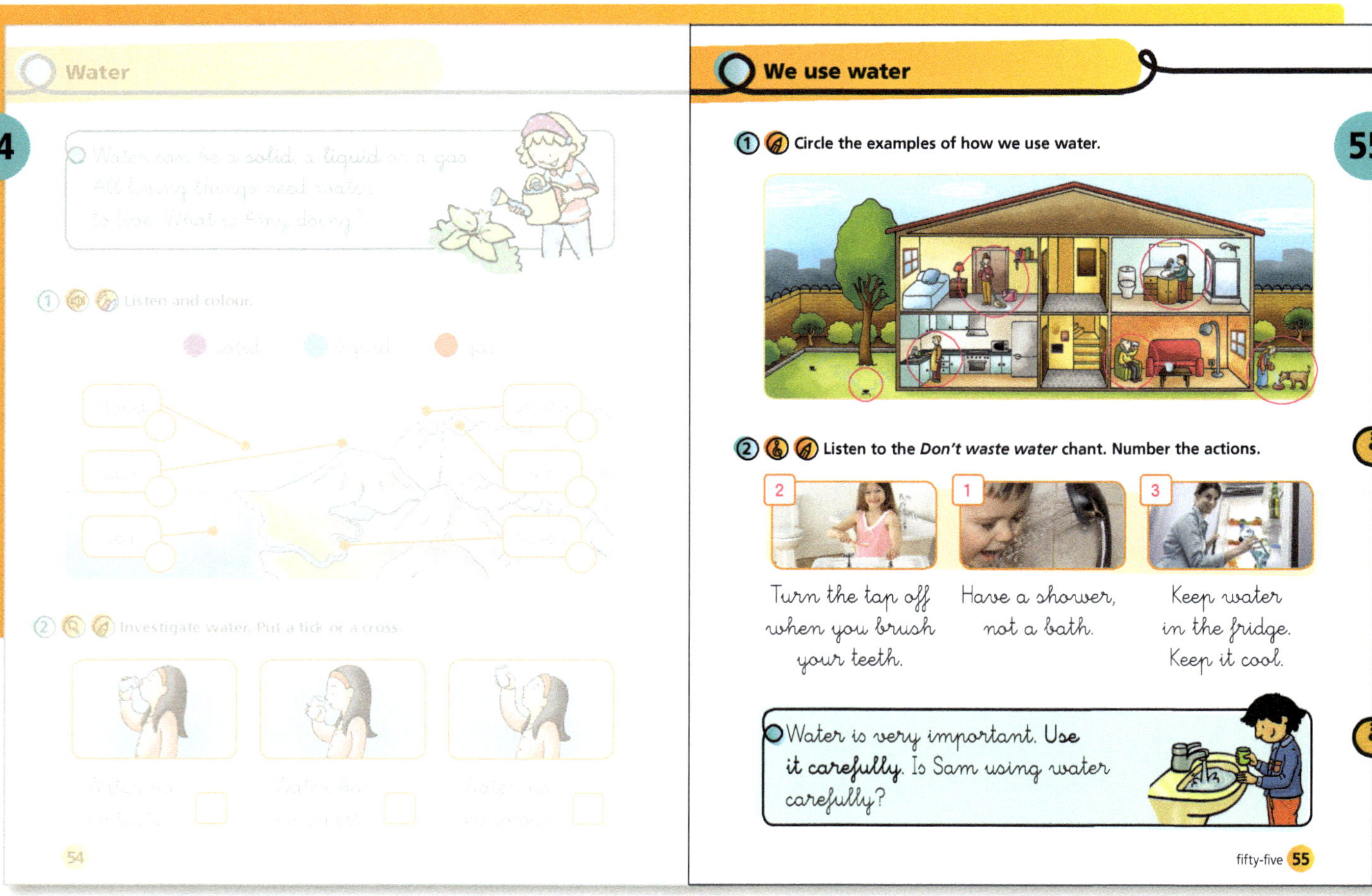

PAGE SUMMARY

Pupils will look at the different ways we use water in our daily lives. They will learn that we must be responsible with our use of water.

LANGUAGE

- We use water for drinking / washing / cooking / cleaning / brushing our teeth / having a shower.
- Turn off, keep, use, don't waste

MATERIALS

Flashcards: (digital) see the *Teachers* section in the digital resources

Additional classroom materials: glass of water, blue card

OPENING ACTIVITIES

- Put up flashcards or pictures of water in different forms (*cloud, river, rain*, etc.) around the room. Name them and have pupils point to the correct card. Encourage pupils to repeat each name together. Draw the *solid, liquid, gas* columns on the board. Take down the flashcards and as you do ask **Solid, liquid or gas?** Have volunteers take the cards and place them in the correct column. Once they are all in place, point to random cards and encourage pupils to say *Snow is a solid / A river is a liquid*, etc.
- Hold up a glass of water and ask pupils to tell you everything they know about water. *It has no taste, smell or colour.*
- Ask pupils what they like to do in the snow and in the rain. Go out and look at the clouds. Remind pupils that water is also a gas. Ask them what shapes or images they can see in the cloud formations.

MAIN ACTIVITIES

- Ask pupils **Do you drink water every day? How many glasses of water do you drink every day?** Remind them that it is good for them to drink plenty of water. Ask the pupils to think about other ways in which we can use water. Ask **What do we use water for?** Use mime to ensure that the pupils include all the different ways in which we might use water in our daily lives. Mime drinking a glass of water and say **Drinking**. Then say **Water is for drinking**. Encourage the pupils to repeat the sentence.

1 Circle the examples of how we use water.

- Tell pupils to open their Pupil's Books on page 55. Ask **What can you see? How are they using water?** Point to each person and ask **What is the man / woman in the bedroom / living room / bathroom doing?** Encourage pupils to reply *He/she is drinking / cooking / cleaning / washing his/her hands / giving water to the dog.*
- Ask pupils to circle all the examples of how we use water. *See answers opposite.* Tell them to name the ways to a partner.
- Ask volunteers to mime one of the actions and ask the rest of the class to guess.

2 Listen to the *Don't waste water* chant. Number the actions.

- Say **Let's look at the photos**. Point to the first photo and ask pupils what they can see. Point to the sentence below and encourage pupils to read it together. Say **If we turn the tap off we don't waste water.** Follow the same procedure for the other two photos. After reading each sentence say **If we have a shower, not a bath, we don't waste water. If we keep water in the fridge to keep it cool, we don't waste water.**
- Draw pupils' attention to the musical note and say **Let's listen to the *Don't waste water* chant.**
- The first time you play the chant, have pupils listen and point to the pictures. Ask pupils to listen again and this time number the photos in the order they hear them in the chant.

CD 1 • Track 59

Don't waste water! Don't waste water!
Have a shower, not a bath [x2]
Turn the tap off when you brush your teeth [x2]
Keep water in the fridge. Keep it cool! [x2]
Don't waste water! Don't waste water!

- Ask pupils **How can we not waste water?** Encourage pupils to repeat the ways they heard in the chant.

Reading. (CD 1. Track 60)

- Focus pupils' attention on the reading box. Say **Let's listen and read.** Play the audio and encourage pupils to follow in their books. Point to Sam and repeat the question **Is Sam using water carefully?** *No.* Ask pupils **Why not?** *Because he's left the tap running for a long time.*

CLOSING ACTIVITIES

- Working in small groups, with their books closed, ask pupils to name ten different ways we use water.
- Remind pupils that water is a natural resource and it is important that we look after it.

EXTRA IDEAS

- Make *Don't waste water!* raindrops. Hand out blue card to each pupil and ask them to cut out a large raindrop shape from it. Write *Turn off the tap! Don't waste water!* on the board and ask the pupils to copy the text onto their raindrops. Tell pupils to decorate their raindrops then hang them around their homes in places to remind them not to waste water.

PAGE 56 Weather

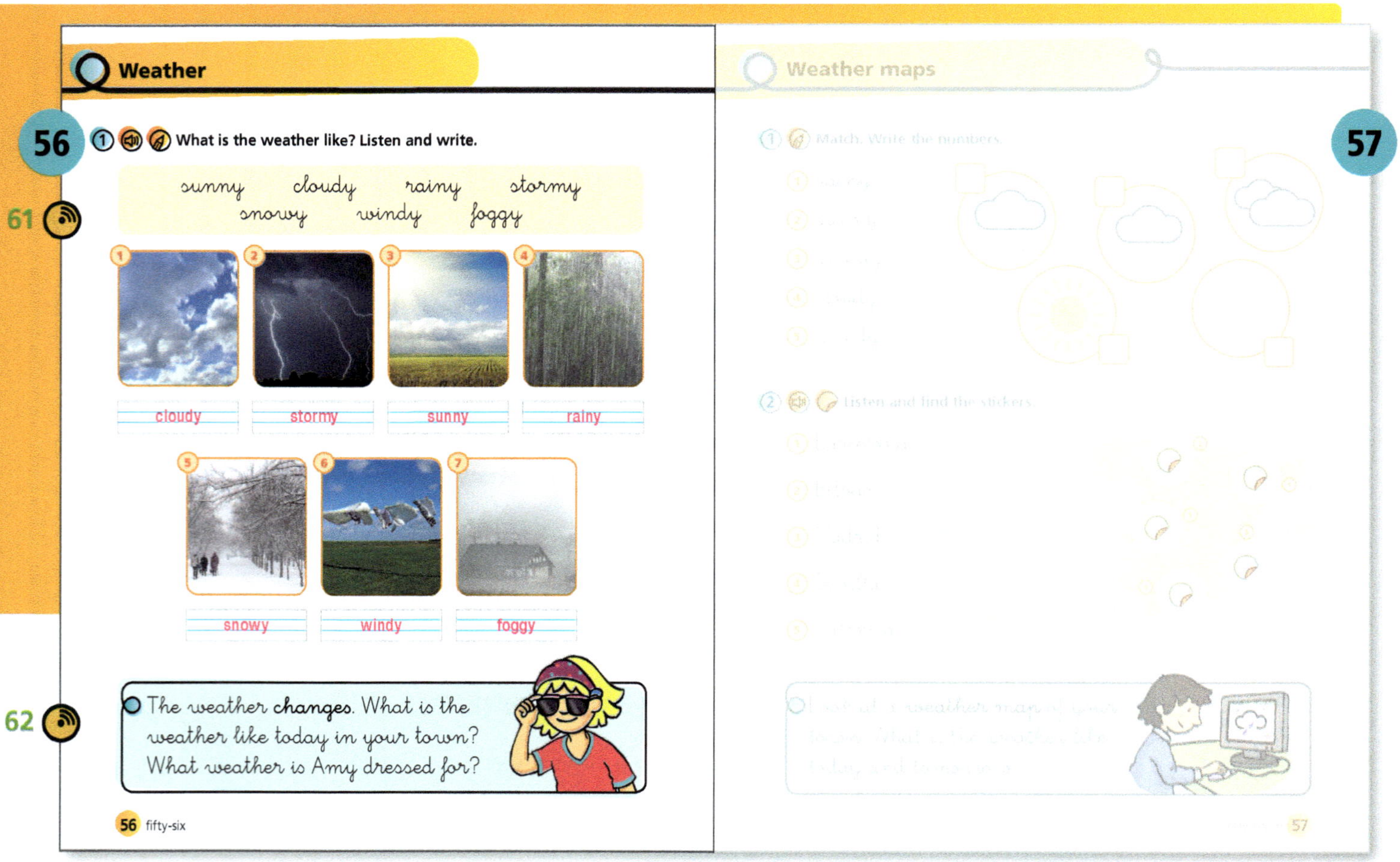

PAGE SUMMARY

Pupils will observe and identify the different types of weather. They will become familiar with the written form of weather words.

LANGUAGE

- Sunny, snowy, cloudy, windy, rainy, foggy, stormy
- What is the weather like?
- What do you wear when it's sunny?

MATERIALS

Flashcards: (digital) see the *Teachers* section in the digital resources

OPENING ACTIVITIES

- Ask pupils to tell you the different ways in which they have used water since the last lesson. Ask **How did you use water yesterday?** Accept short answers such as *Washing (my hands), brushing my teeth,* etc. Ask **Did you turn off the tap?**
- Play *Raindrop race*. Divide the class into two teams. Draw a large window on the board with two panes of glass (as two columns) and write the numbers 1–5 down the length of one side of the window. Cut two raindrops out of paper and write *drip* on one and *drop* on the other. Allocate a raindrop to each team and tell them this is their team name. Stick the two raindrops at the top of the window on the board, one on each pane. Explain that the first raindrop to make it to the bottom of the window is the winner. Ask questions and move the raindrops down when a team answers correctly. **What colour is water? Can you smell / taste water? Is water a liquid? What is a cloud / snow made of? Do plants / chairs need water? Is water for reading?** etc.

MAIN ACTIVITIES

- Introduce the topic of the weather (pupils should be familiar with some weather vocabulary). Point to the window and ask **What is the weather like?** Hold up weather pictures or flashcards one by one, leaving the flashcard of the appropriate weather for the day until last. Ask **Is it sunny / windy / snowy?** etc. Place each flashcard on the board and write the weather vocabulary. Encourage pupils to read each word with you.
- Talk to pupils about recent weather, e.g. **What was the weather like yesterday / on Monday?** Use mime to convey meaning if necessary.
- Explain that sometimes the weather is more extreme. Say **Sometimes it's snowy**. Show the *snowy* picture and ask pupils to repeat after you. Repeat for *foggy* and *windy*.
- Play *Quick flash*. Hold the seven weather flashcards facing you. Quickly, turn the pile around to face the pupils, then turn it back again. Pupils say which type of weather they saw on the top card. If they are correct, say **Yes, that's right. It's (foggy)** and stick the flashcard up on the board. If the pupils guess incorrectly, say **No, try again** and flash the card again for them to see.

1 What is the weather like? Listen and write.

- Tell pupils to open their Pupil's Books on page 56 and look at the weather photos. Point to photo 1 and ask **What is the weather like?** *Cloudy*. Ask pupils to point to the word *cloudy* in the word box and read it together. Ask **Is it cloudy today?** Have pupils look out the window. Repeat the procedure for each photo.
- Say **Now let's listen and write**. Play the audio and pause after each word to allow time for pupils to write the word under each photo. Encourage them to read the words to each other when they have finished.

CD 1 • Track 61

1. Cloudy – cloudy	5. Snowy – snowy
2. Stormy – stormy	6. Windy – windy
3. Sunny – sunny	7. Foggy – foggy
4. Rainy – rainy	

- Take the flashcards down from the board and have pupils read the weather words without the visual prompts. *See answers opposite.*

Reading. (CD 1. Track 62)

- Focus pupils' attention on the reading box. Say **Let's listen and read**. Play the audio and encourage pupils to follow in their books.
- Ask pupils to tell you again what the weather is like but this time to write it on a mini whiteboard or on a sheet of paper. Have them hold up their weather words and check the spelling.
- Ask what weather Amy is dressed for. *Sunny weather.* Ask pupils **What do you wear in sunny / snowy / rainy weather?** Stick the weather flashcards on the board and draw simple clothes pictures beside each one. Encourage pupils to say *I wear (boots) when it's (rainy).*

CLOSING ACTIVITIES

- Ask pupils if they ever watch the weather forecast on the television. Encourage them to do so when they get home.
- Ask pupils **What do you like to do when it's windy / rainy / snowy / stormy?** Encourage them to suggest *flying a kite, jumping in puddles / playing games / building snowmen,* etc.

EXTRA IDEAS

- Have pupils draw a picture of themselves dressed for a particular type of weather.
- Read *Mr Wolf's Week* by Colin Hawkins which reviews days of the week, weather and clothes to wear for each type of weather.

PAGE 57 Weather maps

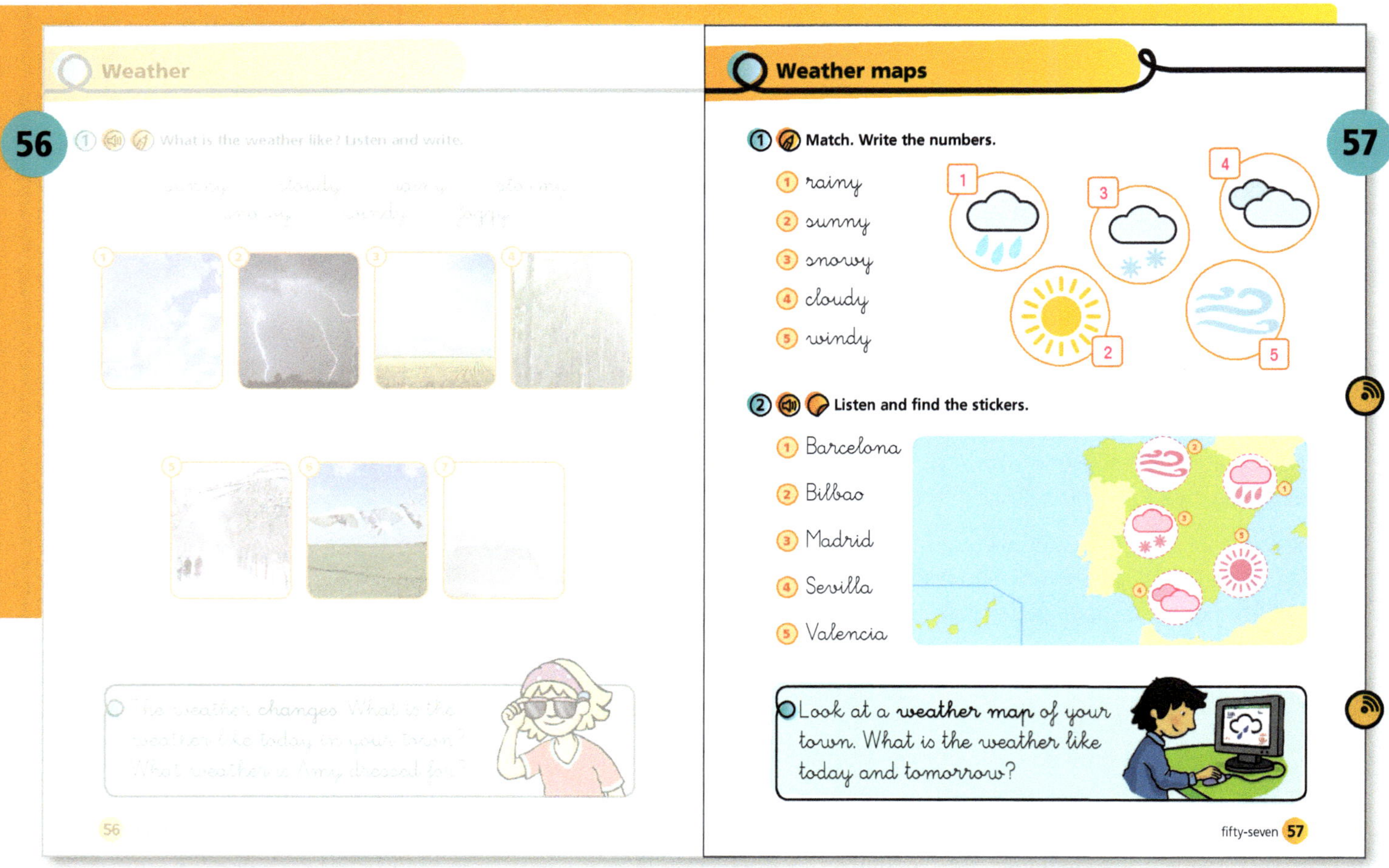

PAGE SUMMARY

Your pupils will identify different weather symbols to represent the weather. They will be able to look at a weather map and talk about the weather forecast.

LANGUAGE

- Sunny, snowy, cloudy, windy, rainy, foggy, stormy
- What is the weather like?

MATERIALS

Flashcards: (digital) see the *Teachers* section in the digital resources

Additional classroom materials: weather maps showing the weather today in the country or your town from newspapers or the internet

OPENING ACTIVITIES

- Spread weather pictures or flashcards on the floor. Ask pupils **What is the weather like today?** Have a volunteer come and stick the corresponding flashcard on the board. Ask what the weather was like yesterday.
- Put all the flashcards up on the board. Show the pupils a weather wordcard. Run your finger under the letters as you say the word, e.g. **Rainy**. Encourage them to read the word together. Choose a volunteer to place the wordcard under the corresponding flashcard. Repeat with the rest of the words. When all the words are in position, point to each one again and read it together.
- Teach pupils a traditional weather rhyme such as *Dr. Foster went to Gloucester; It's raining, it's pouring, the old man is snoring; Rain, rain go away, come again another day.*

MAIN ACTIVITIES

- Explain to pupils that we can use symbols to represent the weather, e.g. on television for the weather forecast or in newspapers. Ask **Do you watch the weather on the television?**
- Draw each symbol similar to those on page 57 on the board, a little at a time, and ask pupils if they can guess what type of weather is represented by each one. Say **Can you guess what type of weather this symbol is for?** Leave *windy* till last, as the others are easily recognisable and *windy* can then be guessed by elimination. Leave the symbols you drew on the board for the pupils to use as a model in the next activity.

1 Match. Write the numbers.

- Tell pupils to open their Pupil's Books on page 57. Point to each symbol and ask **What is the weather like?** Say **Let's read the words.** Encourage pupils to read the weather words together.
- Point to the *rain* symbol and ask **What number?** *Number 1.* Have pupils write it in the box. Ask the question for each of the symbols. *See answers opposite.*

2 Listen and find the stickers.

- Say **Let's look at the map. What country can you see?** *Spain.* Say **Let's read the names of the cities.** Point to city number 1. Read the word and encourage pupils to follow by running their finger under the word. With a more confident class you could ask if they recognise the city names.
- Draw pupils' attention to the map and ask **What city is number 1?** Elicit the name of the city. Repeat the step and elicit the city name for each number.
- Explain that pupils are going to listen and find the sticker for each city on the map. Play the audio once and have pupils listen and tell you the weather for each city. Ask **What is the weather like in Barcelona / Bilbao / Madrid?** etc. Play the audio a second time and have pupils find the stickers. *See answers opposite.*
- Review the activity by asking **What is the weather like in ...?** for each city.

CD 1 • Track 63

1. Today it's rainy in Barcelona. Can you find the sticker?
2. Today it's windy in Bilbao. Can you find the sticker?
3. Today it's snowy in Madrid. Can you find the sticker?
4. Today it's cloudy in Sevilla. Can you find the sticker?
5. Today it's sunny in Valencia. Can you find the sticker?

Reading. (CD 1. Track 64)

- Say **Let's listen and read.** Play the audio and encourage pupils to follow in their books.
- Hand out weather maps for today and tomorrow, either from the internet or photocopied from newspapers. Point to the different cities and elicit the weather.
- Look at maps with a weather forecast for your town. Ask what the weather is like for today and tomorrow. Ask if the weather forecast is correct for today.

CLOSING ACTIVITIES

- Write the weather words on the board with the vowels missing, e.g. *w_ndy, s_nny.* Have pupils notice how the words all end in *y*. Ask pupils to complete the words on a mini whiteboard or in their notebooks. Ask volunteers to come and write in the missing vowels and others to draw the weather symbols next to the completed words.

EXTRA IDEAS

- Give a *Weather symbol* dictation. Give each pupil a sheet of paper. Show them how to fold the paper into eight squares and number them. Tell pupils to draw the symbol for the type of weather you say in the correct square. Start with the weather symbols (*windy, sunny, cloudy, rainy, stormy, snowy, foggy*), but you can also test their ability to adapt the symbols by saying **sunny and cloudy, very cloudy, very rainy**, etc.

PAGES 58-59 Let's investigate and Make a difference

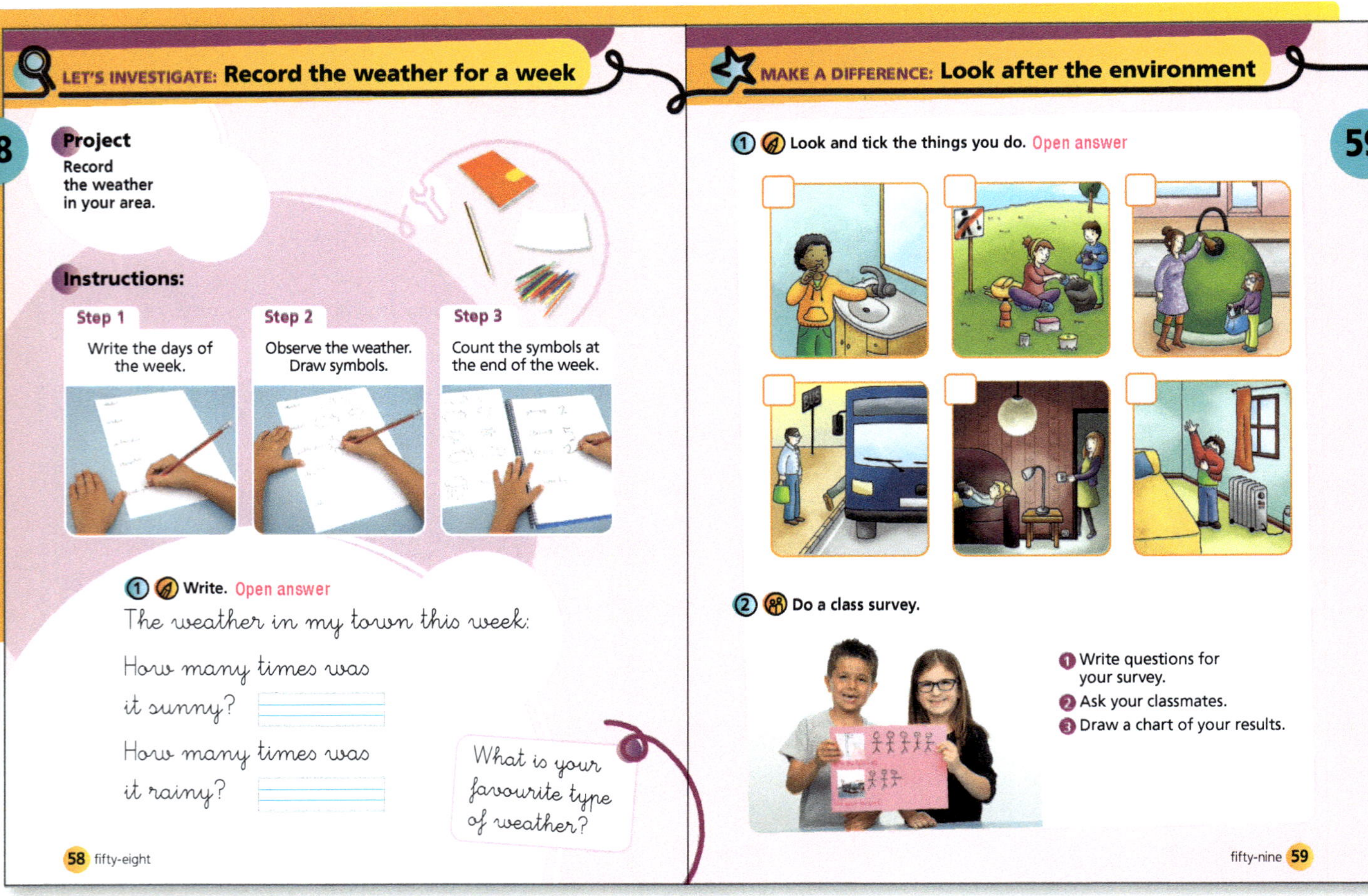
58

LET'S INVESTIGATE: **Record the weather for a week**

Project
Record the weather in your area.

Instructions:

Step 1 Write the days of the week.

Step 2 Observe the weather. Draw symbols.

Step 3 Count the symbols at the end of the week.

① Write. Open answer

The weather in my town this week:

How many times was it sunny? ______

How many times was it rainy? ______

What is your favourite type of weather?

58 fifty-eight

59

MAKE A DIFFERENCE: **Look after the environment**

① Look and tick the things you do. Open answer

② Do a class survey.

1. Write questions for your survey.
2. Ask your classmates.
3. Draw a chart of your results.

fifty-nine 59

PAGE SUMMARY

Pupils will observe and keep a record of the weather for a week. They will consider how we can be more responsible as regards the environment and will carry out a survey to see how environmentally conscious pupils in the class are.

LANGUAGE

- Weather, sunny, snowy, cloudy, windy, rainy, foggy, stormy
- Monday, Tuesday, Wednesday, Thursday, Friday, Saturday, Sunday
- What is the weather like?

MATERIALS

Flashcards: (digital) see the *Teachers* section in the digital resources

Additional classroom materials: weather maps from newspapers or the internet

Pages 58 and 59 allow pupils to take a closer look at the environment around them. The ***Let's investigate*** page encourages pupils to keep a weather record for a week. Pupils will value the use of simple symbols to make an easy visual representation of the week's weather.

The ***Make a difference*** page encourages pupils to observe peoples' behaviour in their immediate environment and decide whether or not they are looking after it. Pupils will conduct a survey to see how responsible their classmates are in relation to the world they live in. Both pages encourage pupils to reflect on and draw conclusions about the results of the activities they participated in.

- Show photos or slides of different local areas and have pupils talk about what they see in groups.
- Make true or false sentences about the pupils' own local area. Have pupils repeat your sentence if it is true and remain silent if it is false.

LET'S INVESTIGATE

⊕ OPENING ACTIVITIES

- Divide the class into seven groups and name each group a day of the week. Tell each group they must listen and mime what you tell them, e.g. **Tuesday wash your hands. Friday swim in the sea. Monday sail in a boat**, etc. Use examples to show the different ways we use water and air. Review these at the end of the activity.
- Play *Run and draw.* Divide the class into three teams. Give the first member of each team a board marker and an area to write on the board. Say **It's rainy**. Pupils must draw the symbol for rain. The first team member to finish drawing gains a point for their team.

MAIN ACTIVITIES

- Ask pupils to open their books on page 58. Say **Let's investigate how we can record the weather for a week**. Read the instructions for step 1 together. Ask pupils to write the days of the week down the left-hand side of an A4 sheet of paper. Read the instructions for step 2 and explain that pupils are going to observe the weather every day that week and draw a symbol or two symbols to show what the weather is like. Ask them to draw the symbol for today now.
- Focus pupils' attention on step 3 and read the instruction. Explain that at the end of the week, they will write the weather words (or draw the weather symbols) in their notebooks and count up how many times it was sunny, cloudy, rainy, stormy, etc. They will then write the number next to the word or symbol.

1 Write.

- Demonstrate that pupils must write each weather word or draw the symbol in their notebooks. Have them look at their weather record and count how many times it was sunny, cloudy, etc. Read the sentences together and have pupils write the number in their books.

⊕ CLOSING ACTIVITIES

- Ask pupils what their favourite type of weather is and why.

MAKE A DIFFERENCE

⊕ OPENING ACTIVITIES

- Ask volunteers to mime activities they do every day. Encourage the rest of the class to name the action.

MAIN ACTIVITIES

1 Look and tick the things you do.

- Have pupils look at each picture and tell you what activity they can see. For each picture ask **What is he/she doing? Is this good behaviour? Why / why not?**
- Ask pupils **Do you do these things?** Say **Tick the box if you do these things**.
- Talk about the importance of not wasting electricity or water, and of looking after the environment by throwing rubbish away in the correct place, recycling, using public transport, etc.

2 Do a class survey.

- Ask pupils to look at the poster to understand what they are going to do. Ask **What can you see?** Tell pupils they are going to work in groups of four to make a survey. Read the first instruction and brainstorm the different questions pupils can ask: *Do you turn the taps / lights off? Do you keep food in the fridge? Do you throw rubbish in the bin? Do you have a shower not a bath? Do you walk / ride a bicycle to school / use public transport?* etc. Encourage two pupils to write the sentences and the other two to draw the pictures.
- Point to and read the second instruction. Put groups together so they can ask each other their questions.
- Read the third instruction and demonstrate how they can record if a pupil from the other group does the activity.

⊕ CLOSING ACTIVITIES

- Ask different groups to report to the class the results of their surveys, e.g. *Three pupils turn off the lights. One pupil rides a bicycle to school.*

PAGES 60-61 Let's remember

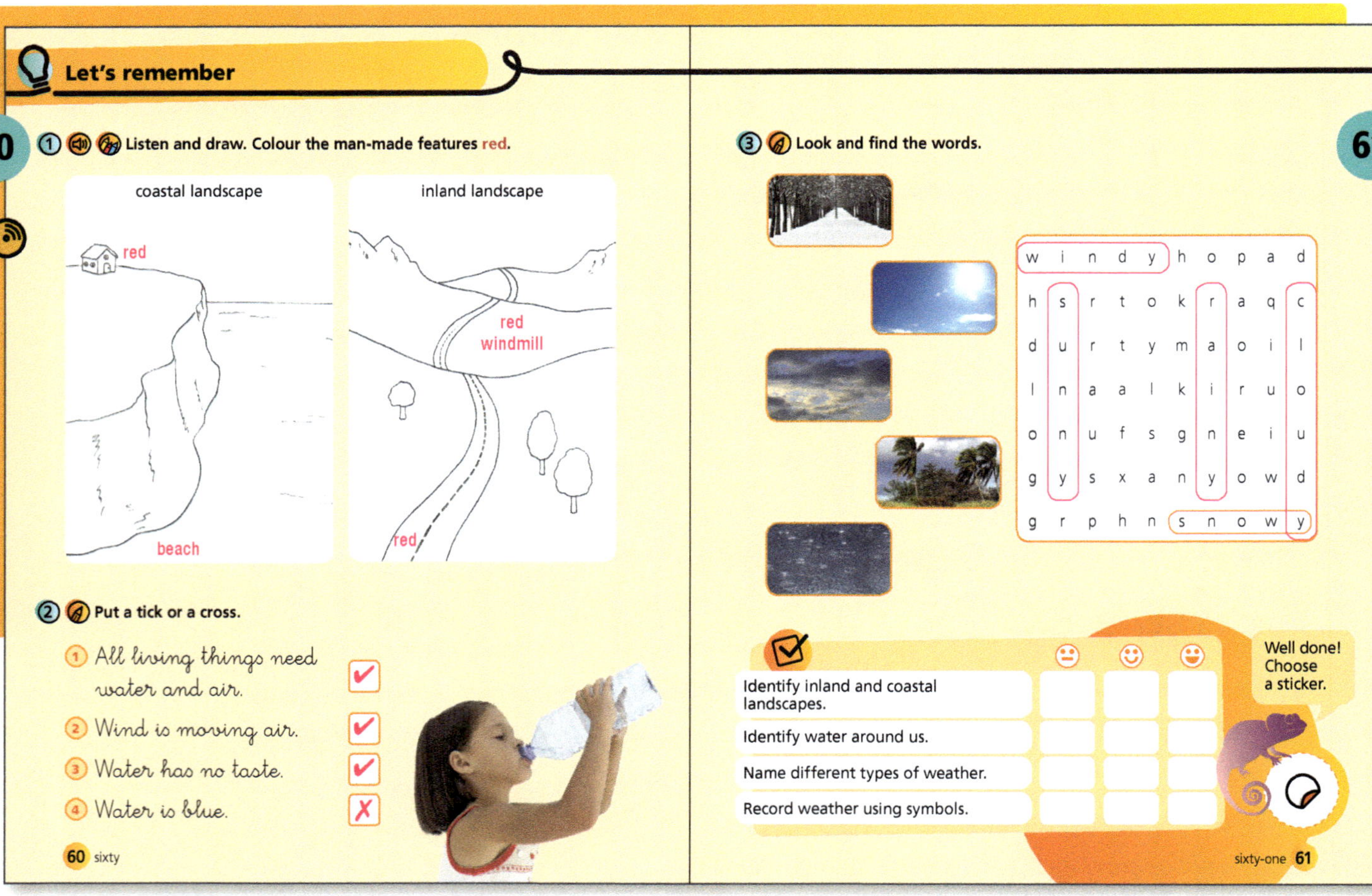

PAGE SUMMARY

Pupils review unit content and undertake a simple self-assessment on the unit content.

LANGUAGE

- Natural, mountain, river, forest, cliff, sea, plain, lake, beach
- Man-made, house, road, park, windmill
- Air, wind, water, solid, liquid, gas, ice, snow, cloud, rain
- Rainy, sunny, snowy, cloudy, windy, foggy, stormy

MATERIALS

Flashcards: digital flashcards for the unit

MAIN ACTIVITIES

1 Listen and draw. Colour the man-made features red.

- Tell pupils to open their Pupil's Books on page 48 and 49 and look at the opening illustration again.
- Use the illustration to review vocabulary for landscape features. Have pupils describe the picture in pairs or small groups. Ask **What have you learned? What do you know?**
- Divide the board into two and write *natural* at the top of one column and *man-made* at the top of the other. Have pupils suggest features to add to each column. Draw simple pictures for each. Give groups a wordcard and have them read their word together. Have a representative from each group come and place the wordcard next to the correct picture in the correct column.
- Ask pupils to turn to page 60. Focus pupils' attention on the black and white scenes. Ask **What can you see?**
- Explain that pupils are going to listen and draw what they hear in the correct scene.

- Play the audio. The first time have pupils listen and repeat what they heard. *Draw a beach / windmill.* Play the audio a second time and pause after each instruction to give pupils time to draw.

> CD 1 • Track 65
> Beach. Draw a beach on the coastal landscape. Windmill. Draw a windmill on the inland landscape. Now colour the man-made features in each landscape red.

- Ask **Is a beach / windmill natural or man-made?**
- Point to the instruction and read **Colour the man-made features red.** Ask pupils to name the man-made features they can see. *House, road, windmill.* Ask pupils to colour them red. *See answers opposite.*
- Have pupils describe the two scenes. *In the coastal / inland landscape there is a house on a cliff / a beach / a road,* etc.

2 Put a tick or a cross.

- Draw a spider diagram on the board with *water* as the central word and eight legs around the sides. Mix some water flashcards with some landscape flashcards and place them all face up on the floor. Name one of the flashcards, e.g. *snow,* and choose a pupil to pick the correct flashcard up. The pupil should decide if it is water or not. Pupils should discard any flashcards that are not water and stick the water flashcards on the board around the spider diagram. Encourage pupils to name the forms of water as they do so. Ask pupils to name the examples of water as a solid, liquid and gas.
- Ask pupils to tell you what else they know about water and how we use it. *We use it to wash with, drink, water plants. It has no taste, smell or colour.*
- Write the beginning of the sentence *All living things need …* and encourage pupils to finish the sentence with the word *water.* Ask pupils what else living things need and elicit *air.*
- Ask pupils to tell you what they know about wind. *It moves air, it moves leaves, windmills,* etc.
- Focus pupils' attention on the sentences. Encourage them to read with you, pointing to each word as they read it. At the end of each sentence ask **Is that right? Tick or cross?** *See answers opposite.*

3 Look and find the words.

- Look out of the window and ask **What is the weather like today?**
- Play *Flash!* Take the weather flashcards and wordcards for the unit. Divide the class in half and do the same with your board. Tell the class you are going to flash a flashcard or wordcard very quickly to one team. If the team guess what is on the card they get a point. You will then flash another card to the other team. Set a time limit.
- Draw pupils' attention to the photos on page 61. Point to each one and ask **What is the weather like?** Have pupils find and circle the words in the wordsearch. *See answers opposite.*

Self-assessment

- Write *The world around us* on the board. Read it out as you do so. Tell pupils that they have learned a lot of things in this unit about landscapes and the weather.
- Focus pupils' attention on the self-assessment table. Read the first sentence together: *Identify inland and coastal landscapes.* Ask pupils if they can name three features of each. Have pupils use their fingers to count and then tell a partner.
- Now read the sentence: *Identify water around us.* Ask pupils to think back to the spider diagram and elicit their suggestions.
- Read the sentence: *Name different types of weather.* Draw symbols on the board as pupils name the different types of weather.
- Finally, together read the sentence: *Record weather using symbols.* Have pupils take out their record sheet and remember the weather for that week.
- After reading each sentence, the pupils should tick the boxes according to whether they have learned a lot *(very happy face),* some things *(happy face)* or a little *(disappointed face)* about landscapes and weather.
- Ask pupils to choose a sticker to show how they feel about their learning in the unit.
- Give individual attention to any pupils who choose the *disappointed* sticker.

Activity book answers

UNIT 4 The world around us

1 Look and write.

l a k e	p l a i n	b e a c h
e a k l	l i n p a	c a e h b
c l i f f	f o r e s t	s e a
f c i f l	s f r e o t	e s a

2 Write the features above in the correct group.

inland landscape	coastal landscape
lake	beach
plain	cliff
forest	sea

3 Trace and colour.

natural   man-made

green house	green tree	red fence
green flowers	red windmill	red bridge

4 Circle the things that need air.

5 Write.

cloud   rain   snow   lake   ice   sea

solid	liquid	gas
snow	rain	cloud
ice	lake	
	sea	

6 Write.

drink   ~~clean~~   hands   wash

We use water to clean the floor.

We use water to wash our hands.

We use water to wash food.

We drink water when we are thirsty.

7 Write.

1 STORMY
2 CLOUDY
3 RAINY
4 SNOWY
5 FOGGY

8 What is the hidden word? S U N N Y

9 Read and draw.

1 It is cloudy in Barcelona.
2 It is snowy in Bilbao.
3 It is rainy in Madrid.
4 It is sunny in Sevilla.
5 It is windy in Valencia.

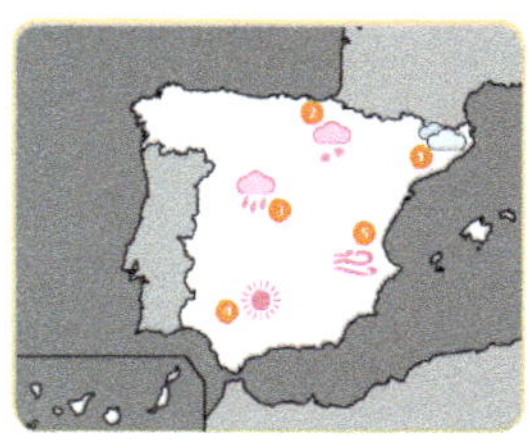

UNIT 4

Let's investigate at home!

Make a weather wheel

1

Cut out two circles.

2

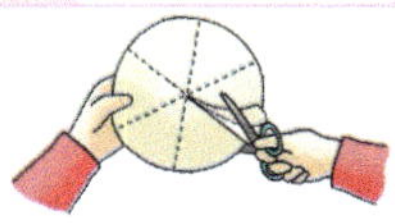

Divide one circle into six parts.
Cut out one part.

3

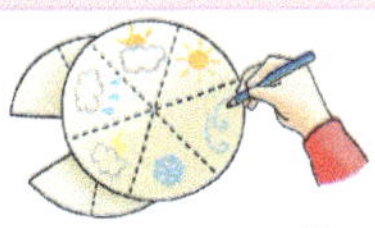

Draw and colour six different types of weather.

4

Fasten the two circles together.
Decorate the top circle.

1 Write. Open answer

What is the weather like today? ____________

What is your favourite type of weather? ____________

Skills check

1 Look and read. Write *yes* or *no*.

Example: There is a man in the bedroom. no

1 Trees are man-made features of a landscape. no

2 A dog needs air to live. yes

3 We use water to wash our hands. yes

4 The weather is snowy in the picture. no

TERM 2 Work together

CONTENT	EVALUATION CRITERIA
The street: characteristics and elements.	Understand the social organisation of their immediate surroundings: the street.
Correct behaviour in the street and road safety.	Respect the basic rules of pedestrians and users of public transport. Observe and recognise street elements essential for a pedestrian.
Introduction to scientific knowledge and its application in the Social Sciences. Collect relevant information using different sources (direct and indirect).	Obtain specific and relevant information, using different sources.
Develop strategies to organise, memorise and remember information obtained through different methods and from different sources.	Develop a capacity for hard work and show perseverance while studying.
Team-building strategies.	Develop a cooperative and adaptive attitude, recognising merit in others' ideas and responding to situations with intuition, an open mind and flexibility.
With help, plan and manage simple projects, showing independence and initiative in order to achieve objectives.	Develop creativity and initiative, improving their capacity to acquire information and ideas and present innovative conclusions.
Correct use of different materials.	Use the materials in a suitable way.
Techniques for intellectual work. Elaboration of diagrams and summaries, memorising and structuring the information received. Reading techniques for Social Science publications.	Employ techniques appropriate to intellectual tasks; produce work and make presentations both individually and as a group, involving research, selection and organisation of texts of a social, geographical or historical nature, while showing autonomy and collaborative skills.
Rights and obligations.	Identify some of their rights and obligations in the context of their city, town or village.

LEARNING STANDARDS	KEY COMPETENCES	PAGES
Identifies and names the different elements in the street.	SOC, LIN	62, 63
Knows and respects the norms of road safety and uses them as a pedestrian and as a user of different means of transport.	SOC, LTL, AUT	62, 63
Identifies and interprets the traffic signs necessary to ensure safety when walking in the street: traffic lights, pedestrian crossing, etc.	SOC, LTL, AUT	62, 63
Looks for, selects and organises information, analysing it and drawing conclusions. Reflects on the process followed and reports on it orally	MST, LIN, LTL	62, 63
Performs academic tasks in a responsible and effective manner.	LTL	62, 63
Uses vocabulary correctly in the presentation of their work.	LTL, LIN	62, 63
Develops a cooperative and adaptive attitude, recognising merit in others' ideas and responding to situations with intuition, an open mind and flexibility.	LTL, SOC	62, 63
Participates effectively and constructively in daily life and develops strategies for conflict resolution.	LTL, SOC	62, 63
Identifies and uses the correct code of conduct for their environment.	LTL, SOC	62, 63
Shows self-confidence, personal initiative, curiosity, interest and creativity in the learning process.	AUT, LTL	62, 63
Shows independence in the planning and carrying out of simple actions and shows initiative when taking decisions.	AUT, LTL	62, 63
Uses the materials in a suitable and careful way, thereby keeping them in good condition.	LTL, SOC	62, 63
Produces work and makes presentations both individually and as part of a group, participating in the research, selection and organisation of texts of a social, geographical or historical nature.	SOC, AUT	62, 63
Identifies some of their rights and obligations in the context of their city, town or village.	SOC	62, 63

PAGES 62-63 Work together: Road safety

PAGE SUMMARY

On these pages pupils will learn about road signs, road safety and how to avoid accidents. The different activities will be carried out following different cooperative learning structures that will provide the optimal learning experience for the pupil and guarantee the involvement of all the members of the group.

LANGUAGE

- Traffic lights, pedestrian crossing, road, stop sign, road sign, pedestrian, pavement
- Inform, prohibit, warn, look, wait, cross, find
- Yes, it is / No, it isn't.
- I agree / I disagree. I think (…).

MATERIALS

Flashcards: (digital) see the *Teachers* section in the digital resources

Additional classroom materials: photos of different road signs

OPENING ACTIVITIES

- Before doing these activities using different cooperative learning structures, you should form the groups. Teachers should form the groups rather than letting the pupils choose their own group members. Remember to form heterogeneous groups of three or four pupils. In heterogeneous groups, the less confident pupils learn from stronger pupils, and the stronger pupils gain a deeper understanding of the subject by teaching it to others.
- Tell the pupils what they will be doing in their groups, what procedures you will follow and what your expectations are. If during these activities any group is having problems, spend some time in class on the relevant team skills.

MAIN ACTIVITIES

1 Look and say what you see. Listen and point.

- This is a *Round robin* activity. Focus pupils' attention on the four pictures on page 62 and ask them to describe what they see.

- Ask pupils to take turns giving their opinions. Ensure that each pupil shares something with their group.
- Ask them to listen to the audio and point to each picture as it is described.

CD 1 • Track 66

1. **Traffic lights. Traffic lights tell the traffic to stop or to go.**
2. **Pedestrian crossing. We use the pedestrian crossing to cross the road.**
3. **Stop sign. A stop sign is a type of road sign.**
4. **Pedestrian. Pedestrians walk on the pavement.**

2 Use the code and colour.

- This is a *Rally robin* activity. Focus your pupils' attention on the eight photos on page 62.
- Ask them to discuss the road signs with their group and decide whether the signs inform, prohibit or warn us. Ensure that each pupil shares something with their group.
- Ask your pupils to take turns giving their opinions. Have them to colour the circles according to the colour code: green for road signs that inform, red for those that prohibit and purple for those that warn. *See answers opposite.*

3 Number the pictures. Tell the story.

- This is a *Timed pair share* activity. Ask your pupils to work in pairs and look at the pictures. Tell them that they have to order the pictures to complete the story and find out how we should cross the road.
- Ask pupils to think independently about the story, choosing the correct order for the pictures. Then tell your pupils to discuss their answers in pairs, ensuring that pupils share their ideas and consider those of others.
- Ask the pairs to share their answers with the class and then number the pictures correctly. *3, 2, 4, 1.*

4 How can you be safe on your bicycle? Put a tick or a cross.

- This is a *Stand up, hand up, pair up* activity. Before doing this activity, review how this particular cooperative structure works.
- Say **Stand up, hand up, pair up as quickly as you can.** Using the zoom on the interactive whiteboard, show pupils the first picture. Ask them if we should do what the picture shows to be safe on our bicycles. Pupils discuss with their partner and share their ideas with the rest of the class
- Repeat the process with the rest of the pictures. Pupils should work with a different partner for each picture and complete the boxes with a tick or a cross. *See answers opposite.*

CLASS PROJECT

- This is a *Rally coach* activity. Focus pupils' attention on the class project. In their groups, they will design a road sign and make a poster for the classroom.
- Ask them to look for information and ideas to use in their design. Once they have designed their road sign, they can label it with short sentences.
- Tell them that when pupil A adds something to the poster, pupil B watches, listens, checks and praises.
- When pupil B adds something to the poster, pupil A watches, listens, checks and praises.
- Once they have finished, ask them to share their results with the class.

CLOSING ACTIVITIES

- Group assessment is essential in cooperative learning to ensure that there is analysis of interactions and promotion of teamwork. Pupils should learn that how they work together affects the quality and quantity of concepts that they learn and understand.
- Ask the pupils to reflect on how they felt in their cooperative groups.
- Then ask the pupils to discuss how the group worked together and identify ideas and actions that helped the group achieve its goals.
- Once they have shared their results, ask them to reflect on how could the project be made better next time. Invite your pupils to share their conclusions with the class.

PAGES 64-65 Review

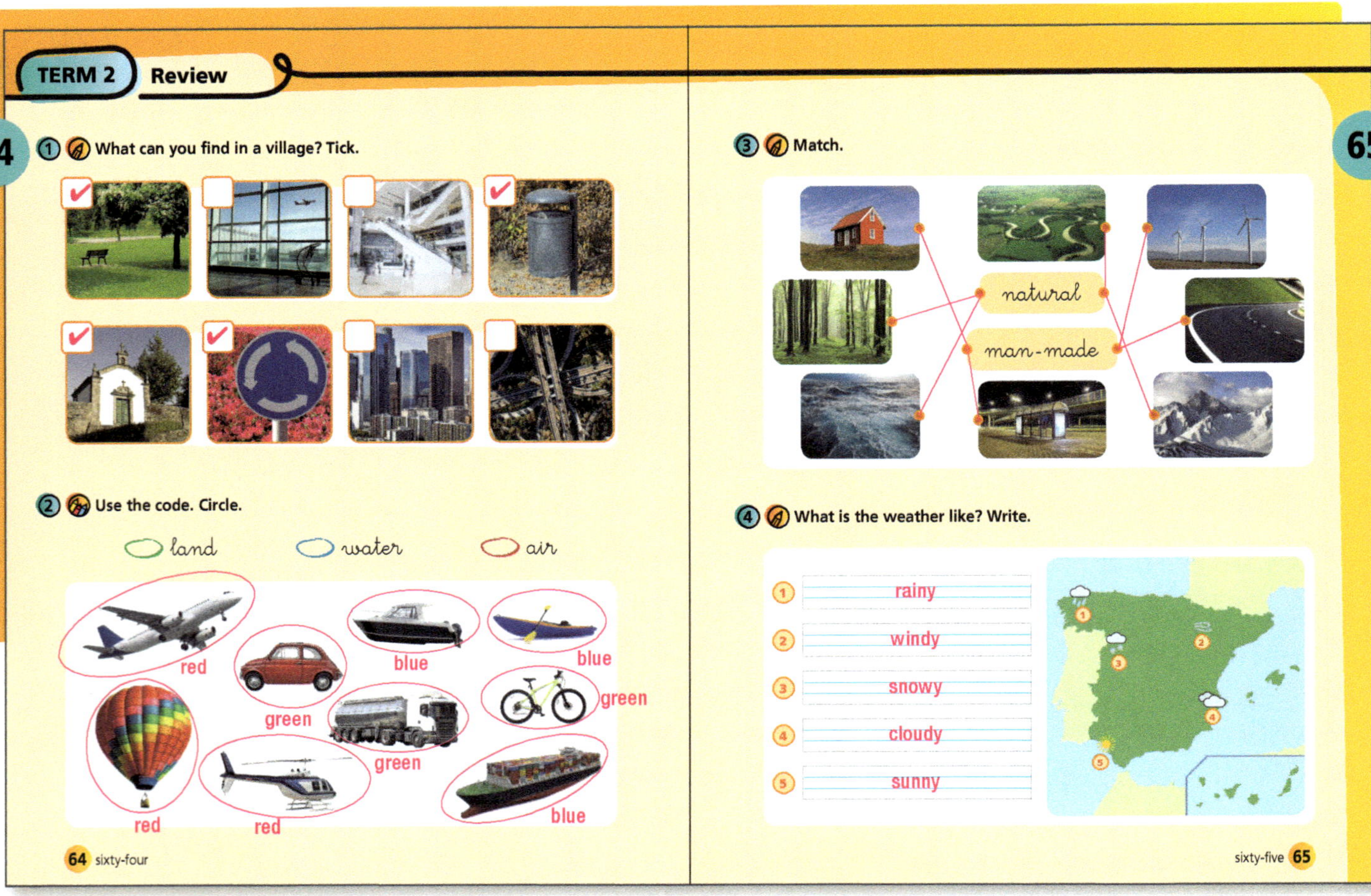

PAGE SUMMARY

Your pupils will use these pages to review content from Term 2 (Units 3 and 4).

LANGUAGE

- Park, airport, shopping centre, bin, church, road sign, building, road, street
- Plane, balloon, car, helicopter, boat, lorry, canoe, bicycle, cargo ship
- House, windmill, bus stop, river, forest, sea, mountain

MATERIALS

Flashcards: digital flashcards for Units 3 and 4

Additional classroom materials: photos of different landscapes, posters and displays pupils have made during Units 3 and 4

OPENING ACTIVITIES

- Tell pupils they are going to review things that they studied in Units 3 and 4.
- Play *Noughts and crosses.* Draw a noughts and crosses grid on the board and write a number in each square. Divide the class into two teams and choose one team to be *noughts* and one team to be *crosses.* Each team takes turns to choose a number, which corresponds to a true or false statement about content from Units 3 and 4. If the team guesses correctly, a team member can come up to the board and replace the number with a nought or a cross. The winning team is the first to get three noughts (or crosses) in a line. Example statements could include: *1. A village is small (T). 2. A cargo ship travels on land (F). 3. We must wait for the green man to cross the road (T). 4. All streets have a name (T). 5. A bridge is a man-made feature (T). 6. We can find beaches inland (F). 7. We can find cliffs on the coast (T). 8. Pencils need water to live (F). 9. Ice is a liquid (F).*

MAIN ACTIVITIES

① What can you find in a village? Tick (✔).

- Ask random pupils questions about where they live, e.g. **What is the name of your street? What is your address? What can you see on your street? How do you come to school? What do you do in a supermarket?** etc.
- Write *city* on one side of the board and *village* on the other. Ask pupils if they can tell you any differences between the two.
- Tell pupils to open their Pupil's Books on page 64. Read the instruction out while pupils follow the words with their finger. Point to each picture and ask **Can you find this in a village?** If the answer is *yes*, have pupils tick the box. *See answers opposite.*

② Use the code. Circle.

- Put pictures or flashcards of different types of transport on the board. Describe one type of transport and have pupils guess which one you are describing, e.g. **It has two wheels. It travels on land. You need to wear a helmet to be safe.** *A bicycle.* Make sure pupils wait until the end of your description to suggest the transport.
- Say **Let's look at activity 2** and read the instruction. Ask **What colour is land / water / air transport?** Encourage pupils to work with a partner to circle the types of transport. Check pupils' answers by asking **What colour is the plane / car / boat?** etc. *See answers opposite.*

③ Match.

- Write *natural* and *man-made* on the board. Ask pupils to look out of the window and tell you what natural things they can see and then what man-made things they can see.
- Focus pupils' attention on activity 3. Point to each photo and ask **Is it natural or man-made?** Ask pupils to draw a line and match the words with the photos. *See answers opposite.*
- Hand out cut-out photos of different landscapes to pupils in groups. Have them talk about the landscape features, transport and things in the street they can see.

④ What is the weather like? Write.

- Ask pupils what the weather is like today. Ask **Is it rainy / stormy / snowy?** etc.
- Put weather wordcards on the board and play *Run and slap!* Divide the class into two teams. The first member of each team comes and stands a metre from the board. Say **Today the weather is (snowy)**. The two team members must run and slap the correct weather word on the board. The first to slap the correct word gains a point for their team. Repeat so that all pupils have a go. Hand out flashcards or pictures and choose volunteers to match a flashcard and a wordcard on the board.
- Focus pupils' attention on the map in their books. Point to each number and ask **What is the weather like?**
- Point to the numbers and lines. Say **Number 1 is …?** and have pupils tell you the weather. Say **Write the word.** Encourage pupils to check the spelling with the wordcards on the board if they are still unsure. Repeat the procedure with the remaining numbers. *See answers opposite.*

⊕ CLOSING ACTIVITIES

- Read *The Town Mouse and the Country Mouse* (one of Aesop's Fables).
- Praise everyone for working well this term.

⊕ EXTRA IDEAS

- Play *Team mime*. Divide the class into two teams. One member of each team sits in a chair facing their team, but with their back to the board. Put a flashcard on the board from Unit 3 or 4. Both teams must mime what is on the flashcard for their team member to guess. The first team member to guess what their team is miming gains a point for their team. Repeat with new team members guessing each time. There should be no speaking, just miming!
- Design a postcard. Have pupils draw a postcard on a sheet of A5 paper or card. On one side they should draw either a coastal or an inland landscape with at least three features of that landscape. Cut a large postbox shape from yellow paper or card and display the postcards around it.

UNIT 5 The Sun and the Moon

CONTENT	EVALUATION CRITERIA
The Earth, the Sun, the Moon and the stars. Day and night.	Observe and understand some characteristics of the Earth, the Sun, the Moon and the stars, describing certain everyday phenomena such as day and night.
The seasons.	Understand the reason why there are seasons.
Introduction to scientific knowledge and its application in the Social Sciences. Collect relevant information using different sources (direct and indirect).	Obtain specific and relevant information, using different sources.
Develop strategies to organise, memorise and remember information obtained through different methods and from different sources.	Develop a capacity for hard work and show perseverance while studying.
Team-building strategies.	Develop a cooperative and adaptive attitude, recognising merit in others' ideas and responding to situations with intuition, an open mind and flexibility.
With help, plan and manage simple projects, showing independence and initiative in order to achieve objectives.	Develop creativity and initiative, improving their capacity to acquire information and ideas and present innovative conclusions.
Correct use of different materials.	Use the materials in a suitable way.
Techniques for intellectual work. Elaboration of diagrams and summaries, memorising and structuring the information received. Reading techniques for Social Science publications.	Employ techniques appropriate to intellectual tasks; produce work and make presentations both individually and as a group, involving research, selection and organisation of texts of a social, geographical or historical nature, while showing autonomy and collaborative skills.

LEARNING STANDARDS	KEY COMPETENCES	PAGES
Identifies some aspects of the Sun and understands its importance for life on Earth.	MST, SOC	66–70
Locates and recognises in images different heavenly bodies such as the Earth, the Sun, the Moon, planets and stars.	MST	68, 69
Differentiates the different parts of the day and describes what happens in each of them.	MST, SOC, LIN	68, 71, 74, 75
Observes certain elements like day and night, and explains orally why they happen.	MST, LIN	68, 71, 74, 75
Identifies the shape of the Earth.	MST	71
Begins to understand the concept of the cardinal points and can identify the difference between land and sea on a map or globe.	MST	71
Knows the months of the year and the seasons they belong to.	MST	70
Looks for, selects and organises information, analysing it and drawing conclusions. Reflects on the process followed and reports on it orally.	MST, LIN, LTL	74, 75
Performs academic tasks in a responsible and effective manner.	LTL	74, 75
Uses vocabulary correctly in the presentation of their work.	LTL, LIN	74, 75
Develops a cooperative and adaptive attitude, recognising merit in others' ideas and responding to situations with intuition, an open mind and flexibility.	LTL, SOC	67, 74
Participates effectively and constructively in daily life and develops strategies for conflict resolution.	LTL, SOC	75
Identifies and uses the correct code of conduct for their environment.	LTL, SOC	75
Shows self-confidence, personal initiative, curiosity, interest and creativity in the learning process.	AUT, LTL	74
Shows independence in the planning and carrying out of simple actions and shows initiative when taking decisions.	AUT, LTL	74
Uses the materials in a suitable and careful way, thereby keeping them in good condition.	LTL, SOC	74
Produces work and makes presentations both individually and as part of a group, participating in the research, selection and organisation of texts of a social, geographical or historical nature.	SOC, AUT	66–75

UNIT INFORMATION

UNIT SUMMARY

In this unit your pupils will talk about what we see in the sky and learn some essential characteristics of the Sun and the Moon. They will understand that the Earth moves around the Sun and that the Moon moves around the Earth. Pupils will talk about the seasons and will understand why we have day and night. They will consider how our activities are different depending on the time of day.

Practical demonstrations and visual support will help pupils understand how the Earth and Moon rotate and why we have day and night. Make sure you concept check as you progress through the unit, and continually recycle new language.

PROJECT

Let's investigate

In the *Let's investigate* activity on page 74, your pupils will use a model of the Earth to investigate why we have day and night.

The pupils need:

- A beach ball
- A torch
- Coloured pencils or felt tips
- Glue
- A4 paper

VALUES AND ATTITUDES

In this unit, encourage pupils to think about what we get from the Sun (heat and light) and how this is important for all living things. Throughout the unit, try to encourage pupils to think about:

- How to protect ourselves in the sunshine.
- Why it is important not to look directly at the Sun.
- How light influences our activities.

Make a difference

The *Make a difference* page in this unit focuses on understanding that we do different activities during the day and at night. In the pairwork activity, pupils will make colourful Sun and Moon mobiles with pictures to illustrate how the Sun and Moon influence the type of activities we do.

EVALUATION MATERIAL

These documents can be downloaded from the *Teachers* section of the digital resources and printed.

The materials include:

- **Unit diagnostic test:** provides an overview of the unit and allows you to assess the pupils' prior knowledge.
- **End-of-unit test:** in addition to the *Review* section at the end of each unit, this summative test can be used to evaluate pupils' progress after studying the unit content.
- **Unit evaluation grid:** based on the evaluation criteria and learning standards of the unit.

DIGITAL RESOURCES

Presentations

- **Unit summary**: a simple slide presentation with text, images and audio to review the main ideas of the unit. It can be used at the beginning of the unit to test pupils' prior knowledge of the unit content or at the end of the unit as a revision tool.
- **Let's investigate**: a slide presentation of the unit's *Let's investigate* page with text, photos and audio. The slide presentation is perfect for a heads-up class, showing the steps one by one. Use this tool to get the pupils to predict the next steps (with their books closed) or to focus their attention on each step as they carry out the project themselves.

Activities

- **Memory game**: useful activity for reviewing key vocabulary and modelling pronunciation.
- **Wordsearch**: use at the end of the unit as a revision activity. Turn it into a game by getting the pupils to work in teams.
- **Spelling**: get a volunteer to come to the board and carry out the activity, but with the help of the whole class.

Song lyrics

Listen to the song *Where the birds fly* and follow the lyrics line by line.

Posters

Attractive and informative posters to display in class. You can use them to review key concepts and vocabulary.

Videos

Use the video links in this unit to present content in a dynamic, real-life context whilst reinforcing the pupils' listening skills.

Teachers

Digital flashcards: a bank of digital images which can be used in a variety of ways in class.

Downloadable pdfs: evaluation tests, evaluation grids, templates, useful links and further information.

PAGES 66-67 The Sun and the Moon

PAGE SUMMARY

The aim of the unit opener is to encourage your pupils' observation skills and invite pupils to explore all the things that are in the sky above them.

Note: Remember that all the CD tracks in Term 3 are found on CD 2.

LANGUAGE

- Sun, Moon, stars, planet, Earth, sky, clouds, heat, light
- Telescope, map, bird, plane

MATERIALS

Flashcards: (digital) see the *Teachers* section in the digital resources

Additional classroom materials: paper plate, skittles, ball

WHAT CAN YOU SEE?

Draw two circles on the board. Write the jumbled letters of the word *Sun* in one, and the jumbled letters of the word *Moon* in the other. Ask pupils what words they make. Explain that *The Sun and the Moon* is the title of the new unit.

Ask pupils what they expect to see in the opening illustration. Encourage them to use their imaginations, e.g. *maybe Sam and Amy are on a rocket to the moon, they meet aliens*, etc. Have them predict where the chameleon might be. *On a star, a spaceship, a space station*, etc.

Have pupils open their books on page 66 and compare their ideas with the illustration. Ask **Can you see the Sun and the Moon?** *The Sun is in the sky and on the mat. There is a picture of the moon on Amy's sister's book*. Ask what other things they can see and if they can name any planets.

Ask **Where is the chameleon?** *On the window box*. Ask what other animals they can see. *A cat, a dog and a bird*. Ask pupils to close their books and tell you what the family members are all doing.

OPENING ACTIVITIES

- Use the zoom to highlight the telescope. Ask pupils if they know the name of this machine and how it helps us. *It makes planets and stars seem closer.* Highlight the Earth on the mat and ask pupils to tell you any interesting information they know about our planet (names of rivers, mountains, countries, continents, etc.).

MAIN ACTIVITIES

1 Do you think it is day or night in the picture? Why?

- Read the question and have pupils follow in their books. Put pupils in groups and tell them to have a close look at the illustration. Pupils should tell you that it is day as the Sun is still in the sky (but that it will soon be night).
- Ask pupils to tell you what they think the family will do once the Sun disappears and it is dark, e.g. *Look through the telescope, Sam and Amy may go indoors, Amy's sister can still read because there is a lamp, Amy's mother will stop watering the vegetables*, etc. Ask pupils if they play outside when it's already dark.

2 What is Sam looking at?

- Ask pupils to point to Sam and say where he is sitting. *On a planets mat.* Point to and read the instruction. Tell pupils to consult with their groups. Listen to each group's suggestions. *He is looking at the planets on the mat.* Ask pupils if they can name any of the planets.

3 Who is not feeling very well? Circle.

- Say **Stand up if you are feeling happy / sad / tired / angry / hot / cold**. Have pupils sit back down between each instruction. Finally, say **Stand up if you are not feeling well**. If a pupil stands up this time, ask them why they are not feeling well.
- Read the question and ask groups to find and circle the person who is not feeling well. Ask groups how they know. *He is coughing or sneezing.* Remind pupils that when they cough or sneeze they should put their hand or a tissue in front of their mouths and noses. Pupils then choose a sticker for their effort of working with a group.

4 Listen and colour the objects you hear.

- Ask pupils what we can see in the sky. *Birds, planes, clouds*, etc. Point to the black and white pictures and read the words together.
- Focus pupils' attention on the musical note. Say **Let's listen to a song**. Play the song twice and tell pupils to colour the objects that they hear.

CD 2 • Track 02
See audio script below.

5 Sing the song and do the actions!

- Say **Now let's listen and do the actions**. Play the song, teach the actions and encourage pupils to copy. Repeat the song and do the actions together.

CD 2 • Track 03
Way up high, in the sky *[hands in air, palms up]*
What can you see? *[point to eye]*
Where the birds fly? *[flap arms]*
Golden Sun *[mime the Sun]*
And grey clouds *[wave hands]*
Above us all, in the sky today *[spin around]*
Way up high, in the sky *[hands in air, palms up]*
What can you see? *[point to eye]*
Where the birds fly? *[flap arms]*
Hundreds of stars *[wiggle fingers]*
And the Moon so bright *[draw a circle]*
Shining down, on us tonight *[spin around]*
Way up high, in the sky *[hands in air, palms up]*
What can you see? *[point to eye]*
Where the birds fly? *[flap arms]*

CLOSING ACTIVITIES

- Ask pupils to close their books and, in groups, describe what they remember from the illustration.
- Ask pupils to find out the names of some of the planets at home.

EXTRA IDEAS

- Make a class Sun. Pupils draw round and cut out their hands, then colour them orange, yellow or red. Stick the hands round a paper plate, with fingers facing outwards, so that the plate is completely covered. Hang up in the classroom.
- Pupils play skittles in teams. Stick numbers on the skittles. When they are knocked over, pupils add up the numbers. The team with the highest number each game scores one point. At the end, the team with the highest score wins.

PAGE 68 High in the sky

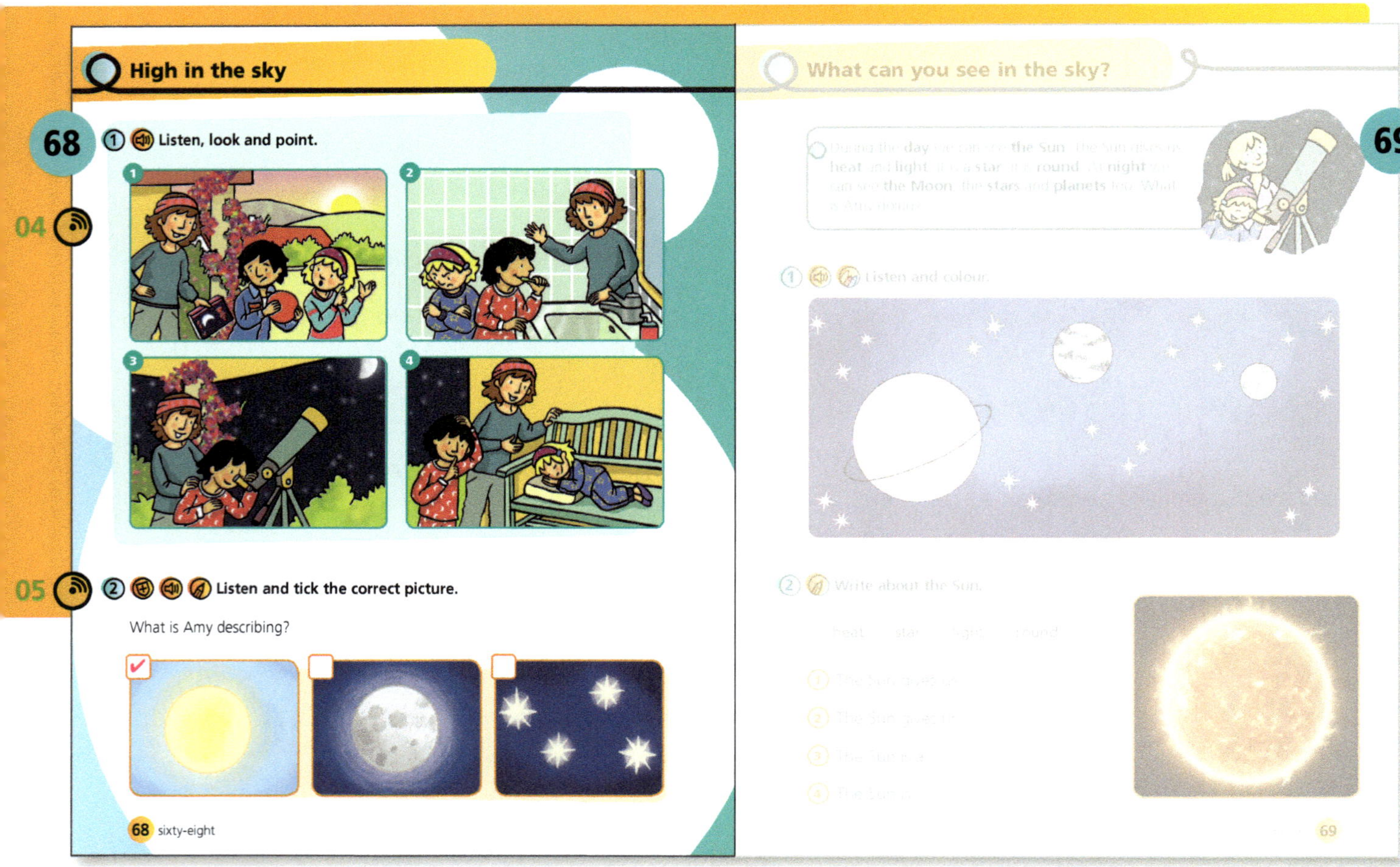

PAGE SUMMARY

Use the story to get pupils interested in and thinking about the theme of day and night, and how this influences some of the things we do.

LANGUAGE

- The Sun, the Moon, stars, planet
- Telescope
- Get ready for bed. It's bedtime. I'm not tired.

MATERIALS

Flashcards: (digital) see the *Teachers* section in the digital resources

Additional classroom materials: white A4 card, white crayons, black paint

OPENING ACTIVITIES

- Play *I Spy* with the opening illustration on pages 66 and 67.
- Can you see it in the sky? Show pupils flashcards or pictures of things you can see in the sky, e.g. *bird, the Sun, the Moon, stars, rainbow, plane, bat, helicopter, planet, clouds, butterfly* interspersed with flashcards or pictures of things that you don't see in the sky, e.g. *plant, cow, grass, flower, elephant, tree, pig, school,* etc. Show the flashcards one by one and ask **Can you see an elephant in the sky? Can you see the Moon in the sky?** etc. Continue showing the flashcards, allowing pupils to decide which things they can see in the sky and which they cannot.

MAIN ACTIVITIES

- Tell pupils they are going to listen to a story about Sam and Amy's bedtime. Ask pupils what their own routine is when they go to bed.

1 Listen, look and point.

- Ask pupils to open their Pupil's Books on page 68. Point to frame 1 and say **Look at the picture**. Ask **Who can you see?** Encourage pupils to say *Sam and Amy, Amy's sister.* Ask **Is it day or night?** *Day, but it's about to get dark.*
- Point to frame 2. Ask **What are the children doing?** *Getting ready for bed.* Ask **How is Amy feeling?** Elicit that she is angry. Ask **Why do you think she is angry?** Accept pupils' suggestions but tell them they will find out when they listen to the story. Finally, look at the last two frames and ask pupils to tell you what they see.
- Say **Let's listen to the story.** Play the audio

CD 2 • Track 04

High in the sky

The children are playing in the garden.

Frame 1

Penny (Amy's sister): **Come on Amy, come on Sam. It's time to get ready for bed.**

Sam: **Ohhh! Already?**

Amy: **But I can see the Sun in the sky. It's not bedtime yet!**

Frame 2

Amy: **I don't want to go to bed. I'm not tired!**

Penny (Amy's sister): **When the Sun goes down, day turns into night. We go to bed at night!**

Frame 3

Penny (Amy's sister): **Let's look at the night sky, before we go to bed.**

Sam: **Wow! I can see the Moon! And the stars!**

Frame 4

Sam: **Hey, where's Amy?**

Penny (Amy's sister): **Sssh! Look! She's asleep! She was tired after all!**

- Play the story again, this time pausing after each frame and asking further questions. Ask why Amy is angry. Elicit that she doesn't want to go to bed. Ask pupils **What does Sam see through the telescope?** *The Moon and the stars.* **Does Amy see the Moon and the stars?** *No.* Elicit that Amy falls asleep on the bench.
- Have pupils notice the difference between the children in frames 1 and 2. *In frame 2 pupils have changed into their pyjamas.* Ask them about the difference between frames 1 and 3. *In frame 1 it is still day, in frame 3 it is night.*

2 Listen and tick the correct picture.

- Point to the first picture and ask pupils what they can see. *The Sun.* Ask **When can we see the Sun, in the day or at night?** *In the day.*
- Point to the second picture and ask what they can see. *The Moon.* Ask **When can we see the Moon, in the day or at night?** *At night.*
- Finally, point to the stars, elicit the name and ask **When can we see the stars, in the day or at night?** *At night.*
- Read the question and have pupils listen and tick what Amy is describing. Play the audio.

CD 2 • Track 05

It is big and round. It gives us heat and light. We can see it during the day.

- Play the audio again and have pupils tell you how Amy describes the Sun. *See answer opposite.*

CLOSING ACTIVITIES

- Ask pupils what time they go to bed and if they like going to bed. Ask pupils what they do just before they go to bed. *Read a book with their parents, drink a glass of milk, have a bath,* etc.
- Have pupils listen to the story again and in groups of three, act out each scene.

EXTRA IDEAS

- Ask pupils what their favourite bedtime book is. Read a bedtime story to pupils connected to the theme of night, e.g. *Whatever Next?* or *Peace at last!* by Jill Murphy, *How to catch a star* by Oliver Jeffers, or *Can't you sleep, little Bear?* by Martin Waddell and Barbera Firth.
- *A starry night.* Give pupils white crayons to draw stars on white card. Have them paint over the stars with black paint. Pupils should see their stars shine in the dark.

PAGE 69 What can you see in the sky?

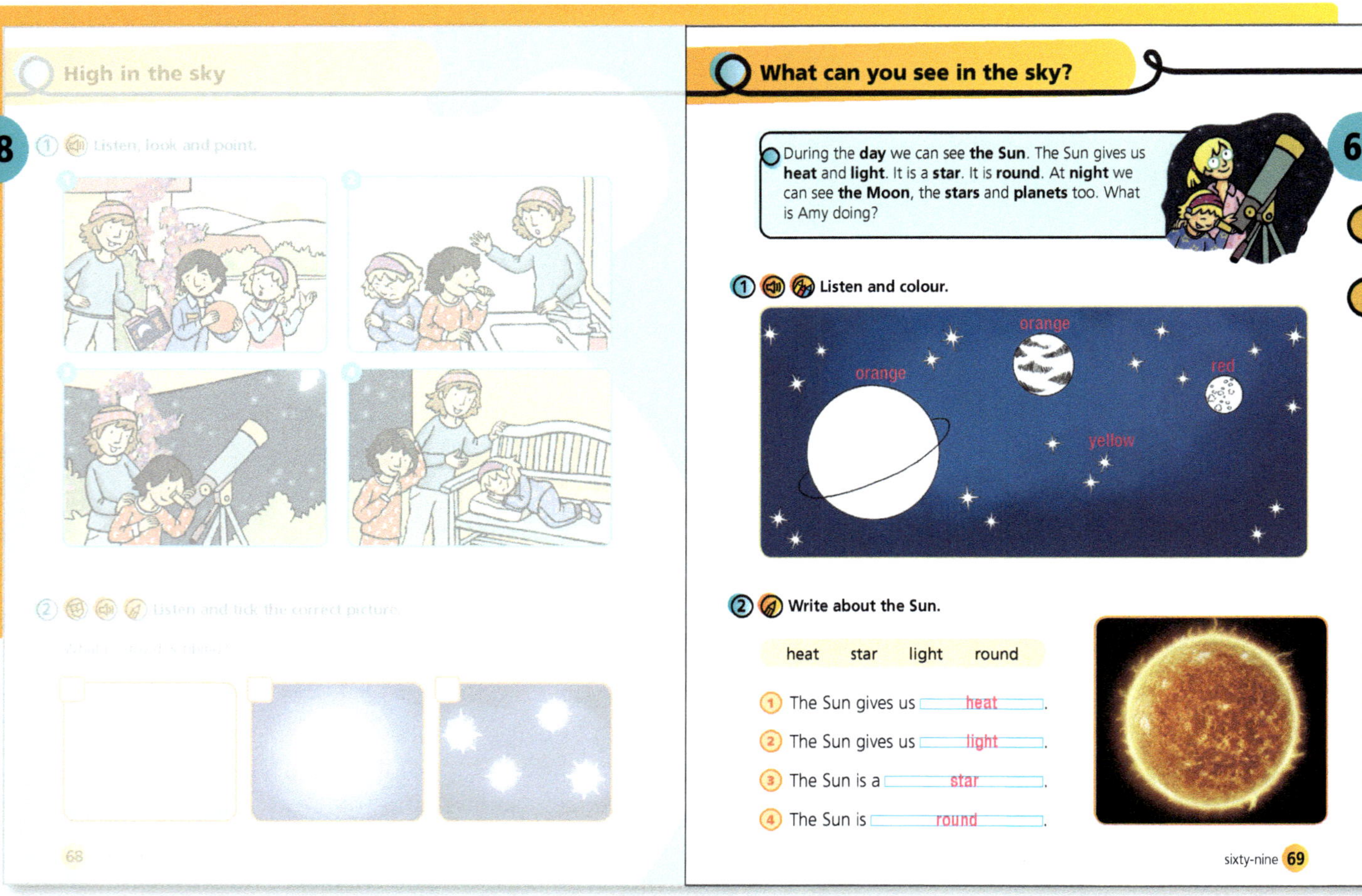

PAGE SUMMARY

Your pupils will learn more information about the Sun.

LANGUAGE

- The Sun, the Moon, stars, planet, night
- Heat, light, round
- The Sun gives us heat and light. The Sun is a star. The Sun is round.

MATERIALS

Flashcards: (digital) see the *Teachers* section in the digital resources

Additional classroom materials: telescope and/or binoculars

OPENING ACTIVITIES

- Pretend you are looking through a telescope at the sky. Ask pupils **What am I doing? What can I see in the sky?**
- Show pupils pictures or flashcards of *the Sun, the Moon, planets* and *stars* one by one and ask them to name each one as you do so. Mix the pictures and stick them face down on the left side of the board. Now show the pupils corresponding wordcards and ask them to read each word aloud. Mix the words and stick them face down on the right side of the board.
- Divide the class into two groups. Ask the first group to choose a flashcard from the left and a wordcard from the right. Turn over the two cards. If the picture and the word match, the group wins a point. If the picture and the word are different, replace the cards as they were on the board. The other group then has their turn. Continue the game until all the pictures and words have been matched. The winning group is the one with the most points.

MAIN ACTIVITIES

- Show pupils *day* and *night* flashcards or pictures and ask them which of the things on the board they see in the day and which they see at night. Draw a Venn diagram on the board. Put the *day* flashcard in one section and the *night* flashcard in the other. Write *both* over the interlocking section. Elicit what things should go in each section, draw a picture and/or write the word, e.g. *(day) the Sun, birds, rainbow; (night) the Moon, stars, bat; (both) plane, helicopter, clouds.*

Reading (CD 2. Track 06)

- Ask pupils to open their Pupil's Books on page 69 and look at the reading box. Say **Let's listen and read about what we can see in the sky**. Play the audio and encourage the pupils to follow in their books.
- Say **Tell me about the Sun**. Elicit the information from the reading box. Encourage pupils to tell you the Sun is round, and gives us heat and light. Make sure pupils understand the word *heat* (mime wiping your brow or rubbing your hands together and putting them up to the Sun to get warm). Ask **Is the Sun a planet?** Encourage pupils to tell you that it is a star.
- Ask pupils what Amy is doing. *Looking through a telescope*. Ask pupils what a telescope is for and see if pupils can tell you that it is for looking at things that are far away.
- Ask pupils if they have ever looked through a telescope or binoculars. Ask what things they looked at through them.

1 Listen and colour.

- Draw pupils' attention to the picture. Ask **Is it day or night?** Ask them how they know it is night. *You can see a planet, the Moon and stars*. Point to each item and ask **What is this?**
- Play the audio and have pupils listen and point to the things they hear. Play the audio a second time. Pause after each instruction and give pupils time to colour the things they hear. *See answers opposite.*

> CD 2 • Track 07
>
> Find the Moon in the picture. Colour it red. Find the two planets in the picture. Colour them orange. Now, look at the stars in the picture. Colour them yellow.

- When they have finished, ask **What colour is the Moon? What colour are the planets / stars?**

2 Write about the Sun.

- Draw the Sun on the board and say **Tell me what you learned about the Sun**. Elicit information from the beginning of the class.
- Focus pupils' attention on the activity and say **We are going to write about the Sun**.
- Read the words in the box together. Point to sentence 1 and encourage the pupils to read with you. Encourage pupils to tell you what the missing word is from the sentence. *Heat*. Have pupils write the word and cross it out from the list in the box. Continue reading and eliciting the words to complete the sentences. *Light, star, round.*
- When all the sentences are complete, read them together as a class.

CLOSING ACTIVITIES

- With books closed, have pupils tell you information about the Sun. Encourage them to begin *The Sun gives us / is …*
- Remind pupils that they must never look directly at the Sun.
- If you have brought in a telescope or binoculars, have pupils take turns looking through them and notice how they make things that are far away seem much nearer.

EXTRA IDEAS

- Have pupils look around the classroom and notice things that are round. *Clock, the top of a plant pot, socket, rings*, etc. Brainstorm what other things are round outside the classroom. *Wheels, road signs, windows*, etc.
- Have pupils draw one thing they can see in the sky. Encourage them to write a sentence below their picture: *I can see (birds) in the sky.*

PAGE 70 We move around the Sun

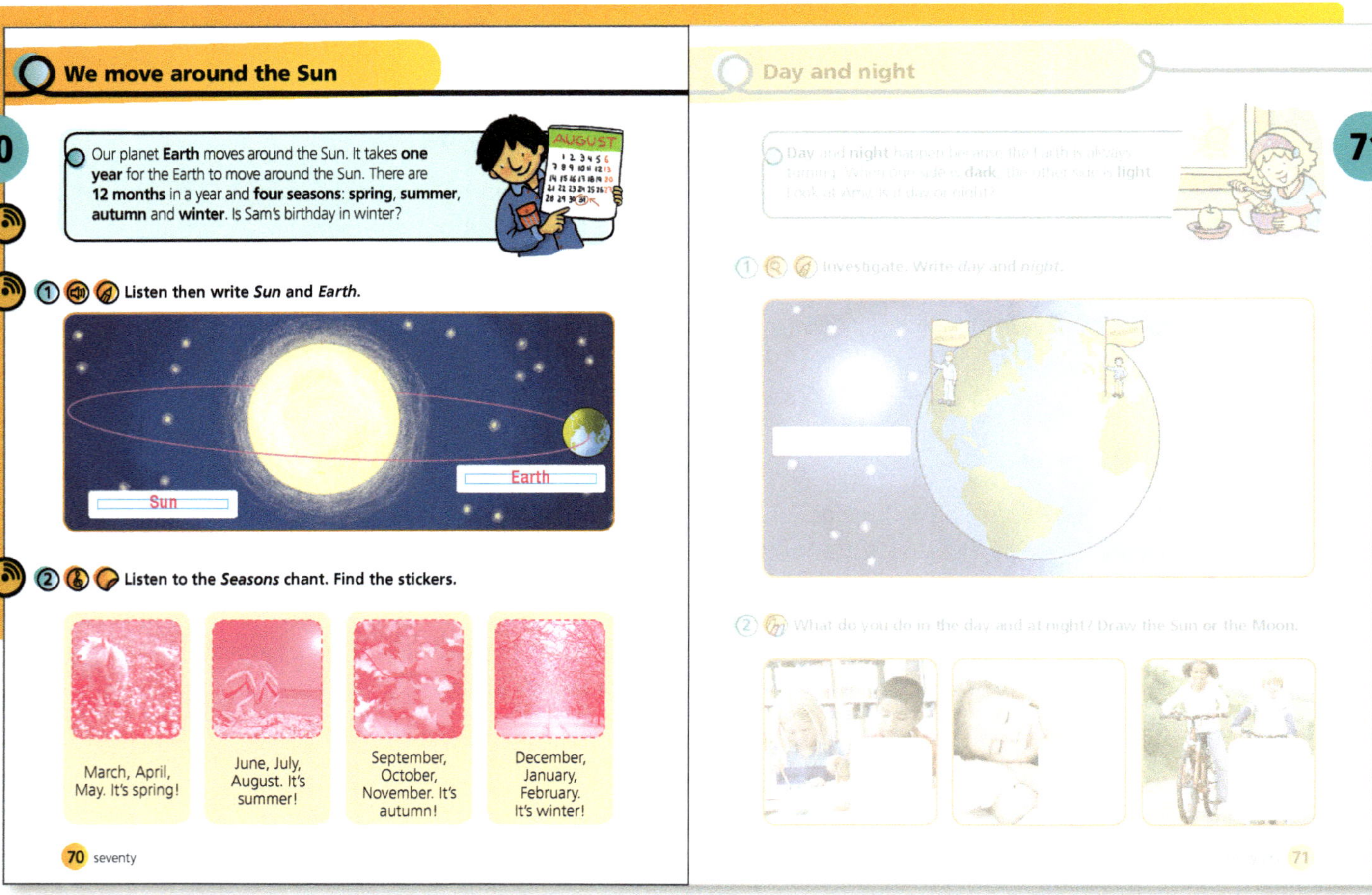

70

We move around the Sun

Our planet **Earth** moves around the Sun. It takes **one year** for the Earth to move around the Sun. There are **12 months** in a year and **four seasons**: **spring**, **summer**, **autumn** and **winter**. Is Sam's birthday in winter?

08

09 ① Listen then write *Sun* and *Earth*.

Sun

Earth

10 ② Listen to the *Seasons* chant. Find the stickers.

March, April, May. It's spring!

June, July, August. It's summer!

September, October, November. It's autumn!

December, January, February. It's winter!

70 seventy

71

Day and night

71

PAGE SUMMARY

Pupils will be introduced to the idea that the Earth moves around the Sun and that this takes a year. Pupils will also review that there are 12 months in a year and that the year is divided into seasons.

LANGUAGE

- Sun, Earth, Moon, planets, stars
- Year, month, seasons, spring, summer, autumn, winter

MATERIALS

Flashcards: (digital) see the *Teachers* section in the digital resources

Additional classroom materials: calendar

OPENING ACTIVITIES

- Ask the pupils **What can you see in the sky at night?** *The Moon, stars, bat, owl, planets*, etc. Ask pupils **What can you see in the sky in the day?** *The Sun, rainbow, birds*, etc. Ask **When can you see the Sun?** *In the day.* **When can you see the Moon?** *At night.*
- Draw a big Sun on the board and say **What can you tell me about the Sun?** Elicit as much information as possible from the previous class.
- Write words on the board from the previous classes with vowels missing, e.g. *S_n, st_r, M_ _n, pl_n_t, _ _rth.* Encourage pupils to spell the words with a partner on a mini whiteboard or in their notebooks.
- Take pupils to the gym or playground. Have pupils jump off a wooden bench and make a star shape with their bodies, arms and legs. Have pupils imagine that they are planets spinning around. Tell them to spin around with their legs and arms apart. Warn them they must not crash into other planets as they spin!

MAIN ACTIVITIES

- Choose two volunteers to come to the front of the class. Tell one pupil **You are the Sun**. Encourage the pupils to 'shine' by opening and closing their hands. Tell the other pupil **You are the Earth**. Show the class how the Earth moves around the Sun by asking the *Earth* pupil to walk around the *Sun* pupil.
- In a space (the playground or gym), have pupils play at being the Sun and Earth in pairs.

Reading. (CD 2. Track 08)

- Ask pupils to open their books on page 70 and look at the reading box. Say **Let's listen and read more information about the Earth and the Sun**. Play the audio and encourage pupils to follow in their books.
- Repeat the sentence **It takes one year for the Earth to move round the Sun**. Show pupils a calendar with the 12 months. As you turn the pages, encourage pupils to name the months of the year. Ask pupils **How many months in one year?**
- Choose the two volunteers from earlier to come to the front of the class to be the Sun and Earth again. This time tell the *Earth* pupil to go round the *Sun* pupil slowly while the class chants the months of the year. Make sure that the *Earth* pupil doesn't complete the full circle before *December* is chanted. Encourage pairs to find a space and practise saying the months of the year as they go round their partner, the Sun.

1 Listen then write *Sun* and *Earth*.

- Focus pupils' attention on the picture and say **Point to the Sun. Point to the Earth**. Play the audio and have pupils listen and tell you the information they heard. Ask pupils to demonstrate what *heat* means.

> CD 2 • Track 09
> **The Earth moves around the Sun. The Sun gives us heat and light.**

- Ask pupils to write the words *Sun* and *Earth* in the correct box. *See answers opposite.*

2 Listen to the *Seasons* chant. Find the stickers.

- Write the word *seasons* on the board. Say **Can you name the seasons?** Encourage pupils to name the four seasons and write them on the board as headings for four columns.
- Ask pupils if they can tell you which months are the spring / summer / autumn / winter months. Encourage pupils to dictate the months of the year to you and indicate under which season you should write them on the board.
- Ask pupils to look back at the reading box and focus their attention on Sam. Ask **Is his birthday in winter?** *No.* Ask pupils to look at the board and tell you what season Sam's birthday is in. *Summer.*
- Focus pupils' attention on the musical note. Say **Let's listen to the *Seasons* chant**. Play the audio and have pupils listen and follow the text about the seasons.

> CD 2 • Track 10
> **March, April, May. It's spring!**
> **June, July, August. It's summer!**
> **September, October, November. It's autumn!**
> **December, January, February. It's winter!**

- Point to the first box and ask **What season is it?** *Spring.* Have pupils find the correct sticker.
- Repeat the question for each box. When all the stickers are in place, play the audio again and have pupils follow the text and join in. *See answers opposite.*

CLOSING ACTIVITIES

- Ask pupils to look at the seasons and the months on the board. Encourage them to tell you what season their birthday is in.
- Ask pupils how long it takes for the Earth to go around the Sun.

EXTRA IDEAS

- Call out the months of the year in a random order and also the seasons. Have pupils jump up if they hear the month or the season of their birthday.
- Ask pupils **What is your favourite season?** Have pupils draw their favourite season. Encourage them to write *My favourite season is (summer).*

UNIT 5

PAGE 71 Day and night

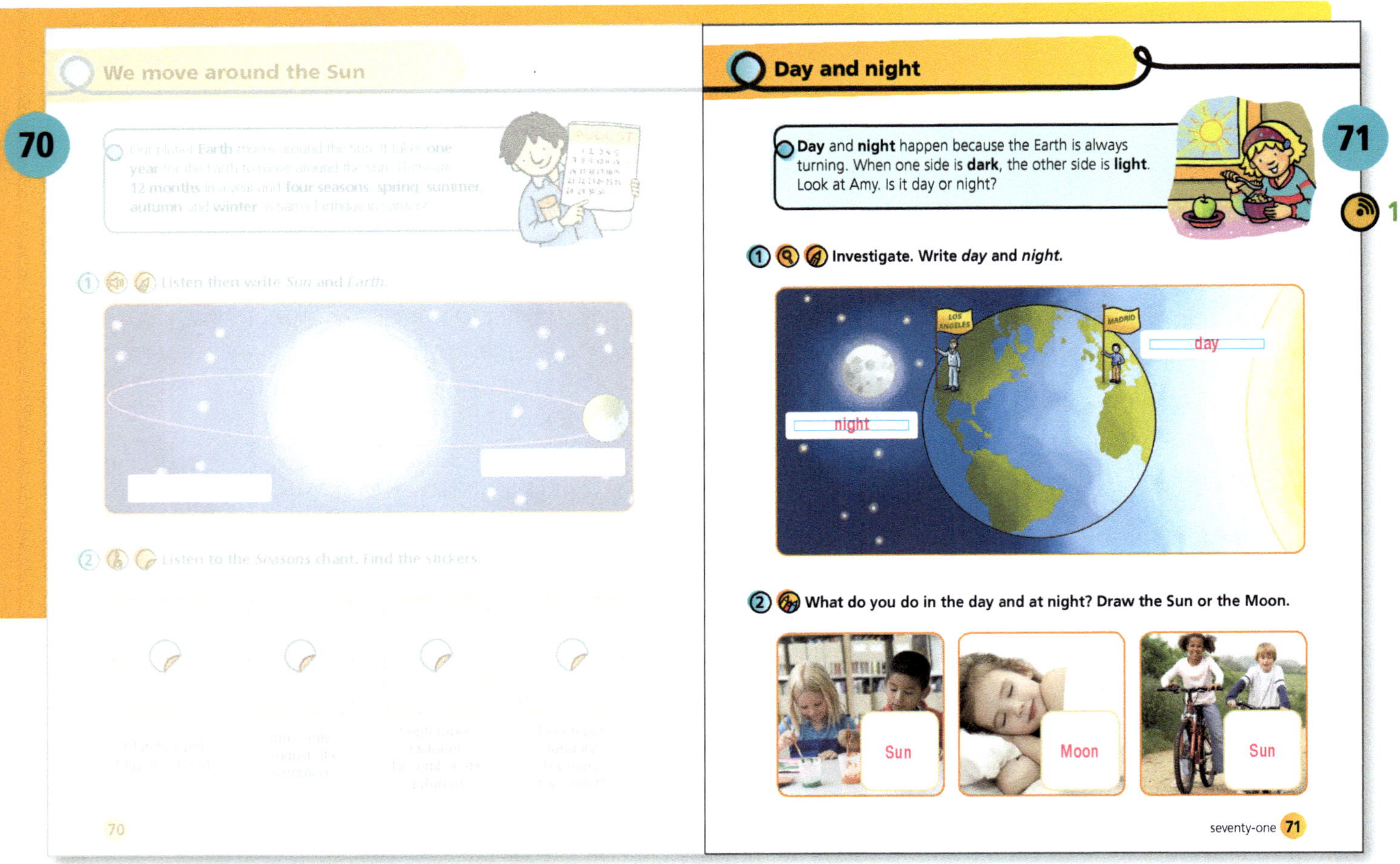

PAGE SUMMARY

Your pupils will understand why we have day and night.

LANGUAGE

- Sun, Earth, Moon, planets, stars
- Day, night, light, dark
- What do you do in the day and at night?

MATERIALS

Flashcards: (digital) see the *Teachers* section in the digital resources

Additional classroom materials: sticky notes, torch, globe

OPENING ACTIVITIES

- Draw a big round Sun on the board with six or seven rays. Ask pupils what they have learnt about the Sun and write a word or phrase on each of the rays, e.g. *star, round, far, big, gives us heat, gives us light*, etc.
- Ask pupils to stand in a line in the order of their birthdays. Point out which side of the room is the beginning of the year and which is the end. Point to each pupil, once they are in order, and ask them to say the month of their birthday.
- Write the name of each season on a card and put each card in a corner of the classroom. Ask pupils to stand next to the season their birthday is in. Encourage pupils to talk about the activities they do their season. Play the *Seasons* chant.

MAIN ACTIVITIES

- Focus pupils' attention on the *night* flashcard or picture. Ask **What can you see in the sky at night?** Encourage pupils to answer *I can see stars, the Moon, clouds, bats, a planet*, etc. Ask **What colour is the sky?** *Black*. Ask **Can you see the Sun?** *No.* **Is it day or night?** *Night.* **Is it light or dark?** *Dark.* **Are the lights on or off in your house at night?** *On.* You can switch the classroom lights on and off to demonstrate meaning.
- Focus pupils' attention on the *day* flashcard or picture. Ask **What can you see in the sky in the day?** Encourage pupils to answer *I can see birds, clouds, the Sun, butterflies, bees*, etc. Ask pupils **Are the lights on or off?** *Off.* Ask **Why?** *Because it is light.* Ask **Can you see the stars?** *No.* **What colour is the sky?** *Blue.*

Reading. (CD 2. Track 11)

- Ask pupils to look at the reading box. Say **Let's listen and read**. Play the audio and have pupils follow in their books.
- Draw a circle on the board and write *Earth* in the centre. Draw another circle on the left, a little away from the first circle. Write *Sun* in the circle. Draw rays from the Sun to the half of the Earth nearest the Sun. Explain how one half of the Earth receives light from the Sun whilst the other half doesn't (colour this other half in with a black marker). Point out that in this half of the Earth it is dark.
- Give each pupil a sticky note. Ask them to write the name of their town on it and stick it on their nose. If you have enough space, group all the pupils together in the centre of the classroom. Tell the pupils they have to imagine they are all the Earth. Hold up a torch and tell them that you are the Sun. Say **It's day in (your town)** and make sure that all the pupils are standing with their sticker facing you. Say **The Earth turns around**. Encourage all the pupils to turn around slowly in an anti-clockwise direction. Say **It's night in (your town)**. Make sure all the pupils are now facing away from you. Say **The Earth turns around. It's day again**.
- Ask pupils to look back at the picture of Amy and ask **Is it day or night?** *Day.*

1 Investigate. Write *day* and *night*.

- Focus pupils' attention on the picture. Say **Point to the Sun. Point to the Earth.** Ask **Where is it light? Where is it dark? Is it day or night in Madrid? Is it day or night in Los Angeles?** Encourage pupils to write *day* or *night* on the corresponding line. *See answers opposite.*
- Using the picture, point out that the Earth is round and is covered with land and water. Ask pupils to point to an example of each. With a more confident class, you could mention that the different areas of land are called *continents* and ask pupils if they know any of their names. You could also test a more confident class on the cardinal points (*north, east, south* and *west*). Use a globe to help you if you have one.

2 What do you do in the day and at night? Draw the Sun or the Moon.

- Ask pupils **What do you do in the day?** Remind them of some of the things they do in the morning before they come to school, e.g. *I have breakfast. I brush my teeth.* Encourage them to think of things they do at school, e.g. *I learn English. I play in the playground.* Ask them to think of things they do at home, e.g. *I have lunch and dinner. I swim. I go to the park.* Remind them that they help with household jobs in the day, e.g. *I tidy up. I lay the table.*
- Ask **What do you do at night?** e.g. *I read a story. I sleep. I look at the Moon and stars.*
- Draw pupils' attention to the photos. Point to each one and ask **Day or night? Sun or Moon?** Have pupils draw the Sun or the Moon in the boxes. *See answers opposite.*

CLOSING ACTIVITIES

- Remind pupils that they must not look directly at the Sun and that they should wear a hat and sun cream when playing outside.

EXTRA IDEAS

- Encourage pupils to mime an activity. The rest of the class have to guess the activity and say whether it is a daytime or nighttime activity.
- Read pupils another bedtime story.

PAGE 72 The Moon moves around the Earth

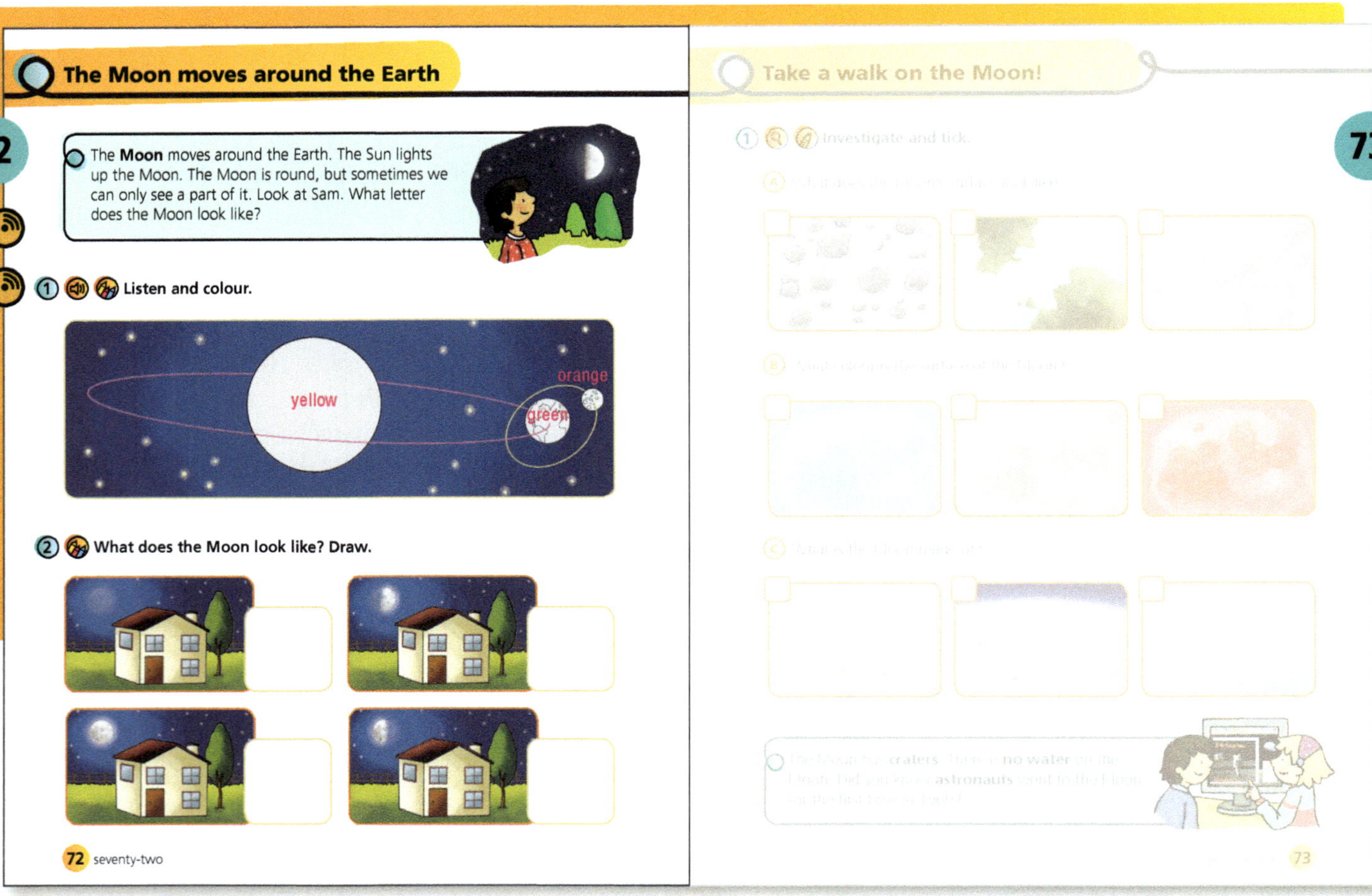

PAGE SUMMARY

Pupils will now learn about the Moon and how it moves around the Earth. Pupils will observe that sometimes we cannot see the whole Moon.

LANGUAGE

- Sun, Earth, Moon, planets, stars
- Day, night, light, dark
- What does the Moon look like?

MATERIALS

Flashcards: (digital) see the *Teachers* section in the digital resources

Additional classroom materials: torch, globe, internet images of the phases of the Moon, black card, chalk, recycled materials

OPENING ACTIVITIES

- Tell pupils to complete the sentences you say with *in the day* or *at night*, e.g. **I have breakfast** ... *in the day*. **I sleep** ... *at night*. **I play football** ... *in the day*. **I go to the park** ... *in the day*. **I swim** ... *in the day*. **I can see the Moon and stars** ... *at night*. **I can see a rainbow** ... *in the day*. **I go to school** ... *in the day*.
- Ask pupils if they remember why we have day and night. *Because the Earth turns around.* Choose a volunteer to be the Sun and give them the torch. Ask the rest of the pupils to stand up in a space. Remind them that their town is their nose. When their nose is facing the Sun, it's day and when their nose is facing away from the Sun, it's night. Encourage all the pupils to turn around slowly and say *It's day / It's night* as appropriate. If you have a globe available, you can use it to show the pupils how the Earth turns around.

MAIN ACTIVITIES

- Repeat the demonstration of how the Earth moves around the Sun. Choose two volunteers to come to the front of the class. Tell one pupil **You are the Sun**. Encourage the pupils to 'shine' by opening and closing their hands. Tell the other pupil **You are the Earth** and ask them to walk around the pupil who is the Sun. Say **The Earth moves around the Sun**.
- Ask for another volunteer. Say **You are the Moon**. Say **The Moon moves around the Earth**. Encourage the *Moon* pupil to move around the *Earth* pupil. Now encourage the *Earth* pupil to move around the *Sun* pupil (at the same time that the *Moon* pupil moves around the *Earth* pupil). Explain that the Sun lights up the Moon so we can see it in the sky.
- Organise pupils into groups of three and have them decide what they are (Sun, Earth, Moon) and how they should move. Walk round and help pupils perform the demonstration.

Reading. (CD 2. Track 12)

- Ask pupils to look at the reading box on page 72. Say **Let's listen and read**. Play the audio and have pupils follow in their books.
- Ask pupils if they have seen the Moon look different at different times. Explain that the part we see is the part which receives light from the Sun.
- Focus pupils' attention on Sam and ask what letter the moon looks like. *The letter D.*

1 Listen and colour.

- Focus pupils' attention on the picture. Say **Point to the Sun / the Moon / the Earth**. Ask **Where do we live?** *The Earth.* Ask for information about the Sun and the Moon.
- Play the audio and have pupils listen. Play the audio again, pausing after each description to allow pupils time to colour the Sun, Earth and Moon. *See answers opposite.*

CD 2 • Track 13

The Earth moves around the Sun. Colour the Sun yellow. We live on the Earth. Colour the Earth green. The Moon moves around the Earth. Colour the Moon orange.

- Ask **What colour is the Earth / Sun / Moon?** *Green / yellow / orange.*

2 What does the Moon look like? Draw.

- Ask pupils to look closely at the Moon in each of the pictures. Point to the first picture and ask **What does the Moon look like?** Say **Draw what you see**. Repeat the question for each picture. Walk round while pupils are drawing and check that they understand the task. *In order, the pictures are: new moon, first quarter, full moon, third quarter.*
- Remind pupils that we can only see the part of the Moon which receives light from the Sun. In the first picture we can't see the Moon very well as there is no sunlight shining on it.

CLOSING ACTIVITIES

- Ask pupils **Does the Earth move around the Sun or the Moon?** *The Sun.* **Does the Moon move around the Sun or the Earth?** *The Earth.*

EXTRA IDEAS

- Look at a chart (from the internet) of the different phases of the moon. Give pupils black card and chalk and have them choose a phase to draw and colour. Make your own display of the phases of the moon in class.
- Build a rocket. Have pupils bring in recycled materials from home (cereal boxes, kitchen paper tubes, wrapping paper, plastic bottles, etc.) to build a rocket to the Moon.

PAGE 73 Take a walk on the Moon!

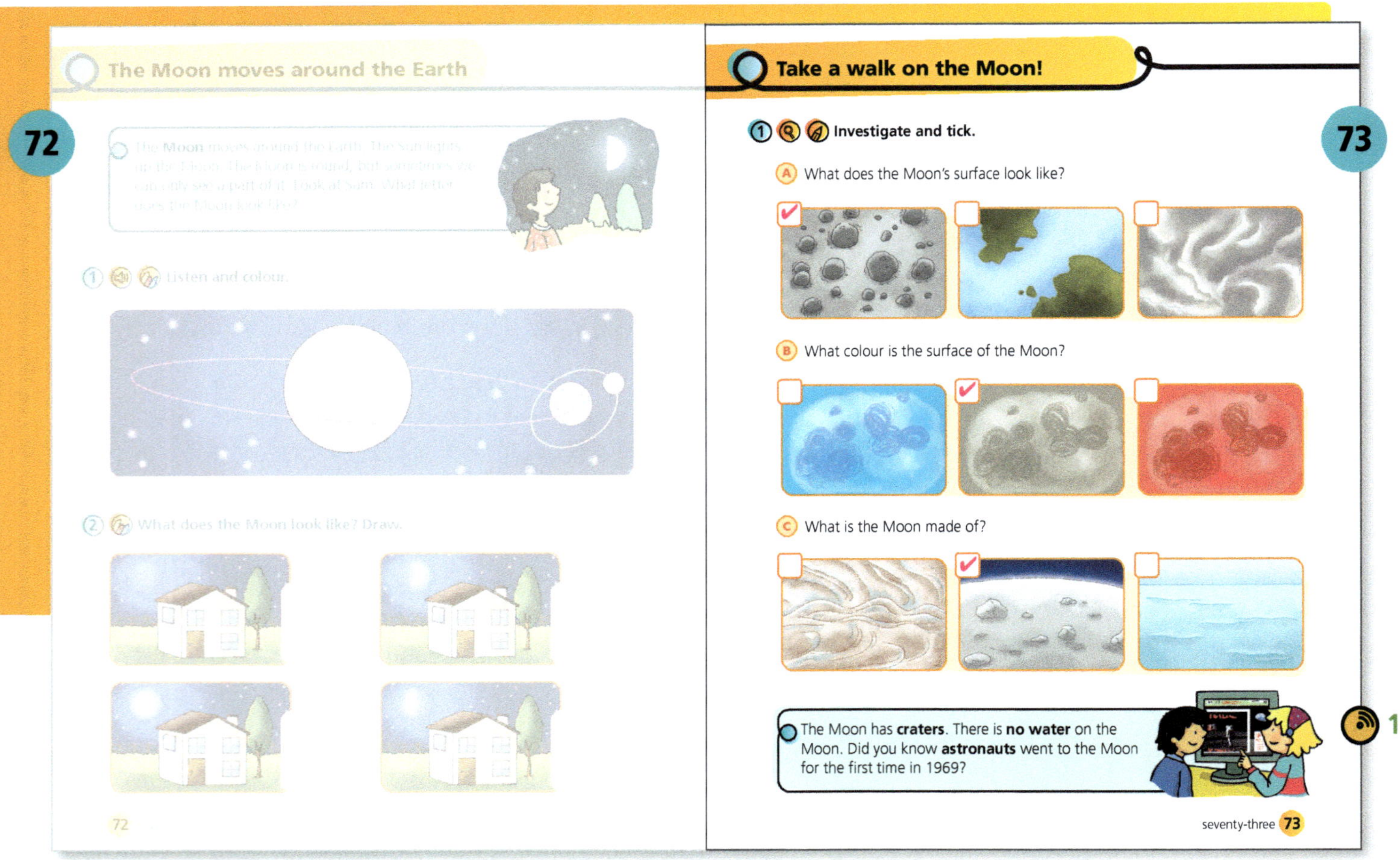

PAGE SUMMARY

Pupils will develop their observation skills and take a closer look at the surface of the Moon.

LANGUAGE

- Sun, Earth, Moon, planets, stars, meteor, crater
- Day, night, light, dark
- What does the Moon's surface look like? What colour is the surface of the Moon? What is the Moon made of?

MATERIALS

Flashcards: (digital) see the *Teachers* section in the digital resources

Additional classroom materials: black and white plasticine, charcoal and white card (or chalk and black card), reference books about the Moon, internet images of the Moon, white and grey paint, black card, potatoes, flour, marbles, footage of Apollo 11 moon landing in 1969

OPENING ACTIVITIES

- *Day and night brainstorm.* Stick up the *day* and *night* pictures or wordcards and encourage the pupils to tell you as many things as they can about day and night, e.g. things they see in the sky in the day / at night, activities they do in the day / at night, animals they can see in the day / at night. Write the sentences the pupils produce under the correct picture or word.
- Put pupils in groups of three and ask them to show you how the Earth and Moon go round the Sun.
- Play *Repeat if true*. Make true or false statements about things pupils have learnt so far in the unit. If pupils think your statement is true, they must repeat it. If they think it is false, they must shake their heads and remain silent, e.g. **The Sun is a star. The Earth has three moons. The Earth has one moon. The Sun gives us light. The Moon gives us heat**, etc.

MAIN ACTIVITIES

- Tell pupils to imagine they are walking on the Moon. Ask **What does the surface of the Moon look like?** Elicit pupils' ideas.
- Ask pupils to draw a picture of what they think the surface of the Moon looks like. Use charcoal on white card or chalk on black card.
- Hand out reference books about the Moon or show pupils images of the Moon's surface from the internet and have pupils compare their drawings with the images they see.
- Ask pupils how we know about the surface of the Moon. Pupils may be able to tell you that we have information from astronauts landing on the Moon, and from satellites, probes and strong telescopes.
- Tell pupils that the big holes on the Moon's surface are called *craters*. Ask pupils to think how they came to be formed. *Meteors crashing into the Moon.*

1 Investigate and tick.

- Tell pupils to open their Pupil's Books on page 73. Ask pupils to look at the first set of pictures (A). Ask **What does the Moon's surface look like?** Point to each picture and ask **The first picture? The second picture? The third picture?** *The first picture.* Ask pupils to tick the first picture.
- Ask pupils to look at the second set of pictures (B). Ask **What colour is the surface of the Moon?** Point to each picture and elicit the answer. *The second picture.* Ask pupils to tick the second picture.
- Finally, ask pupils to look at the third set of pictures (C). Ask **What is the Moon made of?** Point to each picture and elicit the answer. *The second picture.* Ask pupils to tick the second picture.
- Ask **How can we describe the surface of the Moon?** Encourage pupils to describe it by asking **Is it rough or smooth? Does it have trees or rocks? Is it red or grey?** Say **That's right. The Moon's surface is rough and rocky. It's grey and has many craters.**
- Write the words *rough, rocky, grey* and *craters* on the board and have pupils copy these onto their pictures.

Reading. (CD 2. Track 14)

- Focus pupils' attention on the reading box. Say **Let's listen and find out more information about the Moon.** Play the audio and encourage pupils to follow in their books.
- Ask pupils what new information they heard. Repeat the audio again if necessary and have pupils tell you that the Moon has no water and that astronauts visited the Moon for the first time in 1969.
- If possible, show pupils a piece of footage of the Apollo 11 landing on the Moon.

CLOSING ACTIVITIES

- Draw a big circle on the board and write *Moon* inside it. Ask pupils to tell you what they have learnt about the Moon. For every piece of information they give you, write it down and draw a crater on the Moon.
- Ask pupils if the Moon always looks the same. Encourage pupils to tell you that it looks different because of the light of the Sun, so sometimes there are parts we cannot see.

EXTRA IDEAS

- Have pupils drop marbles into a bowl of flour. Tell them to notice how the marbles make *craters* in the flour.
- Make a plasticine Moon. Give each pupil some white plasticine and a little bit of black plasticine. Have pupils roll and blend the plasticine colours together. Ask pupils how they can make craters on the Moon. Encourage pupils to use different circular objects to create craters, such as bottle tops, pencil ends or fingertips.
- Paint a picture of the Moon. Have pupils use white paint on black card to create the Moon. Encourage pupils to create craters by using potatoes cut in half and dipped in grey paint.

PAGE 74-75 Let's investigate and Make a difference

LET'S INVESTIGATE: **Is it day or night?**

74

Project:

Use a model of the Earth to investigate day and night.

Instructions:

Step 1
Stick a picture on one side of the ball.

Step 2
Shine the light on the ball. Turn the ball.

Step 3
See how the light changes.

① Look and write.

What is the boy in Los Angeles doing?
He is going to school.

What is the boy in Tokyo doing?
He is sleeping.

Have you been to a different country?

74 seventy-four

MAKE A DIFFERENCE: **My day and night**

75

① Tick the things you do in the day and at night. Open answer

I enjoy playing with my friends.

I learn lots of things at school.

I relax and talk to my family.

I read and go to bed. Sleep well!

② Make Sun and Moon mobiles.

1. Cut out and decorate the Sun and the Moon.
2. Draw pictures of day and night activities.
3. Stick them on the Sun and the Moon.

seventy-five 75

PAGE SUMMARY

Pupils will use a model of the Earth to investigate and help their understanding of why we have day and night.

LANGUAGE

- Earth, Sun
- Day, night, light, dark
- Stick, shine, see
- What is he doing?

MATERIALS

Flashcards: (digital) see the *Teachers* section in the digital resources

Additional classroom materials: inflatable beach ball, torch, white card or paper plates, magazines

Pages 74 and 75 allow pupils to gain a better understanding of why we have day and night. The ***Let's investigate*** page encourages pupils to carry out a simple demonstration to understand how part of the Earth receives light, whilst another part of the Earth is in darkness.

The ***Make a difference*** page encourages pupils to review the different activities we do during the day, when it is light, and the activities we do at night, when it is dark.

- Show photos or slides of the Earth. Ask pupils to tell you what they see. *Land, water, countries, continents, oceans*, etc.
- Play *Stand up if true*. Make true or false sentences about the Sun. Have pupils stand up if the statements are true and sit down between statements. **We can see the Sun in the day. Don't look directly at the Sun. The Sun is a planet. Living things need sunlight. The Sun gives us water**, etc.

LET'S INVESTIGATE

⊕ OPENING ACTIVITIES

- Say **The Earth moves around the Sun**. Ask pupils how long it takes the Earth to move around the Sun. *A year.* Ask pupils how many months there are in a year. *12 months*. Call out the months and have pupils stand up when they hear their birthday month.
- Review the names for the seasons on the board. Have pupils tell you which months correspond to the different seasons.

MAIN ACTIVITIES

- Ask pupils to open their books on page 74. Say **Let's investigate why we have day and night**. Check pupils' knowledge from previous lessons by asking them what they know.
- Read the instruction for step 1 together. Hand out beach balls to pairs (or groups) of pupils. Encourage pupils to draw and stick their picture on the side of the ball.
- Read step 2 and hand out torches. Have one pupil shine the torch on the picture on the ball. Explain that this represents light from the Sun. You could do this as a class activity, with pupils taking it in turns to come to the front of the class with their ball and pictures.
- Switch off the lights in the classroom. Ask pupils what they notice when they shine the torch on one side of the ball. *The other side doesn't have light*. Explain that this is the same when the Sun shines on the Earth. Explain that when the Earth is facing the Sun we have day. On the half of the Earth that doesn't receive light, it is night.
- Have pupils turn their ball slowly and notice how the light changes so that the picture no longer receives any light.

1 Look and write.

- Focus pupils' attention on the map. Point to each boy in the picture and ask **What is the boy doing in Tokyo / Madrid / Los Angeles?** Ask pupils **Where is it night?** *Tokyo*. Help pupils complete the sentences. *See answers opposite*.

⊕ CLOSING ACTIVITIES

- Ask pupils if they have been to different countries.

MAKE A DIFFERENCE

⊕ OPENING ACTIVITIES

- Ask volunteers to mime activities they do every day. Encourage the rest of the class to name the action and say if it is an activity we do during the day or at night (or both, e.g. *watching TV, brushing teeth*).

MAIN ACTIVITIES

1 Tick the things you do in the day and at night.

- Have pupils look at each photo. Point to the sentence under each photo and read together. Encourage pupils to tick what they do.
- Point to random pupils and ask **What do you do in the day / at night?**

2 Make Sun and Moon mobiles.

- Ask pupils to look at the photo and ask what they can see.
- Point to and read the instructions. Have pupils work in pairs to decide if they are going to decorate the Sun or the Moon.
- Encourage pupils to draw or cut out pictures of daytime or nighttime activities to stick on their Sun or Moon.

⊕ CLOSING ACTIVITIES

- Ask pupils to show their mobile to the class and describe the activity they have drawn or cut out.
- Hang the mobiles in the classroom from the ceiling.

PAGE 76-77 Let's remember

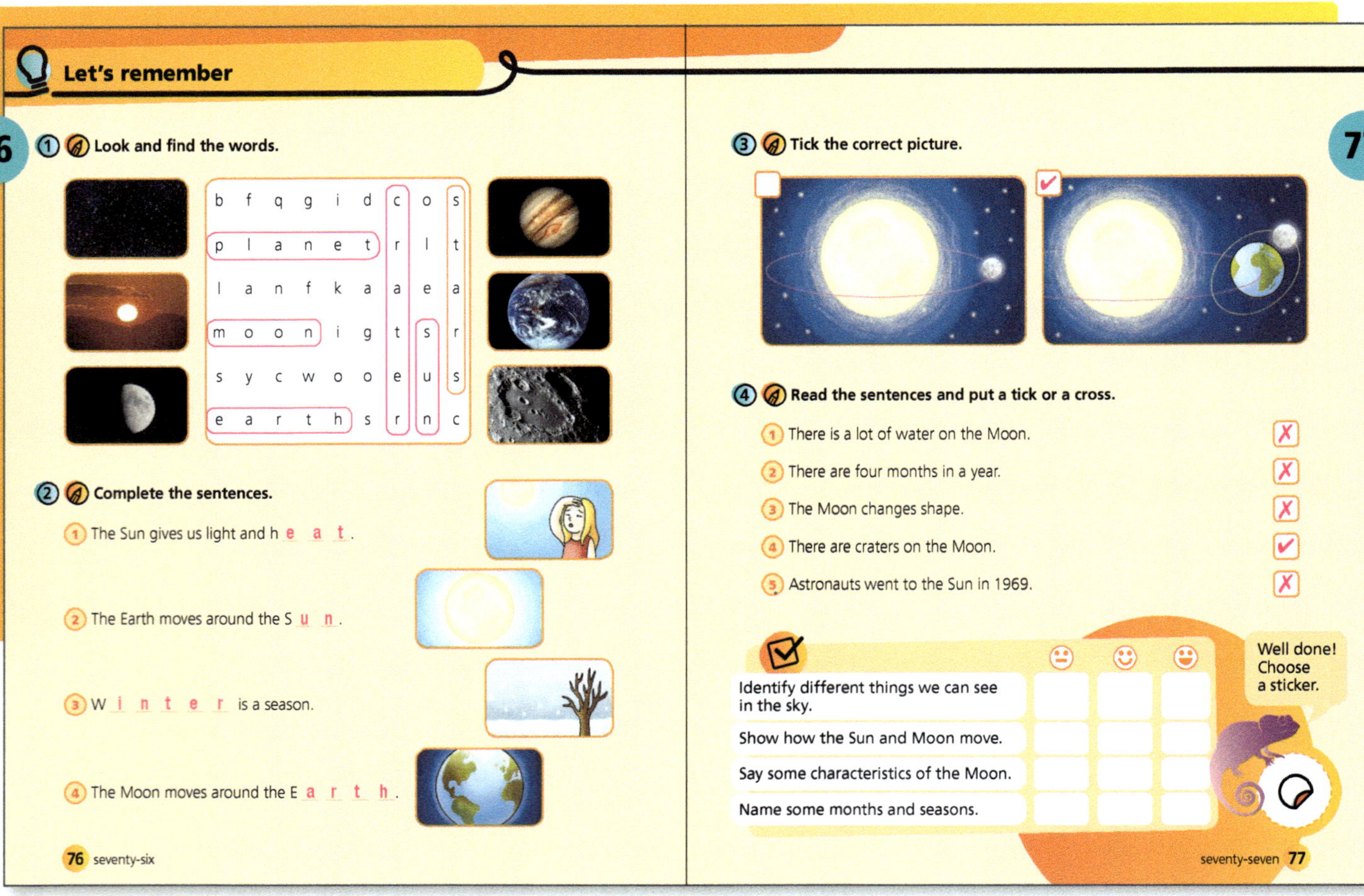

Let's remember

76

① Look and find the words.

b	f	q	g	i	d	c	o	s
p	l	a	n	e	t	r	l	t
l	a	n	f	k	a	a	e	a
m	o	o	n	i	g	t	s	r
s	y	c	w	o	o	e	u	s
e	a	r	t	h	s	r	n	c

② Complete the sentences.

1 The Sun gives us light and h e a t.

2 The Earth moves around the S u n.

3 W i n t e r is a season.

4 The Moon moves around the E a r t h.

76 seventy-six

77

③ Tick the correct picture.

④ Read the sentences and put a tick or a cross.

1 There is a lot of water on the Moon. ✗

2 There are four months in a year. ✗

3 The Moon changes shape. ✗

4 There are craters on the Moon. ✔

5 Astronauts went to the Sun in 1969. ✗

Identify different things we can see in the sky.			
Show how the Sun and Moon move.			
Say some characteristics of the Moon.			
Name some months and seasons.			

Well done! Choose a sticker.

seventy-seven 77

PAGE SUMMARY

Pupils review unit content and undertake a simple self-assessment on the unit content.

LANGUAGE

- Sun, Earth, Moon, stars, planet, day, night
- Heat, light, round
- Spring, summer, autumn, winter
- The Sun gives us heat and light. The Sun is round. The Sun is a star.
- The Moon has craters.

MATERIALS

Flashcards: digital flashcards for the unit

OPENING ACTIVITIES

1 Look and find the words.

- Draw a big circle on the board and ask **What is it?** Elicit as many things as possible that it could be. Encourage pupils to use their imaginations. *A planet, the Sun, an orange, a wheel, an eye, a hole, a zero, a plate*, etc.
- Tell pupils to open their Pupil's Books on pages 66 and 67 and look at the opening illustration again. Have them describe the picture in pairs or small groups. Ask **What have you learnt? What do you know now?**
- Ask pupils to turn to page 76. Focus pupils' attention on the photos around the wordsearch. Point to each photo and ask **What is it?** Encourage pupils to find and circle the words in the wordsearch. *See answers above.*
- Have pupils close their books. Ask them to work in pairs with a mini whiteboard or notebook between them and spell *stars, Sun, Moon, planet, Earth* and *crater.*

② Complete the sentences.

- Draw the Sun with six rays, as you did earlier in the unit, and elicit six pieces of information. There is no need to write them on the board this time.
- Draw the Moon with four craters. Ask pupils to tell you four pieces of information about the Moon.
- Focus pupils' attention on the first picture in the activity. Ask **How is she feeling?** *Hot.* Ask **Why?** *The Sun is hot/gives us heat.* Read the sentence together and encourage pupils' suggestions for the last word. Ask a volunteer to come and spell the word on the board. *Heat.*
- Point to the second picture and ask what pupils can see. *The Sun.* Read the sentence together and again encourage suggestions for the last word. Ask a volunteer to come and spell the word on the board. *Sun.*
- Point to the third picture and ask pupils what season they think it is. Ask pupils if they know which months are the winter months. Read the sentence together. Ask a volunteer to come and spell *winter* on the board.
- Finally, point to the last picture and elicit what pupils can see. Read the sentence together. Ask a volunteer to come and spell *Earth* on the board. *See answers opposite.*

③ Tick the correct picture.

- Have pupils look at the first picture. Ask **What can you see?** Encourage pupils to tell you that they can see the Moon moving around the Sun. Ask **Is that right?** *No.*
- Point to the second picture and again ask pupils what they can see. Encourage pupils to tell you that they can see the Moon moving around the Earth, and the Earth moving around the Sun. Ask **Is that right?** *Yes.* Say **Tick the correct picture**. *See answer opposite.*
- Ask pupils to remember how they demonstrated the Moon moving around the Earth, and the Earth (and Moon) moving around the Sun. Encourage them to act out the sequence again in groups of three.

④ Read the sentences and put a tick or a cross.

- Read the instruction and have pupils follow in their books. Read the first sentence and ask **Tick or cross?** *Cross.* Say **That's right. There isn't any water on the Moon.**
- Read the second sentence and ask **Tick or cross?** *Cross.* Say **That's right. How many months are there in a year?** *12.* Have pupils chant the months of the year.
- Read the remaining sentences together and ask if they need a tick or a cross. *3. Cross: the Moon doesn't change shape, but sometimes we can only see a part of it; 4. Tick; 5. Cross: astronauts went to the Moon in 1969.*

Self-assessment

- Write *The Sun and the Moon* on the board. Read it out as you do so. Tell pupils that they have learned a lot of things and how impressed you are with everything they have learned.
- Focus pupils' attention on the self-assessment table. Read the first sentence together: *Identify different things we can see in the sky.* Ask pupils to name ten things we can see in the sky with a partner.
- Now read the sentence: *Show how the Sun and Moon move.* Ask pupils to remember their movements around each other to demonstrate this.
- Read the sentence: *Say some characteristics of the Moon.* Have pupils whisper a characteristic to their partner.
- Finally, read the sentence: *Name some months and seasons.* Have pupils chant the months and say the seasons as a class.
- After reading each sentence, the pupils should tick the boxes according to whether they have learned a lot (*very happy face*), some things (*happy face*) or a little (*disappointed face*) about the Sun and the Moon.
- Ask pupils to choose a sticker to show how they feel about their learning in the unit.
- Give individual attention to any pupils who choose the *disappointed* sticker.

Activity book answers

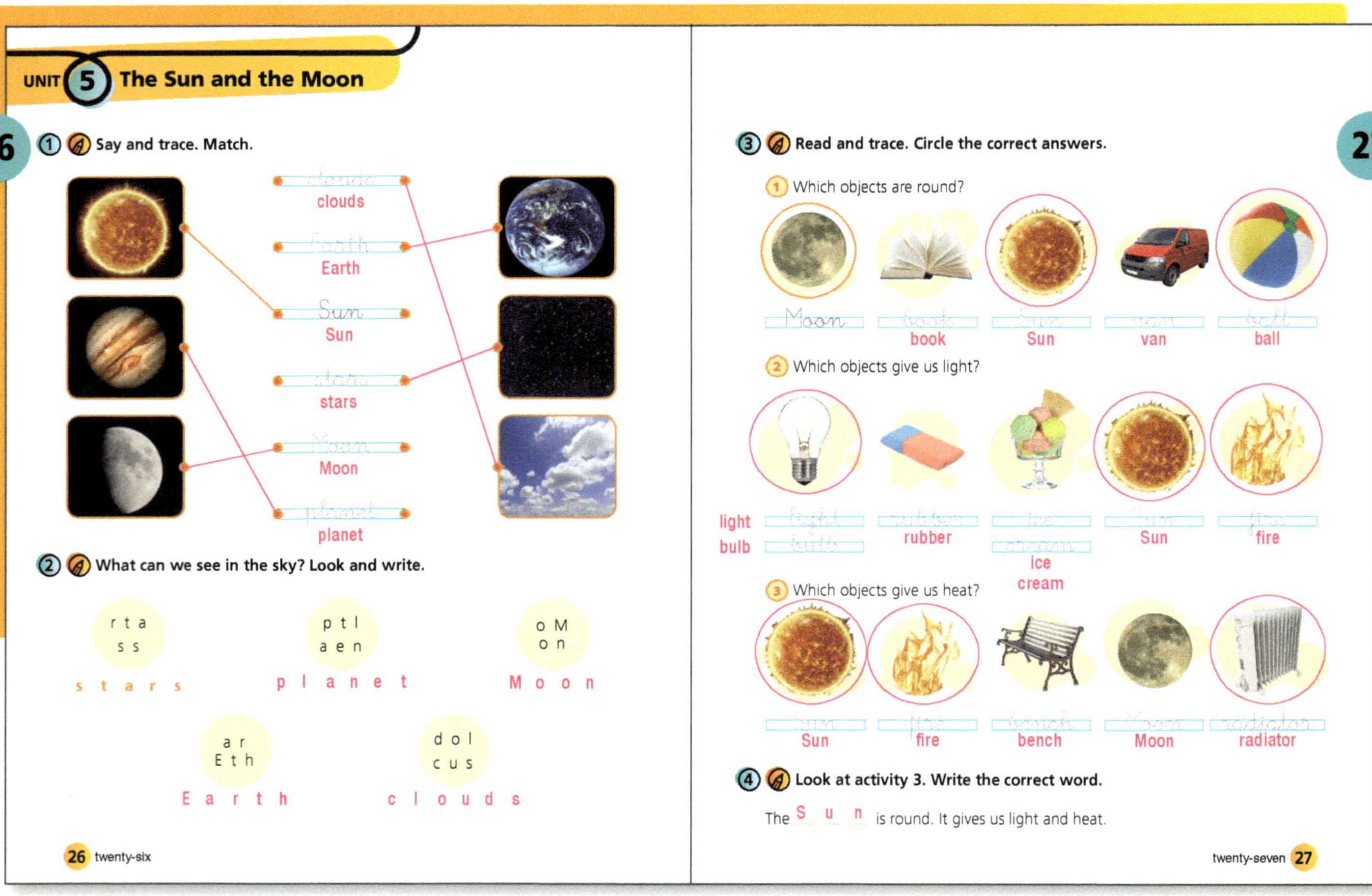

UNIT 5 The Sun and the Moon

26

① Say and trace. Match.

clouds — Earth — Sun — stars — Moon — planet

② What can we see in the sky? Look and write.

rta ss — s t a r s

ptl aen — p l a n e t

oM on — M o o n

ar Eth — E a r t h

dol cus — c l o u d s

26 twenty-six

27

③ Read and trace. Circle the correct answers.

1 Which objects are round?

Moon, book, Sun, van, ball

2 Which objects give us light?

light bulb, rubber, ice cream, Sun, fire

3 Which objects give us heat?

Sun, fire, bench, Moon, radiator

④ Look at activity 3. Write the correct word.

The S u n is round. It gives us light and heat.

twenty-seven 27

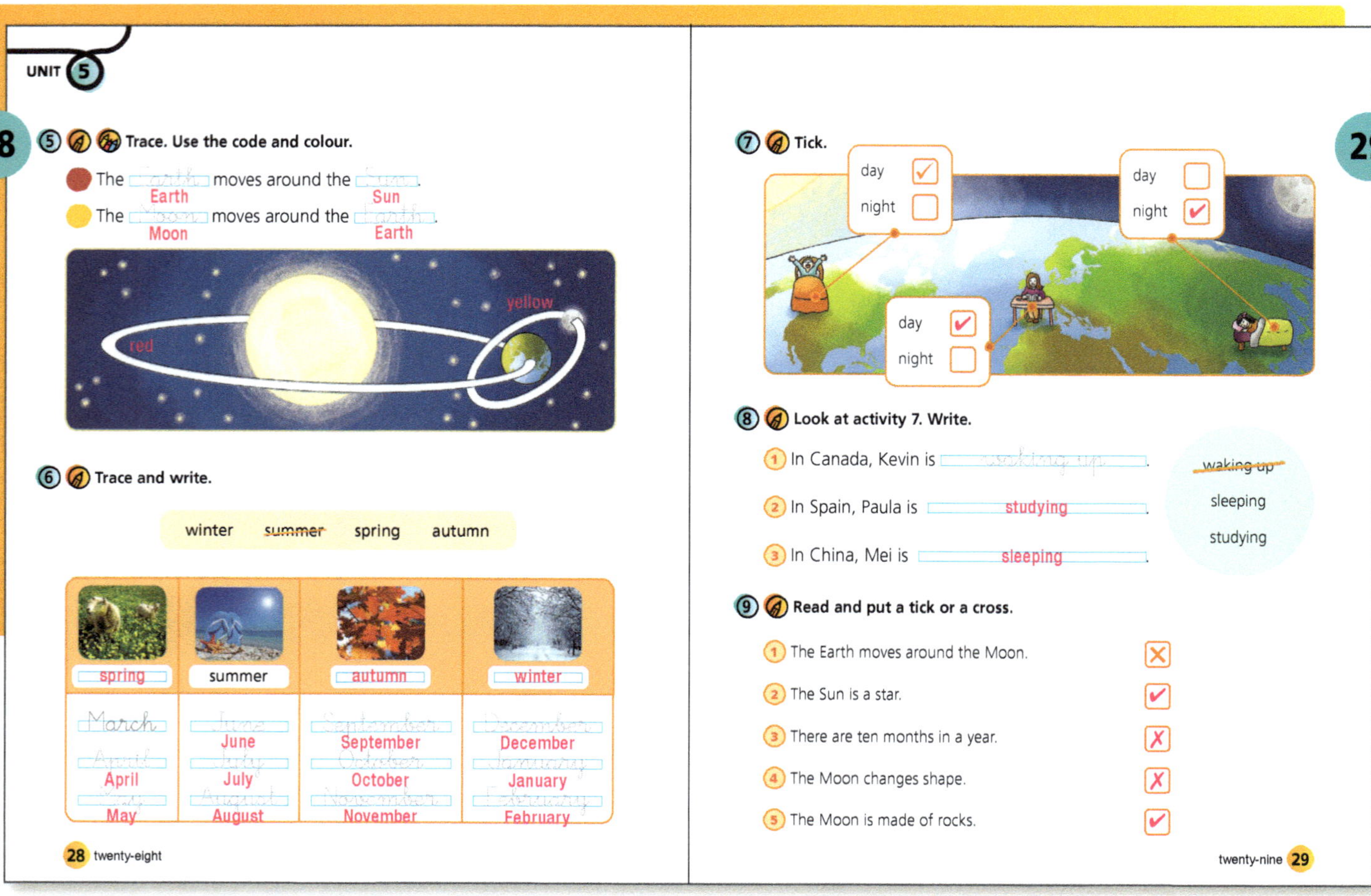

UNIT 5

28

⑤ Trace. Use the code and colour.

The Earth moves around the Sun.

The Moon moves around the Earth.

red — yellow

⑥ Trace and write.

winter ~~summer~~ spring autumn

spring	summer	autumn	winter
March	June	September	December
April	July	October	January
May	August	November	February

28 twenty-eight

29

⑦ Tick.

day ✔ night — day night ✔ — day ✔ night

⑧ Look at activity 7. Write.

1 In Canada, Kevin is waking up.

2 In Spain, Paula is studying.

3 In China, Mei is sleeping.

~~waking up~~ sleeping studying

⑨ Read and put a tick or a cross.

1 The Earth moves around the Moon. ✗

2 The Sun is a star. ✔

3 There are ten months in a year. ✗

4 The Moon changes shape. ✗

5 The Moon is made of rocks. ✔

twenty-nine 29

UNIT 5

Let's investigate at home!

Record the moon for a month

1 

Make a calendar.

2 
Observe the moon every night.

3 

Draw a picture of the moon on your calendar.

4 

Colour and decorate your calendar.

1 Write *yes* or *no*.

Does the moon always look round? no

Does the moon give us heat? no

Skills check

1 Read. Choose a word or phrase from the box and write.

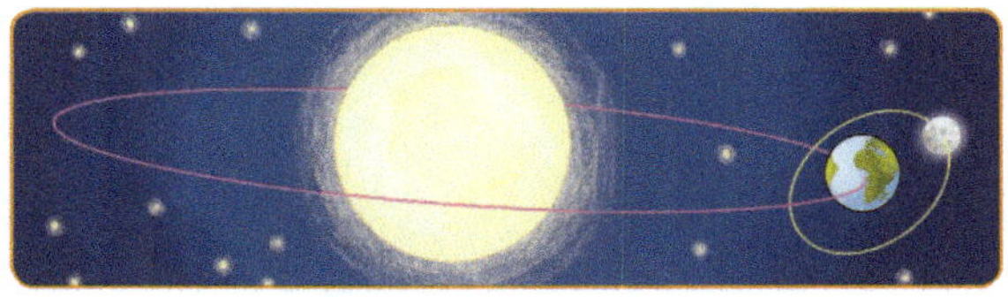

We live on the Earth. During the day we can see the (1) Sun. In the morning I wake up and I (2) go to school ______. At night we can see the (3) Moon. We can also see lots of (4) stars. At night I (5) go to bed.

stars

go to bed

Sun

crater

summer

Moon

go to school

Earth

UNIT 6 Time

CONTENT	EVALUATION CRITERIA
Time. Basic notions: before, after, past, present, future, duration.	Begin the reconstruction of memories of the recent past, from family sources.
Units of measurement: day, week, month and year.	Order family events using simple observation methods and units of measurement (day, week, month, year).
Days of the week. Months and seasons of the year.	Use the calendar to represent the passing of time and locate important days or dates.
Events in the past and the present.	Sequence events applying the basic units of measurement and express some examples of how things change over time.
Historical sources.	Identify historical events through objects.
Introduction to scientific knowledge and its application in the Social Sciences. Collect relevant information using different sources (direct and indirect).	Obtain specific and relevant information, using different sources.
Develop strategies to organise, memorise and remember information obtained through different methods and from different sources.	Develop a capacity for hard work and show perseverance while studying.
Team-building strategies.	Develop a cooperative and adaptive attitude, recognising merit in others' ideas and responding to situations with intuition, an open mind and flexibility.
With help, plan and manage simple projects, showing independence and initiative in order to achieve objectives.	Develop creativity and initiative, improving their capacity to acquire information and ideas and present innovative conclusions.
Correct use of different materials.	Use the materials in a suitable way.

LEARNING STANDARDS	KEY COMPETENCES	PAGES
Investigates, with help, certain events in the history of their family and collects simple facts connected to their family.	SOC, CUL	78–81, 86
With help, produces a simple family tree of their own family.	SOC, LTL, AUT	81
Organises the history of their family through a photo album.	SOC, LTL, CUL	80
Uses oral sources and information from objects and family memories to reconstruct the past.	SOC, CUL, LTL	81, 86
Orders chronologically certain events of their personal life, using basic units of measurement: hour, day, week, year.	SOC, LTL	80, 83–86
Classifies different images according to different notions such as: before, now, after.	SOC, CUL, LTL	80, 82, 86, 87
Orders activities according to notions of time such as: before, after.	SOC, LTL	83
Establishes a chronology based on family relationships and the age of each member and identifies the concepts of past, present and future.	SOC, LTL	80, 81, 86
Locates and places important dates on a calendar.	SOC, LTL, MTS	85
Knows the days of the week and understands the idea of yesterday and tomorrow.	SOC, LTL	84
Knows the months of the year, can place them on the calendar and knows what comes before and after.	SOC, LTL	85
Differentiates the seasons of the year and gives an oral explanation of their characteristics.	SOC, LIN, MTS	85
Locates on a simple timeline their own personal history from birth until today.	SOC, LTL, CUL, MTS	86
Uses basic notions of time (before, after, at the beginning, at the end) to tell events of their daily life in chronological order.	SOC, LTL, LIN, MTS	86
Understands how things change with time.	SOC, CUL	82
Understands the past through historical sources in their immediate environment.	SOC, CUL, LTL	79, 80, 82, 86, 87
Identifies events in the past and the present and their relation to their lives.	SOC, CUL	82
Looks for, selects and organises information, analysing it and drawing conclusions. Reflects on the process followed and reports on it orally.	MST, LIN, LTL	78–80, 86, 87
Performs academic tasks in a responsible and effective manner.	LTL	86, 87
Uses vocabulary correctly in the presentation of their work.	LTL, LIN	86, 87
Develops a cooperative and adaptive attitude, recognising merit in others' ideas and responding to situations with intuition, an open mind and flexibility.	LTL, SOC	79, 87
Participates effectively and constructively in daily life and develops strategies for conflict resolution.	LTL, SOC	79
Identifies and uses the correct code of conduct for their environment.	LTL, SOC	79
Shows self-confidence, personal initiative, curiosity, interest and creativity in the learning process.	AUT, LTL	86, 87
Shows independence in the planning and carrying out of simple actions and shows initiative when taking decisions.	AUT, LTL	86
Uses the materials in a suitable and careful way thereby keeping them in good condition.	LTL, SOC	86

UNIT INFORMATION

UNIT SUMMARY

In this unit your pupils will study different aspects of time. They will extend their knowledge and understand how we measure time in minutes, days, months and years. They will also consider how places, people and things change over time. The unit touches on the importance of things from the past and the value of a family tree that allows us to know who our older family members are.

Most pupils will be familiar with the vocabulary of days, months and names of family members but will need support reading and writing, as well as understanding the concept of change, progress and growth over time.

Make sure you review, recycle and concept check as you progress through the unit, and continually provide visual support and encouragement.

PROJECT

Let's investigate

In the *Let's investigate* activity on page 86, your pupils will make a timeline to help them understand changes and important events in their life so far.

The pupils need:

- Their notebooks
- A pencil
- Coloured pencils, crayons or felt tips
- A3 paper (one sheet per pupil)
- Scissors
- Ruler
- Glue or sticky tape

Show pupils how they will need to cut a sheet of A3 paper in half lengthways, then stick the two strips together. Before the lesson, make sure you tell pupils to bring in photos of when they were babies, when they started school or any other important moments in their lives. Photos could be photocopied if pupils don't want to stick the actual photo on their timeline.

VALUES AND ATTITUDES

In this unit pupils will consider the value of learning things from our grandparents and the importance of things from the past. Throughout the unit, try to encourage pupils to think about:

- Why the past is important.
- What we can learn from older members of our family.
- How we can stay in touch with family members.

Make a difference

The *Make a difference* page in this unit focuses on appreciating and valuing things from the past. It aims to show how the past, present and future are connected by encouraging pupils to make a time capsule with things that are special to them now, which they will view again at a future date.

EVALUATION MATERIAL

These documents can be downloaded from the *Teachers* section of the digital resources and printed.

The materials include:

- **Unit diagnostic test:** provides an overview of the unit and allows you to assess the pupils' prior knowledge.
- **End-of-unit test:** in addition to the *Review* section at the end of each unit, this summative test can be used to evaluate pupils' progress after studying the unit content.
- **Unit evaluation grid:** based on the evaluation criteria and learning standards of the unit.

DIGITAL RESOURCES

Presentations

- **Unit summary**: a simple slide presentation with text, images and audio to review the main ideas of the unit. It can be used at the beginning of the unit to test pupils' prior knowledge of the unit content or at the end of the unit as a revision tool.
- **Let's investigate**: a slide presentation of the unit's *Let's investigate* page with text, photos and audio. The slide presentation is perfect for a heads-up class, showing the steps one by one. Use this tool to get the pupils to predict the next steps (with their books closed) or to focus their attention on each step as they carry out the project themselves.

Activities

- **Memory game**: useful activity for reviewing key vocabulary and modelling pronunciation.
- **Wordsearch**: use at the end of the unit as a revision activity. Turn it into a game by getting the pupils to work in teams.
- **Spelling**: get a volunteer to come to the board and carry out the activity, but with the help of the whole class.

Song lyrics

Listen to the song *Time* and follow the lyrics line by line.

Posters

Attractive and informative posters to display in class. You can use them to review key concepts and vocabulary.

Videos

Use the video links in this unit to present content in a dynamic, real-life context whilst reinforcing the pupils' listening skills.

Teachers

Digital flashcards: a bank of digital images which can be used in a variety of ways in class.

Downloadable pdfs: evaluation tests, evaluation grids, templates, useful links and further information.

PAGES 78-79 Time

PAGE SUMMARY

The aim of the unit opener is to encourage your pupils' observation skills and guide them to notice the clues that suggest the passing of time. The pages serve as an introduction to the rest of the unit.

LANGUAGE

- Clock, watch, calendar, timetable, photo, poster, radio, ink, pen, wooden toy, record, photo album
- Child, adult, grandmother, grandfather
- Spring, summer, autumn, winter
- Monday, Tuesday, Wednesday, Thursday, Friday, Saturday, Sunday

MATERIALS

Flashcards: (digital) see the *Teachers* section in the digital resources

Additional classroom materials: clock with moveable hands, paper plates, card, fastener

WHAT CAN YOU SEE?

Play *Hangman* with the word *time*. Ask pupils what they think of when they see or hear this word. Have them share their ideas with you and help them express themselves in their own language. Ask for further information, e.g. if pupils mention clocks and watches, ask if they can tell you what time they get up / go to bed / start school, etc. If pupils talk about free time, ask what activities they do in their free time.

Ask pupils to open their Pupil's Books on pages 78 and 79. Ask them to work with a partner and notice things that may be connected to the passing of time. Ask pupils who they can see in the classroom apart from children. *Grandparents*. Ask **Why do you think the children's grandmothers and grandfathers are in the class?** *To talk about the past / when they were young.*

Ask pupils what things they can see on the tables. Use the zoom on the interactive whiteboard to focus on the objects and talk about them. Ask pupils to close their books and tell you where the chameleon is. *On a table, next to a photo.*

⊕ OPENING ACTIVITIES

- Ask pupils to tell you what things in the illustration tell you that the unit is about time. *Days of the week, poster of the seasons, clocks, old toys and objects, old photos, grandparents*.
- Ask pupils what day of the week it is today, what day it was yesterday and what day it is tomorrow. Ask pupils how many days there are in a week. Explain that there are about four weeks in a month. Ask pupils if they remember how many months there are in a year.
- Ask **What months are in spring / summer / autumn / winter?** Point to random pupils and ask what season their birthday is in. Ask **How old are you now? How old will you be on your next birthday?**

MAIN ACTIVITIES

1 Find Amy. What is she looking at?

- Point to activity 1 and encourage pupils to read the question with you. Ask pupils to work in groups to find Amy and what she is looking at. If pupils only answer that she is looking at a photo, encourage them to tell you who they think is in the photo. *The grandfather when he was young.*
- Point to the photo of the young tennis player and ask **Who is that?** *Grandmother when she was young.* Ask the groups to now find Sam. Ask **What is Sam looking at?** *A photo album.* Ask pupils if they have photo albums at home. Encourage pupils to bring in a photo for the next class of when they were a baby.

2 What time is it in the picture?

- Check how well pupils can tell the time. Using a clock with moveable hands, ask pupils to tell you the times on the hour, e.g. *one o'clock, two o'clock, three o'clock*, etc. as you turn the hands.
- Check pupils know the difference between the big hand and the small hand on a clock. Ask pupils to look at the clock on the wall in the illustration. Have pupils notice that the big hand has passed the 12. Count the minutes and explain that we say that it is five minutes past 11. Explain that the second clock in the illustration is called a digital clock and doesn't have hands. On a digital clock you can easily see the minutes.
- Look at the clock in your classroom. Ask **What time is it?** Have pupils work out the time together.

3 Who is not a good pupil? Circle.

- Ask groups to brainstorm how to behave well in class. *Lining up correctly, tidying up, sharing, putting rubbish in bins, not running*, etc.
- Read the question and have groups look to find the answer. *The boy is leaning back on his chair and can fall.* Have pupils circle the boy and talk about why this is not good behaviour.

4 Listen and circle the objects you hear.

- Ask pupils to look at the photos and read the word under each picture. Focus pupils' attention on the musical note and say **Let's listen to a song**. Tell pupils that they are going to listen to the song twice and circle the things that they hear.

CD 2 • Track 15
See audio script below.

5 Sing the song and do the actions!

- Say **Now let's listen and do the actions**. Play the song, teach the actions and encourage pupils to copy. Repeat the song and do the actions together.

CD 2 • Track 16

Count the hours on your watch *[point to your watch]*
Time passes, tick, tick, tock *[mime clock hands]*
Count the days on a calendar *[count then draw square in air]*
Time passes, tick, tick, tock *[mime clock hands]*
Time, time, time *[flash hands]*
Child to adult *[crouch down then jump in air]* [x2]
Time passes and we change *[spin around]*

⊕ CLOSING ACTIVITIES

- Ask pupils what time the class ends.
- Have pupils name the ways we can see time pass.

⊕ EXTRA IDEAS

- Help pupils learn how to tell the time. Focus on time on the hour and half past the hour first.
- Have pupils make a clock with a paper plate, two hands made from card, and a fastener.

UNIT 6

PAGE 80 Sam's family album

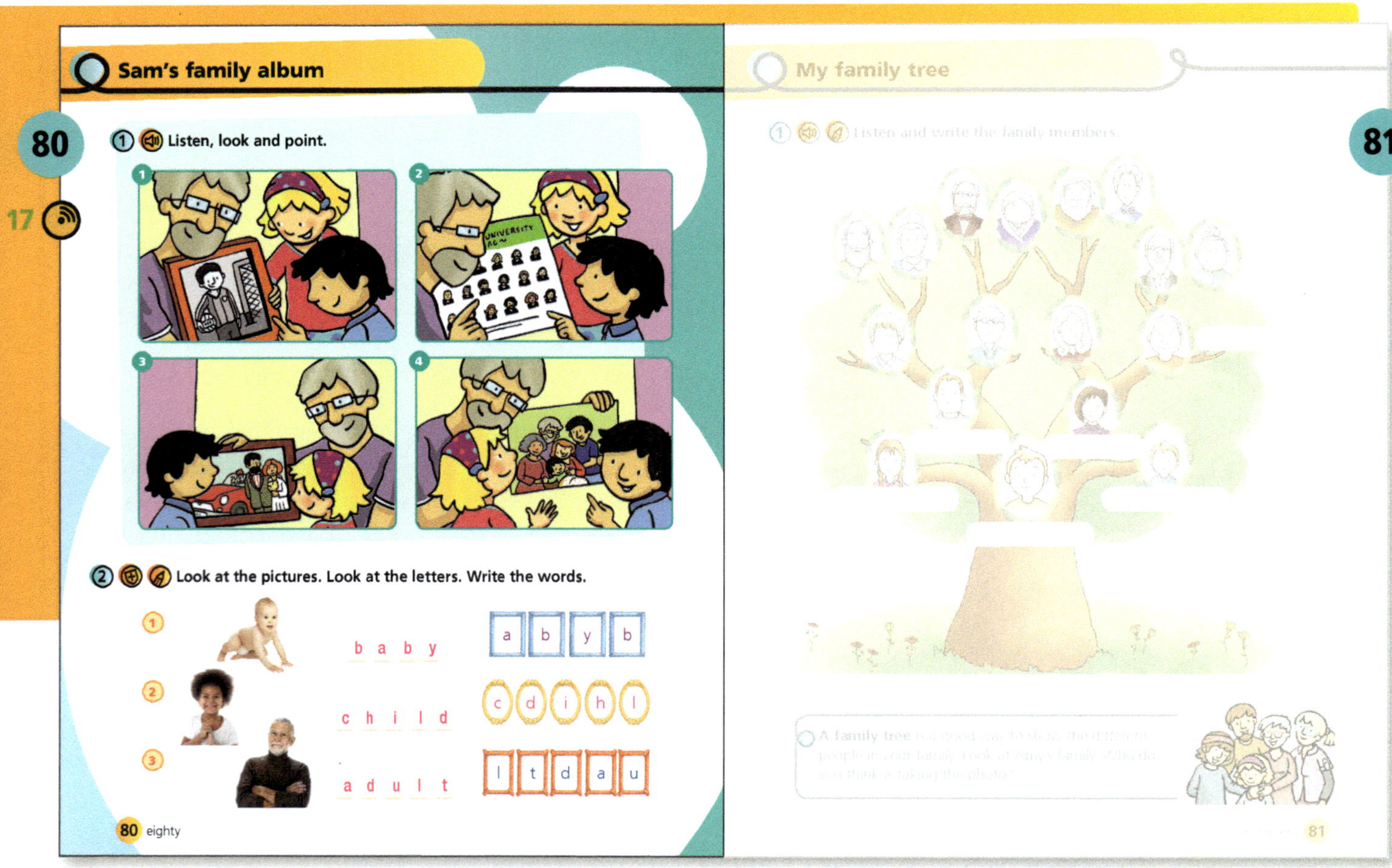

PAGE SUMMARY

Use the story to talk about special events in our lives and how we grow older over time.

LANGUAGE

- Photo album, grandad, grandma
- Young, old, baby, child, adult
- University, wedding day, 60th birthday
- I loved football.
- Did you meet at university?

MATERIALS

Flashcards: (digital) see the *Teachers* section in the digital resources

Additional classroom materials: digital camera, photos pupils have brought in of when they were babies

OPENING ACTIVITIES

- Play *What's the time, Mr Wolf?* Go out to the playground or gym. Choose a confident pupil to be Mr Wolf and stand at one end with their back to the rest of the class. The rest of the class stand some way behind Mr Wolf. Encourage the class to slowly approach Mr Wolf and chant *What's the time, Mr Wolf?* Mr Wolf should turn around and answer a time, e.g. *It's 11 o'clock*. Pupils continue to chant the question, moving closer each time, and Mr Wolf continues to answer with a time. Suddenly, Mr Wolf should turn round and respond instead *It's dinner time!* He must then run and try to tag someone. When he does, the person tagged then becomes the new Mr Wolf and the game starts again. The first time you play, demonstrate how to be Mr Wolf.

MAIN ACTIVITIES

- Tell pupils they are going to listen to a story about Sam's family album. If they brought in photos of when they were babies, encourage pupils to show them to the rest of the class and talk about them.

1 Listen, look and point.

- Ask pupils to open their Pupil's Books on page 80. Point to frame 1 and say **Look at the picture**. Ask **Who can you see?** Encourage pupils to say *Sam and Amy*. Explain that the grandfather they see is Sam's grandfather (or, more informally, grandad). Ask what they can see in the photo and elicit that it is Sam's grandad when he was young. Ask **What did he like to play?** *Football.*
- Explain that the photos show the grandad's life. In frame 2, explain that a university is where students go to study after they finish school.
- Say **Let's listen to the story**. Play the audio.

CD 2 • Track 17

Sam's family album

The children are looking at photos with Sam's grandad.

Frame 1

Sam: **Who's in that photo, grandad?**

Grandad: **That's me! I was seven or eight years old. I loved playing football.**

Amy: **Wow. You look so young!**

Frame 2

Grandad: **This is a photo of when I finished university.**

Sam: **And look, there's grandma! Did you meet at university then?**

Grandad: **Yes, we did.**

Frame 3

Grandad: **And this is our wedding day.**

Sam: **What a cool car!**

Amy: **You both look very happy.**

Frame 4

Grandad: **And look, this is my 60th birthday.**

Amy: **Who's the baby?**

Sam: **I know who that is! That's me!**

- Play the story again, this time pausing after each frame and asking further questions, e.g. **Where did grandad meet Sam's grandma?**

2 Look at the pictures. Look at the letters. Write the words

- Point to the first photo and ask pupils what they see. Encourage pupils to have a go spelling the word *baby* on a mini whiteboard or in their notebooks. Have a volunteer spell the word on the board. Ask the rest of the class **Is that right?**
- Explain that when a baby grows, we don't call him or her *baby*, we call them the next jumbled-up word. Tell pupils to look at the photo and the letters and elicit the word *child*.
- Finally, explain that when we grow up, we change from being a child to being the next jumbled-up word. Elicit the word *adult*. Encourage pupils to have a go at the spelling before writing in their books. *See answers opposite.*

CLOSING ACTIVITIES

- Hand out pictures or flashcards of *baby*, *child* and *adult* to three volunteers. Ask them to stand in order of age. Discuss how we change over time.
- Hand out wordcards to three different volunteers and have them stand in front the correct picture. Read the words together.
- With volunteers back in their seats, ask pupils to close their books and spell *baby*, *child* and *adult*. You may like to show how we spell these words in the plural (*babies*, *children*, *adults*).

EXTRA IDEAS

- Make a *Me now and me as a baby* display. Take photos of pupils. Ask pupils to bring in photos of themselves as babies and create a display, adding them to the photos you have taken of pupils now. Encourage pupils to add sentences, e.g. *My name is Juan. Now I'm six years old.*
- Invite a grandmother and grandfather to come in to class (with objects and photos) and talk to pupils about life in the past. Although the visit would be in their own language, you can talk about the visit afterwards in English.

PAGE 81 My family tree

PAGE SUMMARY

Your pupils will talk about their families and understand how a family tree helps us see who is in our family.

LANGUAGE

- Family tree, great-grandparents, grandparents, grandma, grandad, mother, father, sister, brother
- Who is this?

MATERIALS

Flashcards: (digital) see the *Teachers* section in the digital resources

Additional classroom materials: two clocks (can be handmade), your own family photos to show and talk about with the class, A3 paper

OPENING ACTIVITIES

- *Clock race*. Divide the class into two teams. Two members, one from each team, come to the front and take a clock each with easily moveable hands. Encourage the rest of the class to chant *What's the time?* Respond with a time, e.g. **It's 8 o'clock**. Have the two members at the front of the class race to show the time on their clocks. The first to do so gains a point for their team. Continue the game with different team members until everyone has had a go at showing the time.
- Ask if any more pupils have brought in baby photos. Have them show and talk about them to the rest of the class. Make sure these photos are added to the display.
- Ask pupils to describe what things they can do now that they couldn't do when they were babies, e.g. *talk, ride a bicycle, eat with a knife and fork, go to school*, etc.

MAIN ACTIVITIES

- Jumble up the letters of the word *family* on the board. Ask pupils to guess and spell the word.
- Encourage pupils to name all the family members they know, e.g. *father, mother, brother, sister, grandad, grandma, cousins, uncle, aunt.*
- Use family pictures or flashcards to build up a family tree on the board. Start by placing a picture of a boy and girl at the bottom of the board. Elicit that they are *brother* and *sister.* Above them, place pictures of *mother* and *father.* Encourage pupils to name who they are. Repeat the procedure with *grandad* and *grandma*, placing them above the mother or the father. Finally, hold up pictures of the *great-grandad* and *great-grandma.* Name them and encourage pupils to repeat the vocabulary after you.
- Point to all the pictures or flashcards and review the names of all the members. Write the names of the family members as pupils name them and write *family tree* as a heading. Point out that we have two sets of grandparents and four sets of great-grandparents and indicate where these members go on the family tree.
- Ask pupils if they have great-grandparents.

1 Listen and write the family members.

- Tell pupils to open their Pupil's Books on page 81. Ask **What can you see?** Encourage pupils to say *a family tree.*
- Focus pupils' attention on the boy in the middle, at the bottom of the family tree. Ask **How many brothers and sisters does he have?** *One sister and one brother.*
- Point to different family members and ask **Who is this?** Encourage pupils to name the different family members.
- Explain that pupils are going to listen and write the names of the missing family members. Play the audio and have pupils listen and follow in their books. Play the audio a second time and pause after each description to give pupils time to write the names of the family members.

CD 2 • Track 18

This is my family tree. Look, there's me in the middle! Write ME.

There's my sister, on the left. Write SISTER.

There's my brother, on the right. Write BROTHER.

There are my father and my mother. They're my parents. Write FATHER and MOTHER.

The four people above them are my grandparents. They're the parents of my parents. Write GRANDPARENTS.

At the top there are eight people. They're my great-grandparents. They're the parents of my grandparents! Write GREAT-GRANDPARENTS.

- When pupils have finished, encourage them to review the family tree with a partner.

Reading (CD 2. Track 19)

- Ask pupils to look at the reading box. Say **Let's listen and read about a family tree**. Play the audio and encourage the pupils to follow in their books.
- Ask pupils to look at Amy's family and tell you who they can see. Ask pupils who they think is taking the photo. *Amy's grandad.*

CLOSING ACTIVITIES

- Draw the framework of a family tree on the board with empty squares. Choose volunteers to take a family member picture or flashcard and place it in an appropriate place on the board. When they are all in place, have other volunteers come and take a wordcard and place it under the correct flashcard. Check continually with the rest of the class that the cards are being placed correctly.
- Show pupils photos of your family. Ask pupils to guess who they think the people are and encourage them to ask questions about them.

EXTRA IDEAS

- Show pupils how to fold and cut A3 paper to make a family paper chain. They can colour and decorate each figure to resemble a different family member and write the names on the back.
- Encourage pupils to bring in photos or draw pictures of their grandparents. Have pupils give mini presentations about them.

PAGE 82 Things change with time

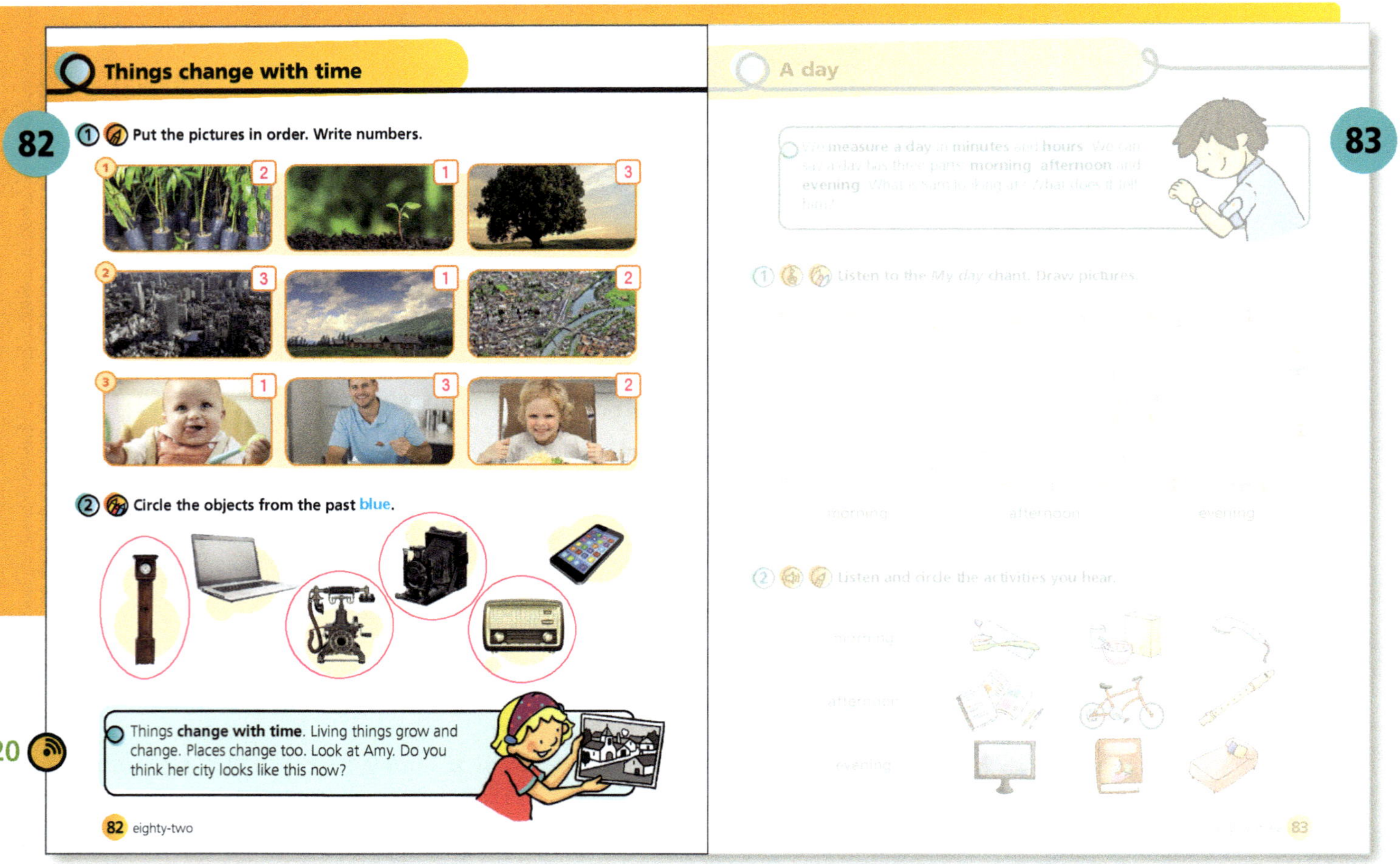
Things change with time

82

1 Put the pictures in order. Write numbers.

1 2 1 3

2 3 1 2

3 1 3 2

2 Circle the objects from the past blue.

Things **change with time**. Living things grow and change. Places change too. Look at Amy. Do you think her city looks like this now?

82 eighty-two

A day

83

20

PAGE SUMMARY

Your pupils will consider and observe how places, objects, people and other living things change over time.

LANGUAGE

- Seed, plant, tree, village, town, city, baby, child, adult
- Past, present
- It changes / grows / gets bigger. We get older.

MATERIALS

Flashcards: (digital) see the *Teachers* section in the digital resources

Additional classroom materials: slide presentation with more examples of things that have changed over time, three board markers, A3 card, magazines (with houses and gadgets)

OPENING ACTIVITIES

- Play *Grandma's footsteps* in small groups out in the playground or in the gym. Choose one pupil in each group to be *grandma* (male or female). Grandma must stand and face a wall, while the rest of the group stand behind an agreed line on the other side of the room. They must try to creep up behind grandma and tap her on the shoulder. At any moment, grandma can turn around. If she sees anybody moving, she will point to them and they must go back to the beginning, behind the line. No one must move while grandma is watching. Whoever manages to tap grandma first, without her seeing them, becomes the next grandma and the game starts again.
- Play *Run and spell*. Divide the class into three teams. Have a member from each team stand in front of the board with a board marker. Say **Spell** ***brother***. The first team member to spell the word correctly gains a point for their team. Repeat the game with each team member and different family words.

MAIN ACTIVITIES

- Introduce the idea of things changing over time with a simple slide presentation showing toys from the past and toys the children play with now. Encourage pupils to think about why the toys are different.
- Continue to develop the theme by showing and comparing pictures of transport in the past and transport now. Ask **How are they different?** *Now they are faster, safer,* etc.
- Compare machines from the past with those of the present, e.g. record players, telephones, cameras, etc.
- Ask pupils how a small village or town can change with time. Encourage pupils to suggest that they get bigger, have more modern buildings, etc.
- Finally, ask pupils how nature / other living things change over time. Encourage them to think about an egg and how it becomes a chick and then a hen. Have pupils think about seeds and how they can grow into trees.

1 Put the pictures in order. Write numbers.

- Tell pupils to open their Pupil's Books on page 82. Focus their attention on the pictures. Say **Let's put the pictures in order to show how they change over time**.
- Give pupils a few moments to look at each set of pictures and consult a partner if they want to.
- Point to the first set of pictures and ask **Which picture is number one? Point and show me**. Have pupils indicate the middle photo. Say **That's right. A plant grows from a seed and starts very small.** Have pupils indicate which is the second photo in the sequence and finally which is the third. Conclude **Over time a seed can grow and becomes a big tree**.
- Repeat the procedure for the next set of pictures, asking pupils to indicate the order before they write the numbers. Conclude that cities start out as just a few houses and grow and grow with time, as more and more people want to work there.
- Finally, look at the last set of photos. Ask pupils **Who can you see?** Encourage them to identify *baby, child* and *adult*. Ask pupils to tell you the order. Then ask them to write correct numbers for all the sets of pictures. *See answers opposite.*

2 Circle objects from the past blue.

- Ask pupils if they can name the objects they see. Say **Some are from the past and some are from now, the present**. Read the instruction and have pupils circle the objects from the past blue. *See answers opposite.*
- Ask pupils if they have any objects from the past in their houses.

Reading. (CD 2. Track 20)

- Ask pupils to look at the reading box. Say **Let's listen and read**. Play the audio and encourage pupils to follow in their books.
- Encourage pupils to describe what they think Amy's city looks like now. *Bigger, tall buildings, flats, lots of cars*, etc.

CLOSING ACTIVITIES

- Ask pupils what things change over time. *People, plants, animals, towns, machines*, etc.
- Replay the images from your slide presentation. Encourage pupils to shout out *Past!* or *Present!* according to the photo they see.

EXTRA IDEAS

- Make *Past and present* posters. Have pupils find pictures of old and modern machines to stick on the correct poster.

PAGE 83 A day

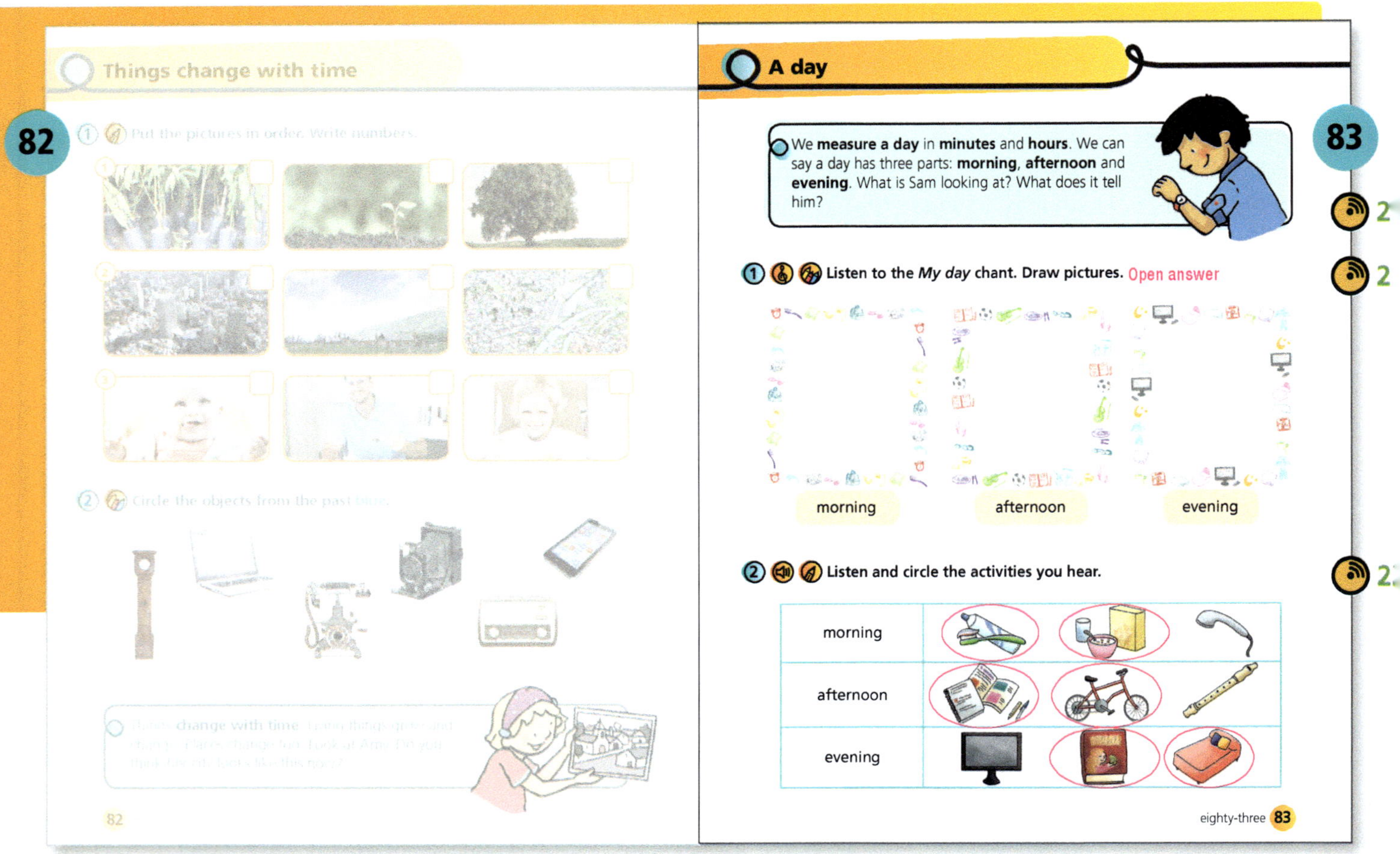

PAGE SUMMARY

Your pupils will understand how we measure days in minutes and hours, and break up the day into morning, afternoon and evening.

LANGUAGE

- Week, day, hour, minute, morning, afternoon, evening, night
- What is the time? What time of day is it?

MATERIALS

Flashcards: (digital) see the *Teachers* section in the digital resources

Additional classroom materials: two clocks, one or two toys or items from the past (from grandparents, a colleague or something at the school), hourglass or timer

OPENING ACTIVITIES

- Play *What's the time Mr Wolf?* Choose a pupil to be Mr Wolf. Have the rest of the class follow Mr Wolf around the playground or gym, chanting *What's the time Mr Wolf?* The pupil playing Mr Wolf must turn around each time and say a time e.g. *It's nine o'clock*. The game continues in this way until Mr Wolf decides he is hungry and responds *It's dinner time!* and tries to tag one of the pupils. If successful, the tagged pupil becomes the new Mr Wolf and the game starts again.
- Play *Clock race*. Two pupils, one from each team, race against each other to move the hands on the clock to show the time you indicated.
- Bring to class one or two items from the past. Show them to your class and encourage them to talk about what they see. Ask pupils to remember the changes over time they learned about in the previous class.

MAIN ACTIVITIES

- Play *How long is a minute?* Tell pupils they are going to guess how long a minute is and ask them to stand up. Tell them that they must sit down when they think a minute has passed. Watch the time yourself so that you can indicate afterwards which pupils were close. Repeat the activity, but this time, have pupils watch an hourglass or wait for a timer to go off.

Reading. (CD 2. Track 21)

- Ask pupils if they know how many minutes are in an hour. Accept their guesses. Tell them there are 60. Indicate on a clock to help pupils understand. Explain that there are 24 hours in a day. Some of the hours are in daylight and some are at night.
- Tell pupils to open their Pupil's Books on page 83 and ask them to look at the reading box. Say **Let's listen and read**. Play the audio and have pupils follow in their books.
- Illustrate the idea of *measuring* with a ruler. Show how we measure objects in centimetres, but we measure a day in hours and minutes.
- Ask pupils to tell you the three sections we can divide a day into. Ask pupils **Is it morning, afternoon or evening now?** Talk with pupils about when one part of the day finishes and another one starts. Explain that afternoon starts after 12 o'clock (midday) and that evening starts after six o' clock or when it starts to get dark.
- Ask pupils what Sam is looking at. *A watch*. Ask what it tells him. *The time*. Ask pupils to put up their hands if they are wearing a watch today. Ask if their watch has hands to tell the time or if it is digital.

1 Listen to *My day* chant. Draw pictures.

- Write *morning*, *afternoon* and *evening* on the board. Point to *morning* and ask for volunteers to stand up and mime an activity for the morning. Ask *What is he/ she doing?* Repeat the miming activity for *afternoon* and *evening*.
- Draw pupils' attention to the musical note. Say **Let's listen to the *My day* chant**. Play the audio and elicit what activities they hear for each part of the day. Play again and pause after each section to allow pupils time to draw pictures.

CD 2 • Track 22

My day, my day
Morning, afternoon, evening
In the morning I wash my face
Then I eat my breakfast
In the afternoon I do my homework
Then I play football
In the evening I watch television
Then I go to bed
My day, my day
Morning, afternoon, evening!

- When pupils have finished their pictures, play the chant one more time for them to join in.

2 Listen and circle the activities you hear.

- Have pupils look at the pictures in each section and elicit what activities they represent.
- Play the audio and ask pupils **What did you hear?** Play the audio again and have them circle the activities.

CD 2 • Track 23

In the morning, I eat my breakfast. Then I brush my teeth. In the afternoon, I do my homework. Then I ride my bicycle. In the evening, I read a bedtime story. Then I go to bed. Good night!

- Ask pupils to tell you one other activity they do in the morning, afternoon or evening.

CLOSING ACTIVITIES

- Ask pupils how we measure a day. Encourage pupils to remember how many minutes in an hour and how many hours in a day.
- Point to the pupils' timetable. Ask **What classes do you have today in the morning / afternoon?**

EXTRA IDEAS

- Tell pupils they have one minute to write their name as many times as possible on a sheet of A5 paper. Set the timer or hourglass. Afterwards, have pupils count.
- Ask pupils fold a sheet of A4 paper into three, write *morning / afternoon / evening* as a title for each section and draw an activity they do at that time of day.

PAGE 84 Days of the week

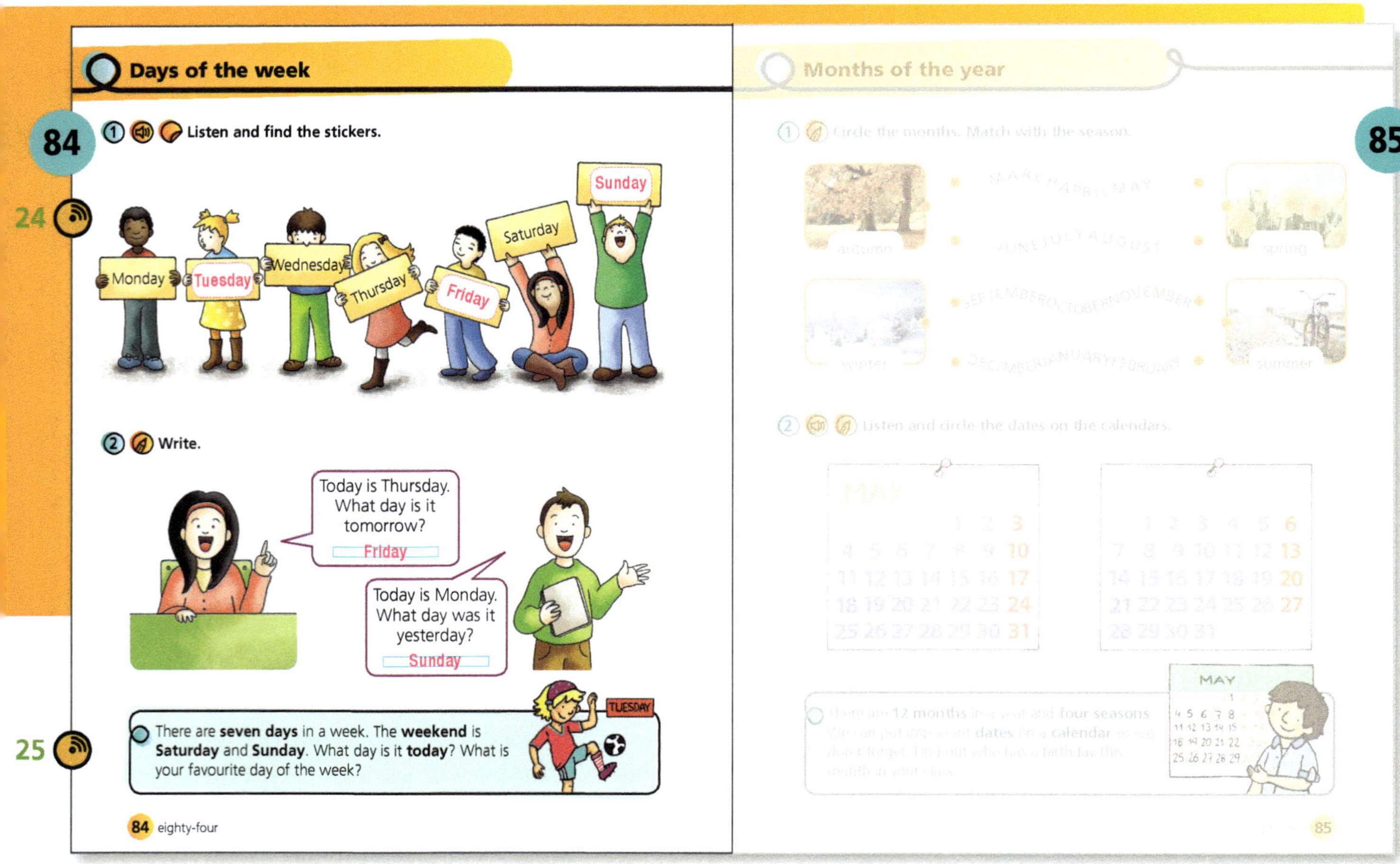

PAGE SUMMARY

Pupils will review the days of the week and their order.

LANGUAGE

- Monday, Tuesday, Wednesday, Thursday, Friday, Saturday, Sunday
- Today is Monday. Yesterday was Sunday. Tomorrow is Tuesday.

MATERIALS

Flashcards: (digital) see the *Teachers* section in the digital resources

Additional classroom materials: hourglass or timer, clocks, old calendars

OPENING ACTIVITIES

- Ask pupils what their favourite time of day is. Create a chain around the class where pupils take it in turns to say *My favourite time of day is the (afternoon) because (I play football).*
- Play *One minute, please!* Hand out an A5 sheet of paper to each pupil. Tell pupils they have one minute to write all the letters of the alphabet. Set the timer or hourglass. Have pupils count up how many letters they wrote. What was the highest number of letters? Did anyone write the whole alphabet?
- Play *One minute, please!* again. This time, ask pupils to line up at the door correctly. Set the timer or hourglass and have pupils see if they can line up in a minute.
- Practise using the clocks (the pupils made) to tell the time.

MAIN ACTIVITIES

- Play *Hangman* with the word *weekend*. Ask pupils to name the days of the weekend. *Saturday and Sunday.* Ask pupils to tell you one thing they love to do at the weekend.
- Shuffle wordcards for days of the week and place them on the board out of order. Ask pupils what day is the first day of the week. *Monday.* Place the *Monday* wordcard apart. Ask pupils which is the next day of the week. Encourage a volunteer to place the *Tuesday* wordcard under the *Monday* wordcard. Repeat the procedure until all seven days are in order.
- Have pupils read the days of the week in order. Ask **What day of the week is it today?** Have pupils tell you and then ask **What day was it yesterday? What day is it tomorrow?**

1 Listen and find the stickers.

- Ask pupils to open their Pupil's Books on page 84. Have pupils read the days of the week and notice the days that are missing. Play the audio. Have pupils follow in their books and find the stickers. *See answers opposite.*

> CD 2 • Track 24
> Monday – Monday; Tuesday – Tuesday; Wednesday – Wednesday; Thursday – Thursday; Friday – Friday; Saturday – Saturday; Sunday – Sunday.

- Have pupils close their books. Ask them work in pairs to spell the days of the week on a mini whiteboard or in their notebooks. When they have had a go at spelling the words, have pupils open their books and check if they spelt the words correctly.

2 Write.

- Hand out jumbled wordcards for days of the week to seven volunteers. Encourage them to show their wordcards and stand in the correct order with *Monday* being the first day.
- Stand behind one pupil, e.g. *Thursday.* Say **Today is Thursday. What day was it yesterday?** Elicit *Wednesday.* **What day is it tomorrow?** Elicit *Friday.*
- Stand behind another pupil, e.g. *Monday*, and repeat the questions. Practise one or two more times.
- Focus pupils' attention on activity 2. Point to and read the first speech bubble together. Elicit the answer and have pupils write *Friday* in the box. Point to and read the second speech bubble. Elicit the answer and have pupils write *Sunday* in the box.
- Have pupils notice that the days of the week in English all begin with capital letters.

Reading. (CD 2. Track 25)

- Ask pupils to look at the reading box. Say **Let's listen and read about the days of the week.** Play the audio and have pupils follow in their books.
- Ask random pupils what their favourite day of the week is and why.

CLOSING ACTIVITIES

- Ask pupils what their favourite day of the week is. Create a chain around the class, where pupils take it in turns to say *My favourite day is (Monday) because (I have Science class!).*

EXTRA IDEAS

- Keep a diary for a week. Have pupils follow instructions to make a simple mini book using A4 paper. Have them write *My diary* on the front of the booklet and each day of the week as a heading for each page. Encourage them to write a sentence for each day as the week progresses beginning with *Today I (...).* Pupils can also add a small picture to accompany their text.
- Hand out old calendars for pupils to look at. Encourage them to count the days and weeks in a month.

PAGE 85 Months of the year

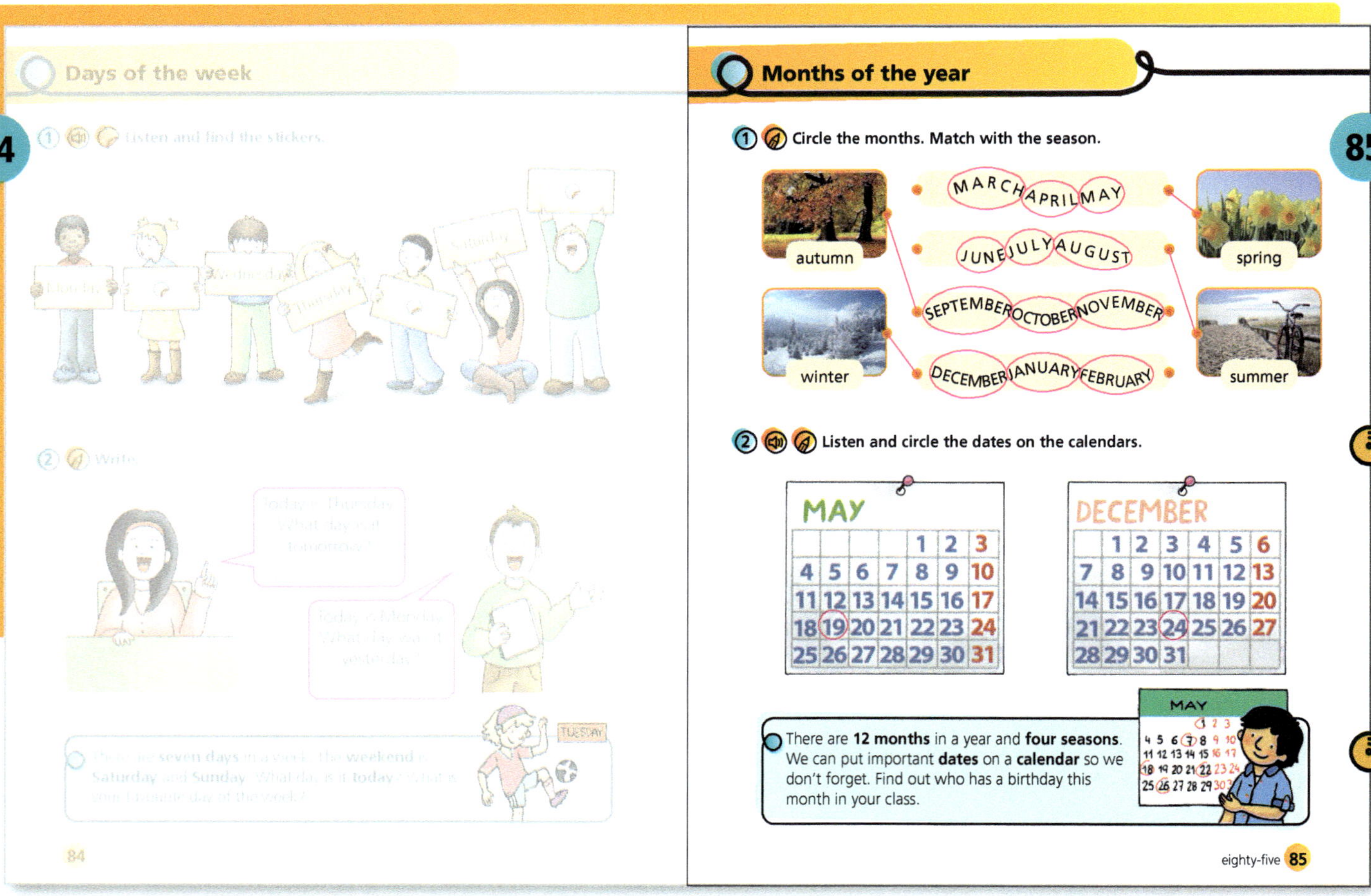

PAGE SUMMARY

Pupils will review the months of the year and the seasons. They will learn how putting dates on a calendar can help us remember special events.

LANGUAGE

- Day, month, year, date, season, calendar
- January, February, March, April, May, June, July, August, September, October, November, December

MATERIALS

Flashcards: (digital) see the *Teachers* section in the digital resources

Additional classroom materials: old calendars, calendar for the current year

OPENING ACTIVITIES

- Ask pupils what day of the week it is today. Ask **What day was it yesterday? What day is it tomorrow?**
- Point to each pupil in turn and name them a day of the week. Once all pupils have a day of the week, ask them to listen carefully and follow your instructions for their day, e.g. **Tuesdays touch your toes. Fridays sit on the floor. Wednesdays stand next to the window. Mondays move your hips. Tuesdays count to ten. Sundays shrug your shoulders. Thursdays fold your arms**, etc. Have instructions ready to keep pupils on their toes and listening for their day of the week.
- Have pupils work in pairs, with one mini whiteboard or notebook between them. Say a day of the week and have pupils spell the word. Put up the wordcard for pupils to check. Repeat the spelling activity with other days of the week.
- Have pupils chant the days of the week in order.

MAIN ACTIVITIES

- Ask pupils **How many days are there in a week?** *Seven*. **How many weeks are there in a month?** *About four*. **How many months in a year?** *12*.
- Call out the months of the year and have pupils stand up when it is their birthday.
- Hand out the jumbled-up wordcards for the months to 12 pupils and ask them to stand in the correct order, starting with *January* on the left. Have the 12 pupils read out their month in order and the rest of the class listen to check that they are correct. Ask pupils to place the months in order on the board.
- Show pupils flashcards or pictures of the different seasons. Elicit the season and ask them what they can see in the picture. Ask **What is the weather like in spring / summer / autumn / winter? What activities do you do in spring / summer / autumn / winter?**
- Put the season pictures on the board and write the name of the season above each picture. Say **Let's match the months with the seasons**. Encourage pupils to come and place a month wordcard under the correct season. Each time a pupil does so, ask the rest of the class **Is that right?** When all the months have been placed under the correct season, ask pupils to tell you what month their birthday is in.

1 Circle the months. Match with the season.

- Tell pupils to open their Pupil's Books on page 85. Focus pupils' attention on the first box of months. Say **Oh dear. All the months are squashed together. Let's circle the months.** Encourage pupils to join you in spelling out the months. Ask them to shout *Circle!* when they say the last letter of the month, e.g. *M-A-R-C-H-Circle!*
- Point to each photo and have pupils read out the name of the season.
- Read out the names of the months in the first box and ask **Which season?** *Spring*. Ask pupils to draw a line between the two. Repeat the procedure for matching the other months and seasons. *See answers opposite*.

2 Listen and circle the dates on the calendars.

- Hand out old calendars to pupils in groups or show a calendar month on the interactive whiteboard. Ask **Why do we have calendars? How can they help us?** *We know what day of the week it is, what month it is, when we need to start school, when it is our birthday, how many days there are until Christmas*, etc.
- Ask pupils to listen and point to the dates you say, e.g. **the fourth / the eleventh / the twenty-second** (only say the month if pupils are all looking at the same month).
- Focus pupils' attention on the two months in their books. Play the audio and have them listen and point to the dates. Play again and have pupils circle the dates. *See answers opposite*. Ask pupils to tell you why the dates are special. *Birthday, Christmas Eve*.

> **CD 2 • Track 26**
>
> Boy: **My favourite day of the year is my birthday! It's on the 19th of May. Circle the 19th of May on the calendar.**
>
> Girl: **My favourite day of the year is Christmas Eve. It's on the 24th of December. Circle the 24th of December on the calendar.**

Reading. (CD 2. Track 27)

- Focus pupils' attention on the reading box. Say **Let's listen and read**. Play the audio and encourage pupils to follow in their books.
- Ask pupils to tell you why it is good to put dates on a calendar. *So we don't forget*.
- Ask pupils what month they can see in the picture of Sam. *May*. Ask pupils to stand up if they have a birthday in May. Ask them to tell you the date.

CLOSING ACTIVITIES

- Remind pupils that the first letter of the days of the week and the months of the year is always a capital letter in English.
- Ask pupils for the exact date of their birthday.

EXTRA IDEAS

- Have pupils come and circle their birthdays on a calendar for the class and write their names.

PAGE 86-87 Let's investigate and Make a difference

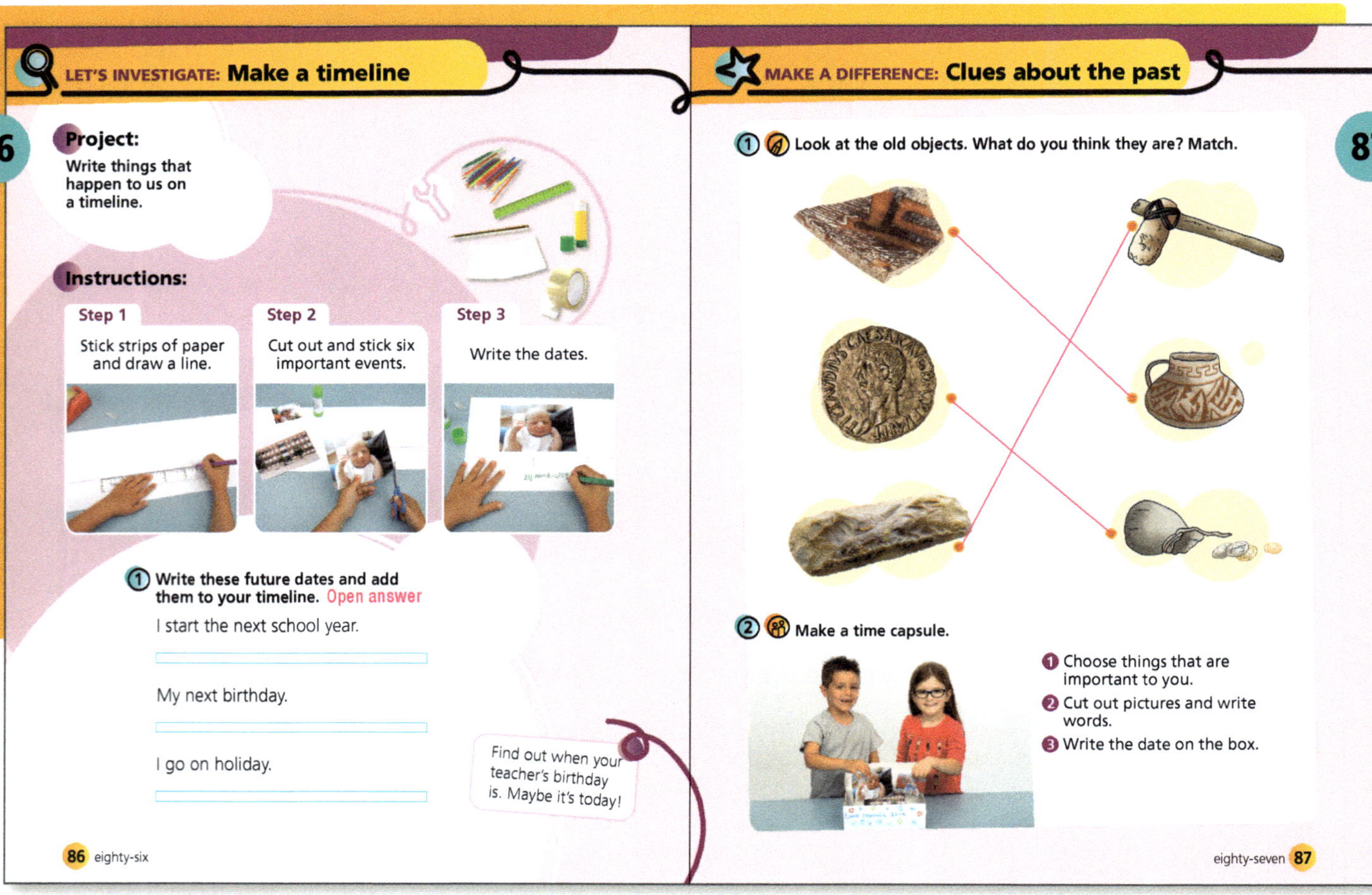

86

LET'S INVESTIGATE: **Make a timeline**

Project:
Write things that happen to us on a timeline.

Instructions:

Step 1
Stick strips of paper and draw a line.

Step 2
Cut out and stick six important events.

Step 3
Write the dates.

1 **Write these future dates and add them to your timeline.** Open answer

I start the next school year.

My next birthday.

I go on holiday.

Find out when your teacher's birthday is. Maybe it's today!

86 eighty-six

87

MAKE A DIFFERENCE: **Clues about the past**

1 **Look at the old objects. What do you think they are? Match.**

2 **Make a time capsule.**

1 Choose things that are important to you.
2 Cut out pictures and write words.
3 Write the date on the box.

eighty-seven 87

PAGE SUMMARY

Pupils will draw a timeline to help them see the important events in their lives and when they happened.

LANGUAGE

- School, birthday, holiday
- When I was born / was 3 years old / started school.
- January, February, March, April, May, June, July, August, September, October, November, December

MATERIALS

Flashcards: (digital) see the *Teachers* section in the digital resources

Additional classroom materials: old calendars, five hula hoops, cardboard boxes, some old and interesting items. Ask pupils to bring in photos of important events in their lives

Pages 86 and 87 allow pupils to connect the past to the present. The ***Let's investigate*** page encourages pupils to draw a timeline to record the important events in their lives up to the present.

The ***Make a difference*** page encourages pupils to look back at the past and appreciate the things that were important and have an impact on the present.

- Hand out the old calendars again to pupils in groups. Write the following numbers spaced out on the board: *12, 30, 7, 31*. Ask pupils to think about what they refer to. *12 months, 30 and 31 days in the months (except February), 7 days in a week.*
- Ask pupils to think in their groups about all the different ways we record or see the passing of time. Have pupils share their ideas. *Calendars, clocks, watches, timers, hourglasses, photo albums, old objects*, etc.

LET'S INVESTIGATE

⊕ OPENING ACTIVITIES

- Have pupils look back to page 80 and the story about Sam's grandad. Ask pupils **What were the important times in his life?** Elicit *being in the football team, going to university, getting married, having children and grandchildren.*
- Lay down four or five hula hoops on the floor in a line with space between them. Tell pupils that the hula hoops are important moments in your life, e.g. Go to the hula hoop furthest away. Say **I was born on 22nd June 1964**. Go to the next hula hoop. Say **My sister was born**. Go to the next hula hoop and say **I started school in 1969**, etc. When you reach the last hula hoop, say **Now I am a teacher at your school**.
- Ask pupils to think about the important things that have happened in their lives so far.

MAIN ACTIVITIES

- Introduce the idea of a timeline. Draw one on the board and add your information from the hula hoops.
- Ask pupils to open their books on page 86. Say **Let's look at the timeline and read the instructions**. Read the instructions together and demonstrate what pupils need to do. Encourage pupils to write the important events first in their notebooks and help them with writing the dates.
- Have pupils add their photos or draw pictures to add to the timeline. Make sure pupils leave space on their timeline for the next activity.

1 Write these future dates and add them to your timeline.

- Encourage pupils to talk about and write the information in their books before adding it to their timeline.

⊕ CLOSING ACTIVITIES

- Encourage pupils to ask when your birthday is.
- Ask pupils what they want to be when they are adults.

MAKE A DIFFERENCE

⊕ OPENING ACTIVITIES

- Ask pupils if they have been to a museum which has things from the past. Ask them to tell you what things they saw. Encourage them to talk about old statues, mummies, dinosaurs, toys, dolls, cars, machines, coins, stamps, etc.
- Ask pupils if they have any old and interesting things at home or at their grandparents' homes. If you have brought any items, show them to the pupils and discuss them. Ask pupils why these old things are interesting to us in the modern world although we may not use them anymore.
- Show pupils images of life in the past (cave dwellers, Victorians) to emphasise changes over a period of time.

MAIN ACTIVITIES

1 Look at the old objects. What do you think they are? Match.

- Have pupils look at each picture of part of an object on the left and ask them to tell you what they think it is. Help them with any vocabulary.
- Ask pupils to match the pictures. *See answers opposite.*
- Ask pupils if the objects are very different from what we use today. Have pupils think about how things are different (materials used, way of making objects).

2 Make a time capsule.

- Ask pupils to look at the photo. Ask **What do you think a time capsule is?** Elicit pupils' ideas.
- Read the instructions and have pupils add photos of themselves and objects (or photos of objects) that are important to them at this moment in time.
- Encourage them to write one or two sentences explaining the things they like and love doing.
- Have them decorate their box and write the date.

⊕ CLOSING ACTIVITIES

- Tell pupils they should put the box away and look at it in the future. They can then observe how they have changed and if the things they like to do are still the same or not.

PAGE 88-89 Let's remember

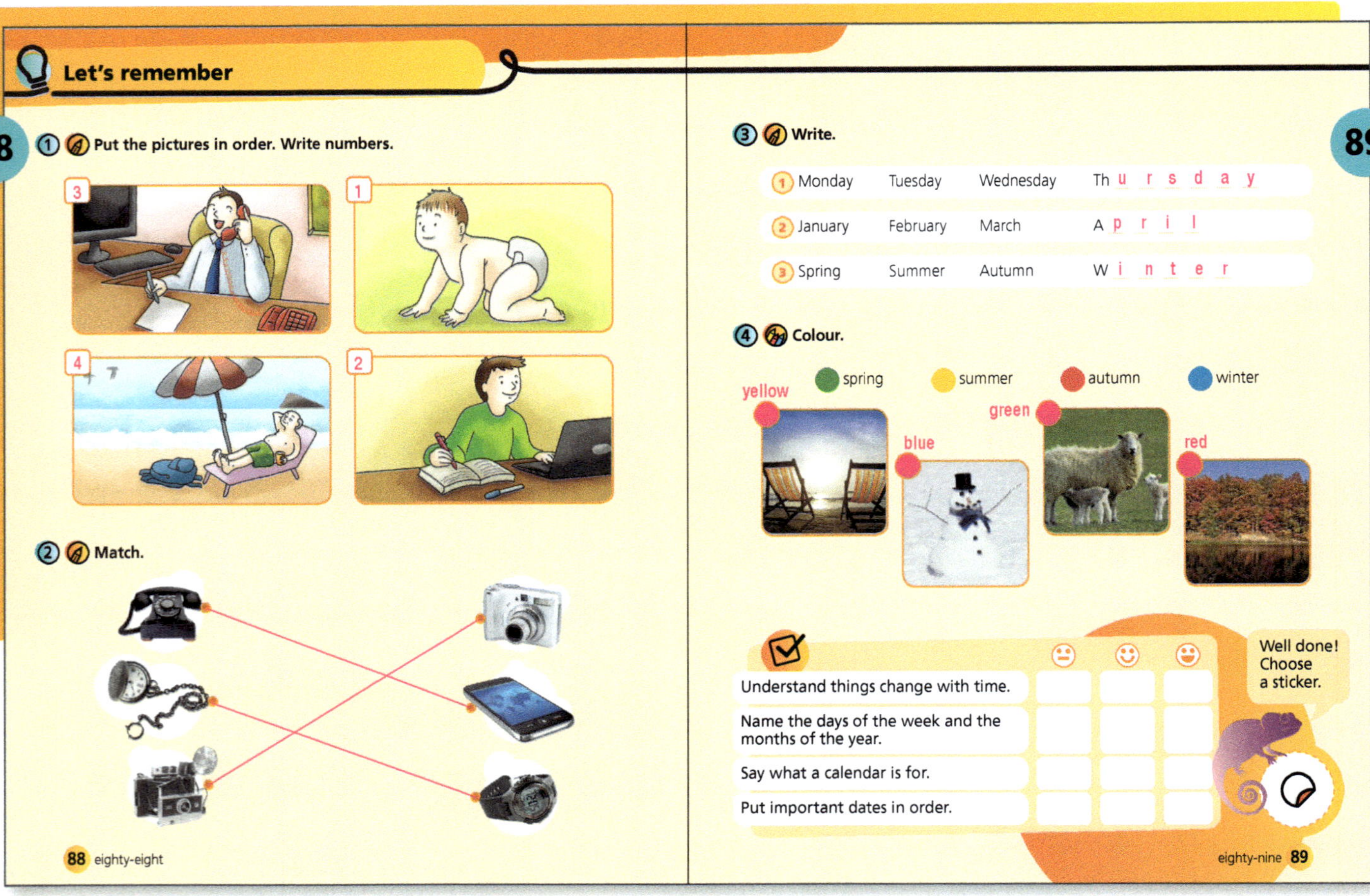

PAGE SUMMARY

Pupils review unit content and undertake a simple self-assessment on the unit content.

LANGUAGE

- Baby, child, adult
- Inventions, telephone, clock, watch, camera
- Days of the week, months of the year, seasons

MATERIALS

Flashcards: digital flashcards for the unit

OPENING ACTIVITIES

1 Put the pictures in order. Write numbers.

- Tell pupils to open their Pupil's Books on pages 78 and 79 and look at the opening illustration again. Have pupils describe what they see in pairs or small groups. Ask **What have you learned? What do you know?**
- Ask pupils to tell you some things that they can do now that they couldn't do when they were babies. *Walk, talk, cycle, use a knife and fork, go to school,* etc.
- Ask pupils to tell you some of the important moments in their lives.
- Play *Guess my word*. Begin to write the following three words (*baby, child, adult*) on the board and encourage pupils to guess the word before you finish spelling it.
- Ask pupils to turn to page 88 and look at the man's life. Say **Let's put the pictures in order. What is number one?** *The baby.* Talk about the pictures and have pupils number them. *See answers above.*

② Match.

- Give each pupil a sheet of paper and tell them they have one minute to draw an important invention. Remind pupils they only have a minute. Tell pupils they must now move around the classroom and find others with the same invention. When they have found others with the same invention, encourage pupils to talk about why they think the invention is important. Write the inventions on the board.
- Focus pupils' attention on the photos and ask them to name the objects they can see. Encourage pupils to talk about how things have changed. *Objects today are smaller, easy to carry, lighter, have more functions*, etc.
- Have pupils match up the photos. *See answers opposite.*

③ Write.

- Play *Action day*. Teach pupils a mime to do for five days of the week (Monday to Friday), e.g. **Monday – move your hips, Tuesday – turn around, Wednesday – wave to a friend, Thursday – bend your knees, Friday – stand still**. Teach the first two mimes, and each time you introduce a new mime, repeat the previous ones to help pupils remember them. Call out the days of the week in a random order and have pupils remember and do the mimes.
- Elicit the names of the seasons and have pupils remember which months correspond to each season. Talk again how the seasons are different and what is special about each one, e.g. *animals are born in spring, people go on holiday in summer, leaves change colour in autumn, it's cold and snowy in winter*, etc.
- Focus pupils' attention on activity 3. Read the words in the first box together and elicit the final word. Encourage pupils to practise the spelling first if they are unsure.
- Repeat the procedure with the months and seasons. *See answers opposite.*

④ Colour.

- Have pupils look at the photos and describe what they see. Ask **Which season is it?**
- Read the names of the seasons and elicit the colour code. Ask **What colour is spring / summer / autumn / winter?** Have pupils colour the circles. *See answers opposite.*
- Ask pupils which is their favourite season and why.

Self-assessment

- Write *Time* on the board. Read it out as you do so. Tell pupils that they have learned a lot of things about time in this unit.
- Focus pupils' attention on the self-assessment table. Read the first sentence together: *Understand things change with time.* Ask pupils to tell a partner what things change with time.
- Now read the sentence: *Name the days of the week and the months of the year.* Ask pupils to run through the names of days and months with a partner.
- Read the sentence: *Say what a calendar is for.* Ask the class to tell you why a calendar is so useful.
- Finally, together read: *Put important dates in order.* Have pupils take out their timeline and tell a new partner one important event in their lives.
- After reading each sentence, the pupils should tick the boxes according to whether they have learned a lot (*very happy face*), some things (*happy face*) or a little (*disappointed face*) about the topic of time.
- Ask pupils to choose a sticker to show how they feel about their learning in the unit.
- Give individual attention to any pupils who choose the *disappointed sticker.*

Activity book answers

UNIT 6 Time

32

① Put a tick or a cross.

1. This is a baby. ✓
2. This is a child. ✗
3. This is an adult. ✗

② Write the family members.

brother mother ~~me~~ grandmother great-grandfather father great-grandmother grandfather sister

1. me
2. brother
3. sister
4. father
5. mother
6. grandmother
7. grandfather
8. great-grandfather
9. great-grandmother

32 thirty-two

33

③ Put the pictures in order. Write numbers.

1. 1, 3, 2
2. 2, 3, 1

④ Write and draw.

computer fridge shoes ~~car~~

Open answer

	past	present	future
car			
shoes			
computer			
fridge			

thirty-three 33

UNIT 6

34

⑤ Match.

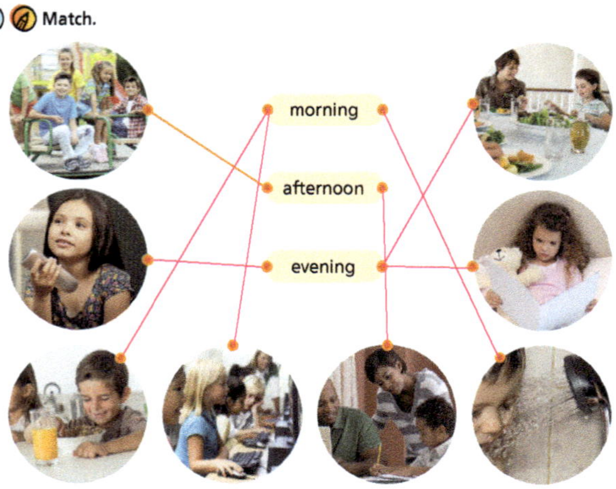

⑥ Write.

Saturday Tuesday Friday ~~Monday~~ Sunday Thursday Wednesday

Monday	Tuesday	Wednesday	Thursday	Friday

weekdays

Saturday	Sunday

weekend

34 thirty-four

35

⑦ Trace and match.

spring summer autumn winter

summer autumn winter

⑧ Colour.

spring summer autumn winter

blue December; yellow June; red September; blue February; green May; green March; yellow July; red October; red November; blue January; green April; yellow August

⑨ Write the correct number.

1. There are f o u r seasons in a year.
2. There are t h r e e months in a season.
3. There are t w e l v e months in a year.
4. There are s e v e n days in a week.

12 7 3 ~~4~~

thirty-five 35

UNIT 6

Let's investigate at home!

Make a four seasons album

1

Cut out your album.

2

Fold on the lines.

3
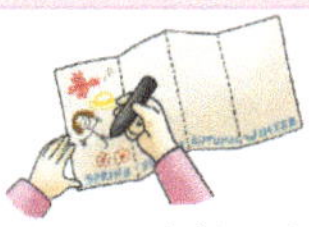
Draw pictures of things from the different seasons.

4

Decorate the cover of your album.

1 **Write.** Open answer

What is your favourite season? ______________________

What is the weather like in your favourite season? ______________

Skills check

1 **Look and read. Write *yes* or *no*.**

Example: The boy is doing his homework. yes

1. The woman is sleeping. no
2. The man is watching television. yes
3. There are three photos on the wall. yes
4. It is Wednesday in the picture. no
5. It is summer in the picture. no

TERM 3 Work together

CONTENT	EVALUATION CRITERIA
Time. Basic notions: before, after, past, present, future, duration.	Begin the reconstruction of memories of the recent past, from family sources.
Units of measurement: day, week, month and year.	Order family events using simple observation methods and units of measurement (day, week, month, year).
Days of the week. Months and seasons of the year.	Use the calendar to represent the passing of time and locate important days or dates.
Events in the past and the present.	Sequence events applying the basic units of measurement and express some examples of how things change over time.
Historical sources.	Identify historical events through objects.
Introduction to scientific knowledge and its application in the Social Sciences. Collect relevant information using different sources (direct and indirect).	Obtain specific and relevant information, using different sources.
Develop strategies to organise, memorise and remember information obtained through different methods and from different sources.	Develop a capacity for hard work and show perseverance while studying.
Team-building strategies.	Develop a cooperative and adaptive attitude, recognising merit in others' ideas and responding to situations with intuition, an open mind and flexibility
With help, plan and manage simple projects, showing independence and initiative in order to achieve objectives.	Develop creativity and initiative, improving their capacity to acquire information and ideas and present innovative conclusions
Correct use of different materials.	Use the materials in a suitable way.
Techniques for intellectual work. Elaboration of diagrams and summaries, memorising and structuring the information received. Reading techniques for Social Science publications.	Employ techniques appropriate to intellectual tasks; produce work and make presentations both individually and as a group, involving research, selection and organisation of texts of a social, geographical or historical nature, while showing autonomy and collaborative skills.

LEARNING STANDARDS	KEY COMPETENCES	PAGES
Investigates, with help, certain events in the history of their family and collects simple facts connected to their family.	SOC, CUL	90, 91
With help, produces a simple family tree of their own family.	SOC, LTL, AUT	90, 91
Organises the history of their family through a photo album.	SOC, LTL	90, 91
Uses oral sources and information from objects and family memories to reconstruct the past.	SOC, CUL, LTL	90, 91
Orders chronologically certain events of their personal life, using basic units of measurement: hour, day, week, year.	SOC, LTL, MST	90, 91
Classifies different images according to different notions such as: before, now, after.	SOC, CUL, LTL	90, 91
Orders activities according to notions of time such as: before, after.	SOC, LTL, MST	90, 91
Establishes a chronology based on family relationships and the age of each member and identifies the concepts of past, present and future	SOC, LTL	90, 91
Locates and places important dates on a calendar.	SOC, LTL, MST	90, 91
Locates on a simple timeline their own personal history from birth until today.	SOC, LTL, CUL, MST	90, 91
Uses basic notions of time (before, after, at the beginning, at the end) to tell events of their daily life in chronological order.	SOC, LTL, LIN	90, 91
Understands how things change with time.	SOC, CUL	90, 91
Understands the past through historical sources in their immediate environment.	SOC, CUL, LTL	90, 91
Identifies events in the past and the present and their relation to their lives.	SOC, CUL	90, 91
Looks for, selects and organises information, analysing it and drawing conclusions. Reflects on the process followed and reports on it orally.	MST, LIN, LTL	90, 91
Performs academic tasks in a responsible and effective manner.	LTL	90, 91
Uses vocabulary correctly in the presentation of their work.	LTL, LIN	90, 91
Develops a cooperative and adaptive attitude, recognising merit in others' ideas and responding to situations with intuition, an open mind and flexibility.	LTL, SOC	90, 91
Participates effectively and constructively in daily life and develops strategies for conflict resolution.	LTL, SOC	90, 91
Identifies and uses the correct code of conduct for their environment.	LTL, SOC	90, 91
Shows self-confidence, personal initiative, curiosity, interest and creativity in the learning process.	AUT, LTL	90, 91
Shows independence in the planning and carrying out of simple actions and shows initiative when taking decisions.	AUT, LTL	90, 91
Uses the materials in a suitable and careful way, thereby keeping them in good condition.	LTL, SOC	90, 91
Produces work and makes presentations both individually and as part of a group, participating in the research, selection and organisation of texts of a social, geographical or historical nature.	SOC, AUT	90, 91

PAGES 90-91 Work together: My family

WORK TOGETHER My family

90

1 Look and say what you see. Listen and point.

28

1 2 3 4

2 How can we communicate with our family? Use the code and colour.

past present

blue purple blue purple

blue purple purple blue

90 ninety

Work in groups. Make decisions together!

91

3 Number the pictures. Tell the story.

4 Clara's son is born.

1 Clara is born.

3 Clara gets married.

2 Clara goes to school.

4 What can we use to measure time? Put a tick or a cross.

✔ ✗ ✔ ✔

Class project

Draw your family tree.
Make a poster for the classroom.

- Use pictures.
- Use text.
- Take photographs.

ninety-one 91

PAGE SUMMARY

On these pages pupils will revise different ways of communicating with our relatives, what a family tree is and how we can measure time. The different activities will be carried out following different cooperative learning structures that will provide the optimal learning experience for the pupil and guarantee the involvement of all the members of the group.

LANGUAGE

- Family, photo, photo album, letter, postcard, family tree, internet, ancestors
- Be born, go to school, get married
- Yes, it is / No, it isn't.
- I agree / I disagree. I think (...).

MATERIALS

Flashcards: (digital) see the *Teachers* section in the digital resources

Additional classroom materials: family photos

OPENING ACTIVITIES

- Before doing these activities using different cooperative learning structures, you should form the groups. Teachers should form the groups rather than letting the pupils choose their own group members. Remember to form heterogeneous groups of three or four pupils. Remind pupils to not only focus on completing the task, but also on maintaining efficient working relationships within the group. Ask them to think about the best way to work together, the need to establish time limits and the importance of expressing approval and asking for help.
- Tell the pupils what they will be doing in their groups, what procedures you will follow and what your expectations are. If during these activities any group is having problems, spend some time in class on the relevant team skills.

MAIN ACTIVITIES

1 Look and say what you see. Listen and point.

- This is a *Round robin* activity. Focus pupils' attention on the four pictures on page 90 and ask them to describe what they see.
- Ask pupils to take turns giving their opinions. Ensure that each pupil shares something with their group.
- Ask them to listen to the audio and point to each picture as it is described.

CD 2 • Track 28

1. We can see photos of our family in a photo album.
2. We can read letters and postcards from people in our family.
3. We can see the different people in our family on a family tree.
4. We can use the internet to investigate our family and ancestors.

2 How can we communicate with our family? Use the code and colour.

- This is a *Rally robin* activity. Focus your pupils' attention on the eight photos in activity 2.
- Ask pupils to discuss with their group and decide how we can use each item to communicate with our family. Ensure that each pupil shares something with their group.
- Ask your pupils to take turns giving their opinions. Have them colour the circles according to the colour code: purple for things we used in the past and blue for things we use in the present. *See answers opposite.*

3 Number the pictures. Tell the story.

- This is a *Timed pair share* activity. Ask your pupils to work in pairs and look at the pictures. Tell them that they have to order the pictures to complete the story and find out what order the important life events happened.
- Ask pupils to think independently about the story, choosing the correct order for the pictures. Then tell your pupils to discuss their answers in pairs, ensuring that pupils share their ideas and consider those of others.
- Ask the pairs to share their answers with the class and then number the pictures correctly. *4, 1, 3, 2.*

4 What can we use to measure time? Put a tick or a cross.

- This is a *Stand up, hand up, pair up* activity. Before doing this activity, review how this particular cooperative structure works.
- Say **Stand up, hand up, pair up as quickly as you can.** Using the zoom on the interactive whiteboard, show pupils the first picture. Ask them if this is an instrument we can use to measure time. Pupils discuss with their partner and share their ideas with the rest of the class.
- Repeat the process with the rest of the pictures. Pupils should work with a different partner for each picture and complete the boxes with a tick or a cross. *See answers opposite.*

CLASS PROJECT

- This is a *Rally coach* activity. Focus pupils' attention on the class project. In their groups, they will draw their family tree for the classroom.
- Ask them to look for or draw pictures and write short sentences on their family tree.
- Tell them that when pupil A chooses a picture and writes a sentence, pupil B watches, listens, checks and praises.
- When pupil B chooses a picture and writes a sentence, pupil A watches, listens, checks and praises.
- Once they have finished, ask them to share their results with the class.

+ CLOSING ACTIVITIES

- Group assessment is essential in cooperative learning to ensure that there is analysis of interactions and promotion of teamwork. Pupils should learn that how they work together affects the quality and quantity of concepts that they learn and understand.
- Ask the pupils to reflect on how they felt in their cooperative groups.
- Then ask the pupils to discuss how the group worked together and identify ideas and actions that helped the group achieve its goals.
- Once they have shared their results, ask them to reflect on how could the project be made better next time. Invite your pupils to share their conclusions with the class.

PAGES 92-93 Review

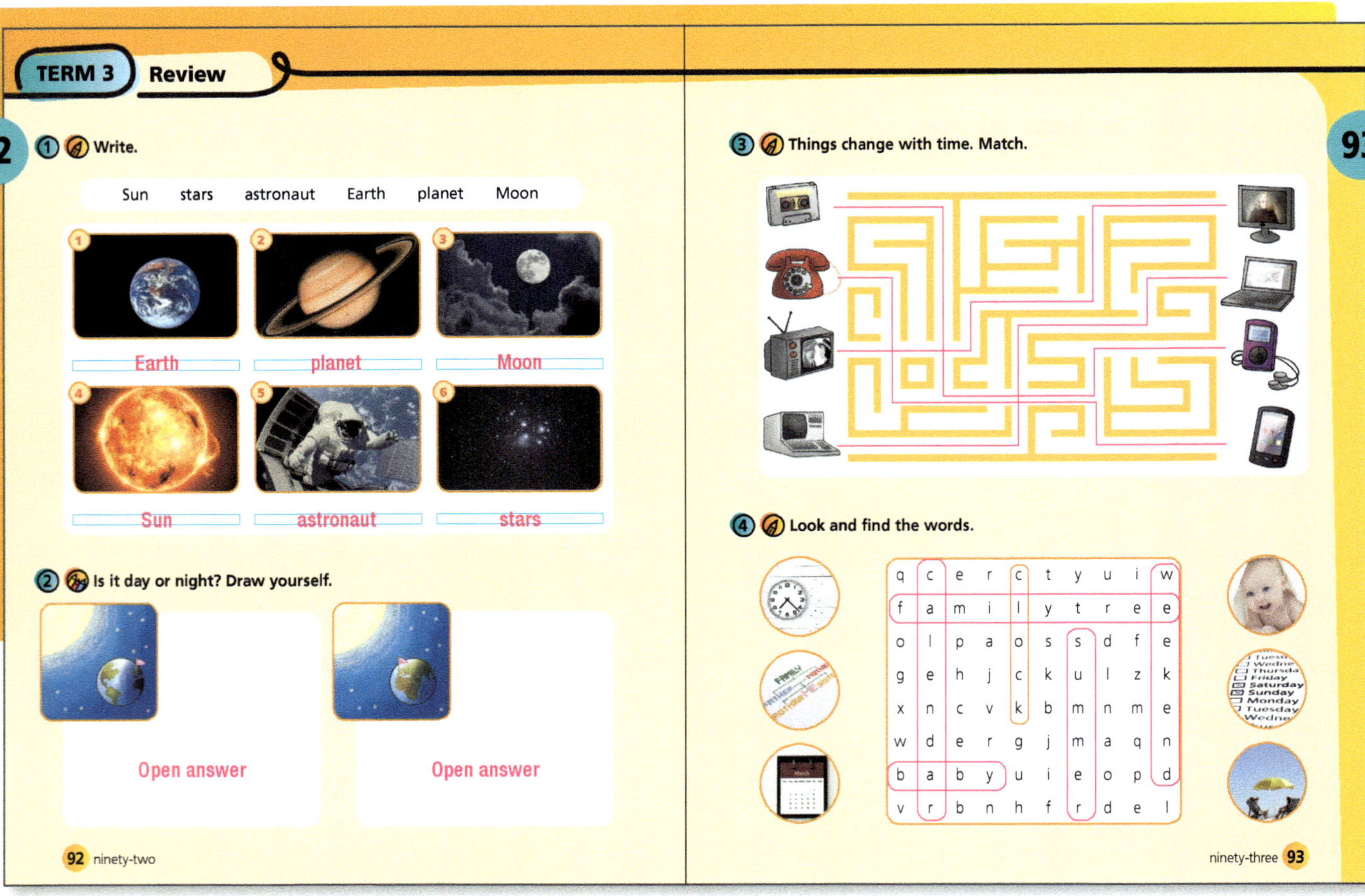

PAGE SUMMARY

Your pupils will use these pages to review content from Term 3 (Units 5 and 6).

LANGUAGE

- Sun, Earth, Moon, planet, stars, astronaut
- Day, night
- Cassette tape, telephone, television, computer, laptop, mp3 player, mobile phone
- Days of the week, weekend, months, seasons, calendar, clock
- Family tree, adult, child, baby

MATERIALS

Flashcards: digital flashcards for Units 5 and 6

Additional classroom materials: hula hoops, torch and globe, posters and displays pupils have made during Units 5 and 6

OPENING ACTIVITIES

- Tell pupils they are going to review things that they studied in Units 5 and 6.
- Play *Backs to the board*. Divide the class into two teams. Ask one pupil from each team to come and sit in a chair facing their team, but with their back to the board. Write a word from Unit 5 or 6 on the board and insist that the two pupils do not turn round. Encourage the teams to mime the word on the board for their team member to guess. The team member who guesses first gains a point for their team. Two new team members then take a turn in the chairs.
- Play *Run and slap!* Write 10 words from Units 5 and 6 around the bottom half of the board where pupils will be able to reach them. Divide the class into two teams. Two pupils, one from each team, come up at a time and stand a metre from the board. Say a word on the board. Pupils race to be the first to slap it. Whoever slaps the word first wins a point for their team.

MAIN ACTIVITIES

1 Write.

- Hand out as many hula hoops as you have. Tell pupils they are going to take it in turns to twirl the hula hoop around their waists. As the first group of pupils twirl, they must call out the names of objects that are round. As the second group of pupils twirl, they must name things we can see in the sky. Finally, as the third group of pupils twirl, they must call out months of the year. Spectators can listen and check the twirlers are naming words appropriate to the category.
- Ask pupils to open their Pupil's Books on page 92 and look at the first activity. Point to each photo and ask pupils what they can see. Ask them to tell you what they learned about the Earth, Sun, Moon and astronauts.
- Read the words in the box together and have pupils write them under the correct photo. *See answers opposite.*

2 Is it night or day? Draw yourself.

- Put pupils in groups of three and ask them to repeat the demonstration they did to show how the Moon moves around the Earth and the Earth moves around the Sun.
- Shine a torch on a globe and have pupils explain about light and dark.
- Say **Let's look at activity 2.** Focus pupils' attention on the first picture. Ask pupils to imagine they are the flag. Ask **Is it day or night?** *Night.* Ask pupils what activity they are doing if it is night. *Sleeping or going to bed.*
- Point to the second picture and repeat the question **Is it day or night where the flag is?** *Day.* Elicit the different activities pupils are doing.
- Ask pupils to now draw themselves to show what they are doing when it is night and when it is day.

3 Things change with time. Match.

- Put pupils in groups of three and have them play *Pictionary.* One group member must think of a modern machine and begin to draw it very slowly. The other two members must guess what it is. The first one of the two to guess the object draws the next picture.
- Ask pupils **What things change with time?** *People, toys, machines, transport, towns,* etc.
- Focus pupils' attention on the maze. Name the objects on the right and encourage pupils to point to the object from the past on the left.
- Ask pupils to draw the line between the two. *See answers opposite.*

4 Look and find the words.

- Repeat the game *Action day* from Unit 6. Remind pupils of the actions for the different days of the week, e.g. **Monday – move your hips, Tuesday – turn around, Wednesday – wave to a friend, Thursday – bend your knees, Friday – stand still.** Call out the days of the week in a random order and have pupils remember and do the action.
- Point to the pictures around the wordsearch and ask pupils to name them.
- Have pupils look at the wordsearch to find and circle the words. *See answers opposite.*

+ CLOSING ACTIVITIES

- Review any displays and art work from this term.
- Praise everyone for working well this term.
- Ask pupils to look back through their books and remember other topics they learned about. Ask them which their favourite unit was and why.

+ EXTRA IDEAS

- *Quiz* time. Prepare a little quiz on the units of the book e.g. *In what unit can we learn about water? In what unit can we learn about transport? In what unit can we learn about being kind to our friends? In what unit do we make a map / family tree?* etc. Read through the questions first and have pupils work in pairs or small groups to find the answers.
- *Spell it!* Hand out letters of the alphabet to groups. Have group members take it in turns to look through the picture dictionary and find words for the rest of the group to spell.

Notes

Notes

Notes

Notes